access to history

Spain 1469–1598

JILL KILSBY

SECOND EDITION

The Publishers would like to thank Robin Bunce, Nicholas Fellows and David Ferriby for their contribution to the Study Guide.

The Publishers would like to thank the following for permission to reproduce copyright material:

Photo credits: p3 Michael David Murphy/Alamy; **p16***l* Portrait of Ferdinand II (1452–1516) King of Spain (oil on panel), Master of the Legend of St. Madeleine (fl.c.1500)/Musee Sainte-Croix, Poitiers, France/Bridgeman Images; **p16***r* Isabella I of Castile or Isabella the Catholic (Madrigal de las Altas Torres, 1451-Medina del Campo, 1504), Queen Consort of Sicily, Queen of Castile and Queen Consort of Aragon, Valencia, Sardinia, Majorca and Queen of Corsica/De Agostini Picture Library/G. Dagli Orti/Bridgeman Images; **p21** TopFoto; **p44** J. Bedmar/Iberfoto/Mary Evans; **p46** Wiliam Perry/Alamy; **p47** http://upload.wikimedia.org/wikipedia/commons/6/65/Arolsen_Klebeband_02_361.jpg?uselang=en-gb; **p54** Library of Congress, LC-USZ62–1784; **p66** Library of Congress, LC-USZ62–113618; **p68** Charles V, Holy Roman Emperor, 1514–16 (oil on panel), Flemish School, (16th century)/Royal Collection Trust © Her Majesty Queen Elizabeth II, 2015/Bridgeman Images; **p95** CAGP/Iberfoto/Mary Evans; **p122** Library of Congress, LC-USZ62–100317; **p124** King Philip II (1527–98) 1550 (oil on canvas), Titian (Tiziano Vecellio) (c.1488–1576)/Prado, Madrid, Spain/Bridgeman Images; **p135** World History Archive/TopFoto; **p159** World History Archive/TopFoto; **p160** Allessandro Farnese, 1884–90 (phototype), German School, (19th century)/Private Collection/© Purix Verlag Volker Christen/Bridgeman Images.

Acknowledgements: see page 212.

Every effort has been made to trace all copyright holders, but if any have been inadvertently overlooked the Publishers will be pleased to make the necessary arrangements at the first opportunity.

Although every effort has been made to ensure that website addresses are correct at time of going to press, Hodder Education cannot be held responsible for the content of any website mentioned in this book. It is sometimes possible to find a relocated web page by typing in the address of the home page for a website in the URL window of your browser.

Hachette UK's policy is to use papers that are natural, renewable and recyclable products and made from wood grown in sustainable forests. The logging and manufacturing processes are expected to conform to the environmental regulations of the country of origin.

Orders: please contact Bookpoint Ltd, 130 Milton Park, Abingdon, Oxon OX14 4SB. Telephone: +44 (0)1235 827720.
Fax: +44 (0)1235 400454. Lines are open 9.00a.m.–5.00p.m., Monday to Saturday, with a 24-hour message answering service.
Visit our website at www.hoddereducation.co.uk

© Jill Kilsby
Second edition © Jill Kilsby 2015

First published in 1989 by
Hodder Education
An Hachette UK Company
Carmelite House, 50 Victoria Embankment
London EC4Y 0DZ

Impression number	10	9	8	7	6	5	4	3	2
Year			2019	2018	2017	2016			

All rights reserved. Apart from any use permitted under UK copyright law, no part of this publication may be reproduced or transmitted in any form or by any means, electronic or mechanical, including photocopying and recording, or held within any information storage and retrieval system, without permission in writing from the publisher or under licence from the Copyright Licensing Agency Limited. Further details of such licences (for reprographic reproduction) may be obtained from the Copyright Licensing Agency Limited, Saffron House, 6–10 Kirby Street, London EC1N 8TS.

Cover photo: © Fine Art Images/Heritage Images/Getty Images
Produced, illustrated and typeset in Palatino LT Std by Gray Publishing, Tunbridge Wells
Printed and bound by CPI Group (UK) Ltd, Croydon CR0 4YY

A catalogue record for this title is available from the British Library

ISBN 978 1471838095

Contents

CHAPTER 1 **Spain 1474–1598**   1
    1 The geographical background   2
    2 The historical background   4
    3 The institutions of Aragon and Castile   6
    4 Religion   7
    5 The growth of the Spanish Empire   8

CHAPTER 2 **Ferdinand and Isabella: Castile and Aragon 1479–1516**   14
    1 Securing the throne 1469–79   15
    2 The Granada War 1482–92   19
    3 Government and administration under Isabella and Ferdinand   22
    4 Religion in the reigns of Isabella and Ferdinand   29

CHAPTER 3 **Ferdinand and Isabella 1479–1516: Europe, the wider world and the end of the reign**   39
    1 Foreign policy   40
    2 The New World: discovery and settlement   50
    3 The closing years of the reign 1504–16   55
    4 Key debate   59

CHAPTER 4 **Charles I: 1516–56**   64
    1 The succession to the Crowns of Aragon and Castile   65
    2 Revolts in Spain 1519–21   70
    3 Key debate   73
    4 Charles's return to Spain 1522   75
    5 The government of Spain   76
    6 Finance   83
    7 Religion and the Church in Spain   86
    8 Foreign policy   90
    9 The New World   96
    10 Spain in 1556   99

CHAPTER 5 **Spain in the sixteenth century: the price revolution and its effects**   103
    1 Evidence for inflation in sixteenth-century Spain   104
    2 Sixteenth-century explanations for inflation   105
    3 Modern interpretations for inflation in this period   108
    4 The social impact of inflation   112
    5 The impact of inflation on agriculture and industry   114

CHAPTER 6 Philip II: 1556–98. Spain: the heart of government 119
1 Philip's early life and character 120
2 The government of Spain 123
3 Finance 128
4 Religion and the Church 131
5 The revolts of Granada and Aragon 139

CHAPTER 7 Philip II: foreign policy and the New World 149
1 Philip's aims in ruling his empire 150
2 The foreign policy of Philip II 151
3 The New World 166
4 Key debate 169
5 Spain in 1598 170

Study guide 175

Glossary of terms 203

Further reading 206

Index 208

Dedication

Keith Randell (1943–2002)

The *Access to History* series was conceived and developed by Keith, who created a series to 'cater for students as they are, not as we might wish them to be'. He leaves a living legacy of a series that for over 20 years has provided a trusted, stimulating and well-loved accompaniment to post-16 study. Our aim with these new editions is to continue to offer students the best possible support for their studies.

CHAPTER 1

Spain 1474–1598

This chapter introduces the reader to some of the issues and problems that emerged during the years 1474–1598. It briefly presents information about how the physical geography of Spain influenced its development; its history before 1474; the way Aragon and Castile developed in different and distinct ways; the position of the three religious groups which lived in Spain in 1474; and how the empire's rapid expansion during the late fifteenth and sixteenth centuries posed unique challenges that the kings and queens needed to deal with. This is covered under the following headings:

★ The geographical background
★ The historical background
★ The institutions of Aragon and Castile
★ Religion
★ The growth of the Spanish Empire

Key dates

711	Islamic conquest of Spain	1516	Charles I King of Castile and Aragon
c.720	Start of the Reconquest in Spain by Christians	1519	Charles I became Holy Roman Emperor as Charles V
1469	Marriage of Ferdinand of Aragon and Isabella of Castile	1520–66	Suleiman the Magnificent became Sultan of the Ottoman Empire
1477	The Habsburg Maximilian I married Mary of Burgundy	1529	Armies of Suleiman stopped outside Vienna
1478	Maximilian became Holy Roman Emperor	1556	Philip II became King of Castile and Aragon
1496	Marriage alliances between Spanish and Habsburg families		

The geographical background

▶ *How did the geographical features of Spain influence the way it developed as a country?*

When we think of Spain today, we tend to picture that part of the coast that borders the Mediterranean and which many seek for its 'sun, sand and sea'. This, however, is only one part of Spain. Another coast borders the Atlantic Ocean. One land frontier is marked by the Pyrenees, and the other by modern-day Portugal. Together Spain and Portugal make up the **Iberian Peninsula**. Although a part of continental Europe, it is very much a distinct unit. There are no easy channels of communication with the other countries of Europe. On the other hand, only 19 kilometres separate it from the coast of north Africa. The peninsula is therefore at a crossroads, between the Mediterranean Sea and the Atlantic, and between the mainland of Europe and Africa.

This is not to say that the peninsula enjoys close links with the world beyond. Geographical factors prevent this being so (see Figure 1.1, page 5). Around the edge is a narrow coastal plain. But a short journey into the interior quickly reveals rivers, valleys and, in particular, mountains. Spain is Europe's most mountainous country after Switzerland. Over one-sixth of the country is more than 1000 metres above sea level. The most important geographical feature in the interior is the *Meseta*, the enormous plateau at its centre. This is almost completely surrounded by high mountain ranges and is therefore remote from both the sea and the neighbouring countries of Portugal and France.

The *Meseta* is an area of extreme climate. Its long, hard winters are followed by short periods of intense heat – what some Spaniards of today refer to as 'nine months of winter and three of hell'. The areas near the Pyrenees are, in contrast, much wetter with no extremes of temperature. The east and south coasts are different again. Here it is very hot with little in the way of a winter, but the area suffers from a lack of rain.

Spain, a country shaped by its geography

Such conditions make for a country in which food cannot easily be grown. In almost every part of Spain, apart from the river valleys and the narrow coastal plains, there are many areas where crop yields are too poor to provide enough food to sustain a large population. It is not surprising therefore, as the Spanish historian Pierre Vilar (1977) has shown, that so many of the maritime areas of Spain have sought to build up trade overseas – across the Mediterranean, over to Africa, or towards the Atlantic – rather than with the less productive central area.

The geography of the peninsula partly explains the way in which the political units in the area came to be formed as they did. Three main divisions can be distinguished: the area forming Portugal, that making **Castile**, and those

 **KEY TERMS**

Iberian Peninsula The land mass occupied by today's Spain and Portugal. It is separated from France by the Pyrenees Mountains and from Africa by the Strait of Gibraltar.

Meseta The vast highland plateau that occupies the interior of Spain at an average elevation of 600 metres.

Castile In the mid-fifteenth century the Crown of Castile occupied the area from Burgos in the north to Toledo in the south, equivalent to the modern-day provinces of León, Madrid and La Mancha.

SOURCE A

How far does Source A reflect the way geographical features affected Spain's history?

The plateau landscape (*Meseta*) in central Spain.

regions which comprised the Crown of **Aragon**. However, there was no kingdom of Spain as there was a kingdom of Portugal. The word 'Spain' was not widely used by those living in the peninsula in the mid-fifteenth century, although there may have been some who referred to themselves as 'Spanish'. Certainly, many foreigners called the people who lived in the Iberian Peninsula by this name. But most of the population thought of themselves as coming from particular parts of the peninsula, identifying first with Castile, Aragon, Catalonia, the **Basque countries** or Portugal. They called themselves not Spanish but Castilians, Aragonese, Catalans, Basque or Portuguese. It was not, however, just geographical factors which led to these groupings. The political history of the various regions also contributed.

KEY TERMS

Aragon In the mid-fifteenth century, the Crown of Aragon consisted of three kingdoms, Aragon, Catalonia and Valencia. In this book the term 'Crown of Aragon' is used to mean all three kingdoms. References to the kingdoms of Aragon, Catalonia or Valencia mean the individual kingdoms.

Basque countries Consisted of Vizcaya, Guipuzcoa, Alava and Navarre and were in the western end of the Pyrenees. In the mid-fifteenth century Navarre, the main Basque country, was partly in Spain and partly in France.

The historical background

▶ *What were the reasons for Castile becoming more important than Aragon by the mid-fifteenth century?*

The only time the Iberian Peninsula had been a single political unit was when it was a province of the Roman Empire – Roman Hispania. It was during this period that it became Christianised. However, in the eighth century, Muslims from north Africa crossed to the peninsula and conquered it. Two centuries later, the Christians recaptured part of the north of Spain, and from the eleventh century onwards began to move south on a slow but definite **Reconquest**. By the end of the thirteenth century, only the kingdom of Granada remained under Muslim rulers.

The Reconquest had partly been a desire to re-establish Christian rule. At the same time, increases in population among Christians in the north, and subsequent pressure on food supplies, had led to a need to expand and acquire more land.

The kingdoms of the peninsula

By the end of the thirteenth century, three major Christian areas had formed in the peninsula. Castile and León had come under one Christian king as the kingdom of Castile; Portugal had become an independent kingdom, and the Pyrenean kingdoms of Catalonia, Aragon and Valencia had become the Crown of Aragon. The small kingdom of Navarre mainly governed itself, although in some matters it was subject to Castile. At the same time, even within these units, there remained great varieties of customs and laws.

The warlike existence of the kingdoms had meant that the nobility, which provided the military leadership in each, held a position of importance. This was true of Castile in particular. The nobles there were **frontiersmen** who fought and won large areas of land from the Muslims. To help in the struggle, three **religious orders of knights** had been formed in the twelfth century – Calatrava, Alcantara and Santiago – whose task was to defend the frontier bordering Muslim territory.

The expansion of Aragon

While most of Castile's interests had been involved in the Reconquest, from the twelfth century, Aragon had begun to direct its energies beyond the peninsula and into the Mediterranean. Majorca and all the Balearic Islands had been conquered. Further conquests had followed over the next two centuries. The most important of these were Sicily, Sardinia and Naples (see Figure 3.1, page 41). Aragon had also taken control of a number of fortified towns in north Africa. Barcelona, in Catalonia, became one of the most important ports in the

KEY TERMS

Reconquest (*Reconquista* in Spanish.) A succession of military campaigns to reclaim Iberian lands from Muslim occupiers. The Reconquest started in the eighth century and ended in 1492 with the capture of Granada.

Frontiersmen Christian men who lived on the frontier of Christian and Muslim Spain; they had to fight to defend and extend Christian lands.

Religious orders of knights Christian military monastic organisations formed to defend and expand the Christian lands of Spain against the Muslims.

Chapter 1 Spain 1474–1598

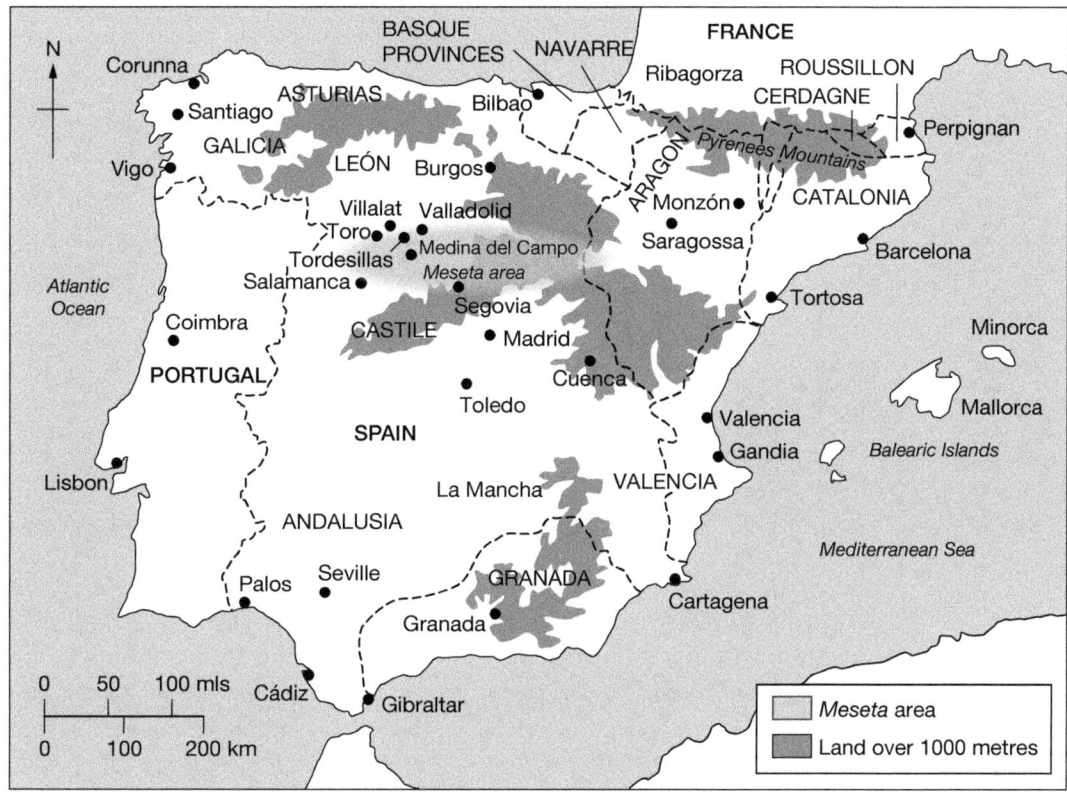

Figure 1.1 The Iberian Peninsula in the fifteenth and sixteenth centuries.

western Mediterranean. The first Spanish overseas empire had been founded and Spanish interest in Italy had been established.

Differences between Castile and Aragon in the mid-fifteenth century

Aragon's power did not last. By the middle of the fifteenth century it was clear that Castile would be the more important in the future. There were several reasons for this:

- Castile was four times larger in size than Aragon. Its population was also greater, possibly 5 million people in contrast to Aragon's 1 million.
- Castile was more unified. It possessed only one **Cortes** (or parliament), one language, one coinage and one administration.
- The Castilian economy had begun to thrive. Trade was mainly in raw materials, above all wool. The wool trade was controlled by the *Mesta*, which was a group of all the producers of wool in Castile. Exports were sent to the markets of northern Europe, particularly Flanders in the Netherlands, where Castilian merchants played a leading role. Castilian ports through which such exports were sent also co-operated with each other.

 **KEY TERM**

Cortes The parliament in each of the kingdoms in Castile and Aragon (called *Corts* in Catalonia).

- In the Crown of Aragon, in contrast, there was no such economic unity. Towns even competed against each other for trade as much as against any rivals outside Aragon. Much economic damage was done to Aragon by a lengthy civil war. In addition, its major port, Barcelona, in the kingdom of Catalonia, was hit by an economic crisis which affected most of the Mediterranean ports after 1350, and which led to bankruptcies and unemployment.

The institutions of Aragon and Castile

▶ *In what ways did the institutions of Aragon and Castile differ?*

Just as Aragon and Castile had developed in different ways, so were the institutions within the two realms different. The Crown of Aragon consisted mainly of the three separate kingdoms of Catalonia, Aragon and Valencia. Each was governed independently, and had its own laws and its own *Cortes*. In contrast, Castile consisted of a number of former kingdoms which held their institutions in common. There were, however, even in Castile, areas which had a great deal of independence. Although the Basque provinces recognised the sovereignty of the King of Castile, their geographic isolation meant that they were virtually independent from the rest of the peninsula. Asturias and Galicia had their own regional governments. In other parts of Castile there were local privileges, particularly those held by the nobility.

The *Cortes*

The *Cortes* was the means by which the political views of the important people in the country were heard. However, the powers held by the *Cortes* in each of the kingdoms were very different. In Aragon, the various *Cortes* sometimes met at the same time and in the same city (*Cortes generales*). More frequently they met separately in their own kingdoms. All laws in the Crown of Aragon (meaning all the kingdoms in Aragon) had to be approved by the individual *Cortes*. The monarch's powers for administering justice, imposing taxes or raising armies were all severely limited by the *fueros* (the laws and privileges possessed by these kingdoms). These were defended by the *justicia* – a law officer with wide powers, who could not be removed from office by the king. In Castile, in contrast, the *Cortes* was weak, and had few powers to prevent a ruler from doing as he or she wished. The Crown here had the right to make and unmake laws without the consent of the *Cortes*.

 **KEY TERMS**

Fueros Aragonese laws and privileges.

Justicia Aragonese law officer in charge of courts and justice, appointed by the Crown for life.

Religion

> ▶ What factors contributed to the growing hostility towards Jews and Muslims by the late fifteenth century?

By the mid-fifteenth century the main religion in the peninsula was Christianity, although there were large communities of both Muslims and Jews. All three felt that they had to coexist if they were to survive economically. At times of peace during the Reconquest, it had been common for Muslims and Christians to visit each other, to trade and even to intermarry.

The historian Henry Kamen (2005) quotes from a Czech traveller in 1466, who was astonished to find that in the household of the Count of Haro there were 'Christians, **Moors** and Jews, and he lets them all live in peace in their faith'.

Within the Christian territories Jews mainly lived in the towns. They were often leading financiers, lending to both the kings of Aragon and Castile. One king of Aragon claimed that, 'our predecessors have tolerated and suffered the Jews in their territories because these Jews are the strong box and treasury of the kings'. Many Jews were important in trade and in professions such as medicine. The Muslims, on the other hand, resided mainly in the countryside, working on the lands of the nobility.

The Christian victories of the Reconquest altered the relationship between the three religious groupings. Although the rulers might continue to show support for Jews and Muslims, there was a general hostility towards them, particularly during times of economic depression and epidemics. Most Jews suffered increasingly during the fourteenth century from **pogroms** (organised massacres). Many were forcibly converted to Christianity. They were then known as **conversos** or 'new' Christians to distinguish them from those who had been Christians for many generations – the 'old' Christians.

 **KEY TERMS**

Moors Muslims who invaded in the eighth century and established a rule that lasted until the fifteenth century in Andalusia.

Pogrom The officially ordered persecution and massacre of a minority group, especially Jews.

Conversos Jews who converted to Christianity, many forcibly, to avoid persecution or expulsion from Spain or Portugal.

Religion in Spain

- *Catholicism (Christianity).* The Catholic Church in the mid-fifteenth century was in need of reform. Its leader was the pope who, in theory, had complete power over the Church from his base in Rome. Many of the popes during this period were more interested in secular rather than spiritual matters. There were frequent complaints about a number of abuses in the Church and the poor education and low standards of many of the clergy.
- *Protestantism (Christianity).* A religion that had splintered off from Catholicism. Up to the early sixteenth century there was only one accepted Christian faith in Europe: Roman Catholicism. In 1517 a German monk called Martin Luther produced a list of complaints of abuses in the Catholic Church. Followers of Luther believed that many of the doctrines and practices of the Catholic Church were unnecessary and 'faith' alone was all that was necessary in one's belief. His ideas spread quickly and Luther's

followers became known as 'Protestants' – a general term referring to anyone who 'protested' against the Catholic Church. The Lutherans were the first of these Protestant Churches. Later others formed such as the Calvinists. Luther and the Protestant German princes who supported his movement were to become a great problem for Charles V (Charles I of Spain). In the reign of Philip II it was the Protestants in the Netherlands who were to be the major problem.

- *Islam*. A follower of Islam is called a Muslim. There were different groups of Muslims in the mid-fifteenth century. The Muslims who lived in Spain were called Moors. In the east was the vast Ottoman Empire, also referred to as the Turkish Empire or Turkey. The Ottomans had overthrown the Byzantine Empire in 1453 when they had conquered Constantinople (present-day Istanbul). During the sixteenth century this powerful empire, under Suleiman the Magnificent, controlled vast areas, including much of southeast Europe, west Asia and north Africa. It struck fear into the heart of most of Christian western Europe.
- *Judaism*. A follower of Judaism is called a Jew. Many Christians in Europe considered Jews to be anti-Christian. By the mid-fifteenth century in Spain they were often treated as scapegoats for any wrongs in society. From time to time this led to massacres and forcible conversions to Christianity.

The growth of the Spanish Empire

▶ *Why did the Spanish Empire grow and what problems developed as a result?*

By the middle of the fifteenth century Castile was in a position from which it could become an important power in Europe. The marriage of Ferdinand of Aragon and Isabella of Castile in 1469 brought most of the peninsula under the same rulers. Other marriages were to further extend the Spanish Empire, or Monarchy, as it was called to distinguish it from the Holy Roman Empire (a collection of hundreds of states in the lands which today make up Germany and beyond). In 1496 two portentous marriages were arranged: those of two children of Ferdinand and Isabella with two children of the Holy Roman Emperor, Maximilian.

The Habsburg connection

Maximilian was the head of the Habsburg family, whose lands lay mainly in Austria. In 1438 a member of this family had become Holy Roman Emperor and from then on members of the family were to hold the title continuously. However, although the title brought prestige, it brought little influence. Power came from the lands the Habsburgs had acquired through a series of

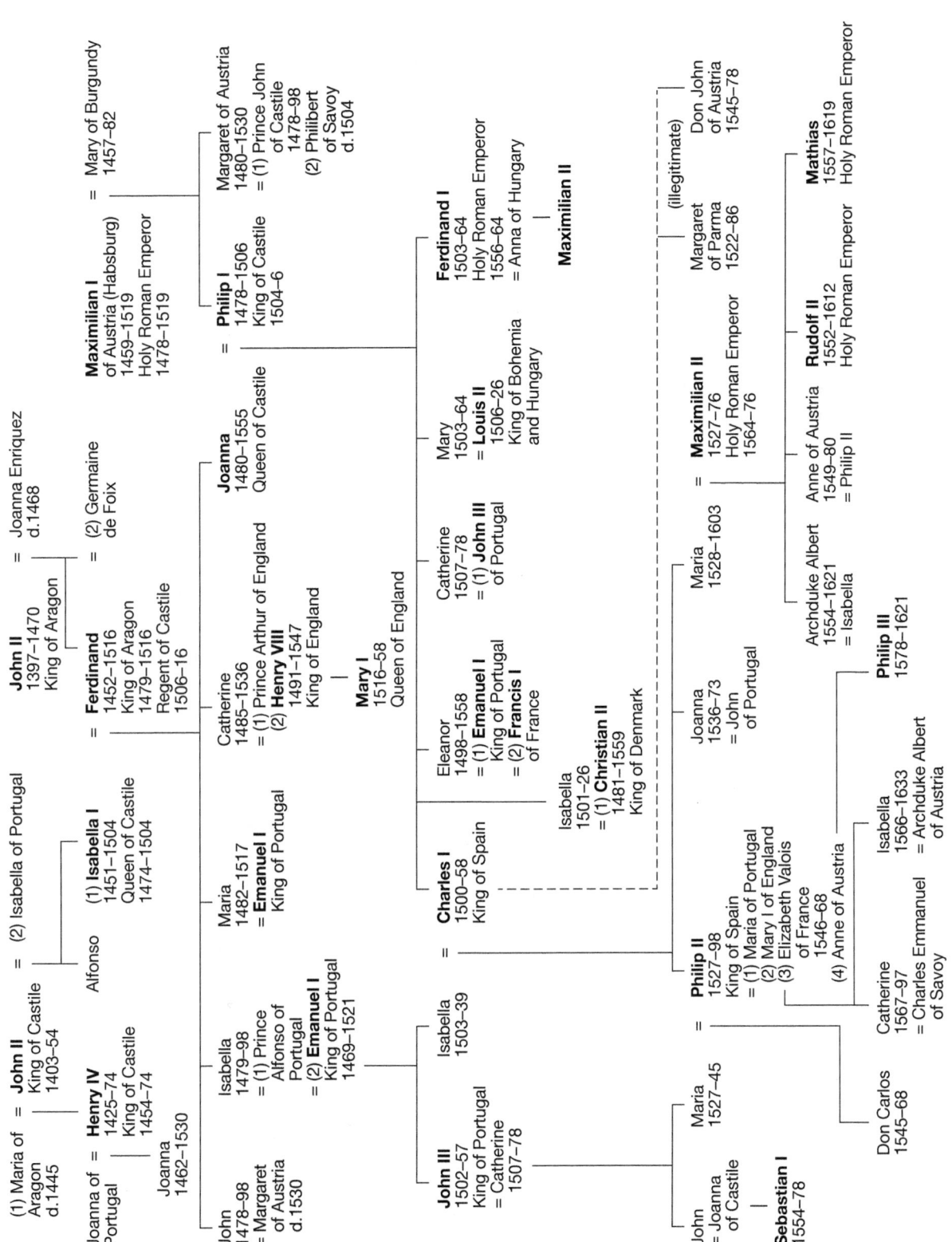

Figure 1.2 A family tree of the rulers of Spain.

advantageous marriage alliances. In 1477 Maximilian had married Mary of Burgundy. As a result, he had obtained much additional land, including Artois, Franche-Comté and the Netherlands.

The marriages of two of the Habsburg children to two of those of Ferdinand and Isabella were eventually to bring a Habsburg to the thrones of Aragon and Castile in the person of Charles I, who was also to inherit the Habsburg lands in northern and central Europe and thereby not only extended his empire considerably but also brought Spanish involvement in the affairs of northern Europe.

The inheritance of Philip II

Charles's son, Philip II, was to inherit the Habsburg lands in Italy, the Netherlands, Spain and Spain's empire in the **New World**, which had been discovered during the reign of Ferdinand and Isabella, and had grown considerably in size by the mid-sixteenth century. In addition, he became ruler of Portugal and acquired the vast Portuguese Empire in the east. Writers of the time commented on the vast extent of the Spanish Empire by the end of the sixteenth century (see Source B).

> **SOURCE B**
>
> **A Castilian's view, written in 1620, of the vast number of lands held by Philip.**
>
> *Now that to the Crown of Spain there have been added Aragon, Portugal, Navarre, and all that is beautiful and splendid in Italy, Flanders, Lombardy, the East and the West Indies, such that with its land and its sea it lies along the whole path of the sun and the sun is scarcely lost to view from this monarchy, now that it is superior in Territories, in riches, unequalled by those of Antiquity, superior in valour, loyalty, and the troth it keeps with its princes, and in firm religion and unswerving devotion to the church … the Ambassador of Spain has a patent claim everywhere and always to lay claim to precedence.*

The problems created by Spain's empire

The sheer size of the lands over which Charles and his successors ruled was to lead to difficulties. The increased power which it gave them led to the Habsburg name being feared and envied throughout this period by the other powers of Europe, particularly France. All countries in western Europe feared a Habsburg takeover. France felt particularly vulnerable as it was almost entirely surrounded by countries which were under Habsburg control. To the northeast were the Netherlands, to the east Franche-Comté and to the south-west Spain itself.

If the other European powers feared Habsburg domination, the Habsburg rulers felt it a matter of pride that they should not lose any of their **patrimony**. At all costs, the lands that they had inherited had to be held on to, and handed to their successors intact.

KEY TERMS

New World A name for the Americas, especially during the time of first exploration and colonisation of the region by Europeans; also called the Indies in contemporary sources.

Patrimony An inheritance or legacy handed down to someone.

? What does Source B show of the extent of Spanish power by the end of the sixteenth century?

Charles I of Spain becomes Holy Roman Emperor

Charles I had not just acquired territorial power. He had also become Holy Roman Emperor as Charles V. This had brought him the responsibility of defending the Roman Catholic religion both against the threat of Islam and against the growing threat of Protestantism even within the very lands over which he ruled.

The duty to defend the Roman Catholic religion against Islam, especially the **Ottoman Empire** ruled over by the Turks, was to have serious repercussions on the ability of the Habsburgs to defend their lands against other Christian rulers and against the Protestant threat. From the fourteenth century, the Ottoman Empire had expanded from Anatolia, into Europe via the Balkans, and into the Middle East via Palestine. In the early sixteenth century, under **Suleiman** the Magnificent, the Turks took the island of Rhodes. Control of the eastern Mediterranean was then theirs. On land they conquered part of Hungary and also controlled north Africa. On all sides the Habsburgs were therefore to feel the Islamic threat. The safety of their lands as well as the defence of the Roman Catholic religion demanded Habsburg action against both the followers of Islam and those of a growing Protestantism.

Defending the faith against Protestantism

At the same time, the growth of Protestantism forced the Habsburgs to strive for the purity of the faith within their own lands. Protection of that faith was a prime consideration in dealing with the component parts that made up their empire and failure to compromise led to long and costly struggles. As a result, the Habsburgs were involved in almost continuous warfare throughout the sixteenth century.

The importance of the army and navy

Defence of Habsburg territories and religion required an effective army and navy. The Habsburgs were generally fortunate in this respect. During the reign of Ferdinand and Isabella the 'Great Captain', Gonzalo de Córdoba, had created a professional army based on the infantry. At the core of this army were the Spanish troops who were to dominate warfare in Europe for much of the sixteenth century, under the skilled leadership of such commanders as the Duke of Alba, Don John of Austria and Alexander Farnese, Duke of Parma. Spain also made a major contribution to the navy, with the Netherlands and the Habsburg states in Italy, in particular Genoa, after contributing additional vessels.

KEY TERM

Ottoman Empire
The former Turkish (and largely Muslim) Empire in Europe, Asia and Africa, which lasted from the late thirteenth century until the end of the First World War.

KEY FIGURE

Suleiman I (1494–1566)
Sultan of the Ottoman Empire from 1520, was known as 'the Magnificent' in the west and 'the Lawgiver' in the east. His armies attacked Hungary, Belgrade and Rhodes before being stopped outside Vienna in 1529; his fleet dominated the eastern Mediterranean. Much of north Africa came under his rule.

The individual nature of each part of the empire

It must be remembered that the empire was never a Spanish one. Each realm considered itself an equal among the others and worthy of equal esteem from its ruler. For the people in each realm, the ruler was their king, their count or their duke. They were not interested in the wider aspects of his rule beyond their realm. Each part of the empire had a different history. Each part had developed different methods of government and had different rights and privileges in relation to its ruler. Their only common elements were loyalty to the ruler and loyalty to the Roman Catholic faith.

At the centre: Castile

In practice, the base of the Spanish Empire became Castile, which was to become under Charles I the most loyal and obedient province in the empire. From the time of Philip II, Madrid became the centre of Habsburg rule and the king was rarely to leave the city. Castile alone bore the high cost of the royal court. Its economic position meant that it could, at least in the sixteenth century, provide much of the financial support needed by the Crown. It was also able until the end of the century to provide much of the manpower needed for the army and navy. The cost to Castile was high. In return, it gained the expensive symbols of royalty – fine buildings, works of art and the elaborate ceremony of the court; and the pride that it was at the heart of one of the greatest empires ever known.

Summary diagram: Keys to understanding Spain 1474–1598

Geography	• Borders on the Pyrenees and Portugal • Mountainous country with different climates • Limit to the areas that can be cultivated for food crops • Tradition of maritime trade
History	• A Roman province • Conquered by Muslims in the eighth century • Gradual north-to-south *Reconquista* by Christians, starting in the tenth century • By the thirteenth century, only Granada remained under Muslim rule • Aragon developed a small empire in the Mediterranean
Religion	• In the mid-fifteenth century Christianity, Judaism and Islam coexisted (*convivencia*)
Politics	• Crown of Castile was unified (one *Cortes*, one language, one coinage, administration and economy) • Crown of Aragon was made up of three separate kingdoms. Aragon, Catalonia and Valencia each had their own laws, *Cortes*, *fueros* and economies
Events	• 1469 – Isabella of Castile married Ferdinand of Aragon • 1474 and 1479 – each became monarch of their respective, separate, realms • Castile and Aragon united by the inheritance of the Habsburg Charles I but remain separate realms
Growth of the Spanish Empire: fifteenth and sixteenth centuries	**Added during the reign of Ferdinand and Isabella (1474–1516):** • Granada 1492 • New World discoveries 1492 onwards • Cerdagne and Roussillon 1493 • Navarre 1515 **Added during the reign of Charles I (1516–56):** • Habsburg lands: north and central Europe, including the Netherlands **During the reign of Philip II (1456–98), consisting of:** • Spain, Italy, Netherlands, New World • Portugal and its empire 1581

 Refresher questions

1 What geographical features of Spain would have an effect on its history?
2 What was the Reconquest?
3 By the mid-fifteenth century what did Aragon's overseas empire consist of?
4 What were the *Cortes*, and how were they different in Aragon and in Castile?
5 What territories are included under the umbrella term 'Crown of Aragon'?
6 What three religious groups were established in Spain in the mid-fifteenth century?
7 Why did many Christians become hostile to Jews and Muslims?
8 Who were the *conversos* or 'new' Christians?
9 Who were the Habsburgs? How extensive was their power in Europe?
10 What was significant about a Habsburg becoming King of Spain?
11 How much unity was there within the Spanish Empire in the mid-fifteenth century?

CHAPTER 2

Ferdinand and Isabella: Castile and Aragon 1479–1516

From the time of her marriage to Ferdinand in 1469, Isabella strove to ensure that she would be recognised as heir to the Crown of Castile. On the death of her half-brother Henry IV in 1474 she proclaimed herself queen. Ferdinand himself became King of Aragon in 1475. The two monarchs were able to secure the throne of Castile for Isabella against attempts to overthrow her and then laid a firm groundwork for establishing their rule. For many Spaniards then and now, it was a 'golden age' in Spanish history. The chapter first considers the marriage and succession to the throne of Castile of Isabella and then considers the problems that Isabella and her husband Ferdinand met and how successfully they dealt with them – in government and administration, finance and religious policies. The chapter examines these themes under the following headings:

★ Securing the throne 1469–79
★ The Granada War 1482–92
★ Government and administration under Isabella and Ferdinand
★ Religion in the reigns of Isabella and Ferdinand

Key dates

1462–72	Revolt in the kingdom of Catalonia	1478	Establishment of Spanish Inquisition
1468	Ferdinand became King of Sicily in his own right (as Ferdinand II)		Ferdinand became King of Aragon on his father's death
1469	Isabella, half-sister and heir to King of Castile, married Ferdinand, son and heir to King of Aragon	1482–92	Granada War
		1492	Expulsion or conversion of all the Jews in Castile and Aragon
1474	Death of King Henry IV of Castile	1499	Muslims in Granada had to convert or leave
	Isabella proclaimed herself Queen of Castile		
	War of Succession between Isabella and Joanna, daughter of King Henry IV of Castile	1502	Muslims in Castile had to convert or leave
		1504	Death of Isabella
			Joanna Queen of Castile and Archduke Philip of Austria ruled Castile
1475	Ferdinand defeated the King of Portugal in Battle of Toro	1506	Death of Philip
1478	Birth of only son John to Isabella and Ferdinand	1507	Ferdinand returned to Castile and became regent

Securing the throne 1469–79

▶ How united were Aragon and Castile at the time of Isabella and Ferdinand's marriage in 1469?

▶ How did Isabella manage to secure the throne of Castile?

The marriage between Isabella and Ferdinand of Aragon

On 19 October 1469, the eighteen-year-old Isabella, half-sister and heir to the King of Castile, secretly married her cousin, the seventeen-year-old Ferdinand, son and heir to the King of Aragon. The events leading to the marriage read like something from a novel – Ferdinand making his way in disguise with only a small escort to Valladolid, where the marriage was to take place; Isabella acting against her half-brother Henry's wishes, in arranging her marriage with Ferdinand. This is not to imply it was a love match. The two had never met before. Both must have felt that the marriage would bolster their chances of becoming rulers in Castile and Aragon, respectively.

The marriage contract between Isabella and Ferdinand was important. It stated how they each would play a part in the government of the kingdoms of Aragon and Castile. Ferdinand's authority in Castile had clear limits:

- He was to respect the customs of Castile; all appointments and decisions were to be in accordance with Isabella's wishes.
- He was to live in Castile and support the policy of reconquering land from the Moors.
- All public decisions were to bear the signatures of both partners.

The contract aimed to dispel fears that an Aragonese was taking over in Castile and would use the kingdom's money and resources to finance Aragonese, rather than Castilian, interests. In fact, after Isabella's coronation in 1474 the terms were slightly modified to make Ferdinand more of an equal in Castile:

- The two monarchs were to dispense justice jointly.
- In 1475 Isabella granted Ferdinand power to act without her in Castile, as though she was present.

Isabella retained considerable powers for herself, however. She alone could grant gifts and favours to the nobles and towns and cities in Castile. She alone was responsible for the administration of Castile and its territories. Isabella needed Ferdinand to secure her rule in Castile, but she was determined that his role would not overshadow her own there.

SOURCE A

? Looking at Source A, and bearing in mind that Isabella and Ferdinand were very conscious of how they were seen as monarchs, what image does each portrait create of the two rulers?

Portraits of King Ferdinand of Aragon (left, painted by the Master of the Legend of St Madeleine c.1500) and Queen Isabella of Castile (right, painted in the sixteenth century by an unknown artist).

The situation in 1469

Both kingdoms were suffering from the effects of civil war. In Castile the nobles had been disputing the power of King Henry IV since 1464. In Aragon, the kingdom of Catalonia had revolted against the rule of Ferdinand's father, **John II**, in 1462. This revolt would not be defeated until ten years later. There was no guarantee, therefore, that either of the newly-weds would succeed to their respective kingdoms. This was particularly the case with Isabella, whose half-brother, King **Henry IV**, had a daughter, Joanna. It was, however, widely believed that Joanna was illegitimate, and Henry had agreed to acknowledge Isabella as his heir. However, his anger at her marriage with Ferdinand led him to acknowledge his young daughter Joanna instead of Isabella. The situation was made more difficult in that Henry did not leave a final will naming his successor.

The fight for the Crown of Castile

When Henry died in 1474 Isabella proclaimed herself Queen of Castile. At the time, Ferdinand was in Aragon and she acted on her own initiative without consulting him. Her proclamation said that she was Queen of Castile and that Ferdinand was her consort. She had been building up her support for the throne over a number of years and she acted first to assume power in Castile. She was proclaimed queen in the important city of Segovia, where one of her supporters controlled the royal treasury.

KEY FIGURES

John II of Aragon (1398–1479)

Ferdinand's father, who in later years would come into conflict with both his Aragonese and Catalan subjects, and with the French king.

Henry IV of Castile (1425–74)

Isabella's half-brother, who ruled during a time of conflict in Castile. It is difficult to establish the facts of his reign because of the propaganda used against him after his death, particularly about the illegitimacy of his daughter Joanna. Historians are now confident that she was legitimate.

At the same time, Joanna also claimed the throne. She, too, had some support in Castile. To strengthen her claim, Joanna became engaged to King Alfonso V of Portugal. A War of Succession broke out in 1475 between the supporters of Joanna and those of Isabella. It took five years for Isabella, with the help of Ferdinand, to gain control of all Castile.

How Isabella gained support

Isabella showed her determination and capabilities in securing the throne for herself. She was supported by a number of the **grandees** such as the **Mendoza family**. In addition, she worked hard to win over those grandees and other nobles who had originally supported Joanna by offering them amnesty and:

- new grants of lands
- grants of titles and royal offices, confirmed or newly given
- reaffirmation of their right to collect financial grants awarded by the Crown since 1464.

Isabella felt obligated to confirm the privileges of loyal nobles. She also secured the backing of large numbers of Castilian cities and towns, for example Toledo, by such means as confirming their privileges. When necessary she was prepared to use force, as when she gained Cordoba. This strategy to gain support worked and the number of defections by supporters of Joanna's camp increased as time went on.

Isabella was also fortunate in the support she received from Ferdinand. His ability in war made him a successful leader of her forces. Like Isabella, he travelled the country galvanising support for their cause. He fortified key strategic points and had an important victory in the Battle of Toro in 1476 over Portuguese forces. In contrast, Alfonso of Portugal failed to show the leadership and military strategy necessary to enable Joanna to replace Isabella. His loss at Toro signified the end of his efforts.

Joanna, following the failure of her claim, went into a convent in Portugal, there to remain for the rest of her life, 'unmarried and a nun'. In the same year, 1479, Ferdinand's father died. Ferdinand and Isabella were now the rulers of Aragon and Castile, respectively.

The qualities which Ferdinand and Isabella brought to their rule

Ferdinand, though one year younger than his wife, had much more experience of politics and military affairs, particularly beyond Spain. As king, he was to prove skilful and pragmatic in his handling of political matters, being described by one contemporary writer as never preaching: 'anything except peace and good faith: and he is an enemy of both one and the other, and if he had ever honoured either of them he would have lost either his standing or his state many times over'.

KEY TERMS

Grandee A Spanish nobleman of the highest rank. During the reign of Charles I the number of grandees was limited to 25.

Mendoza family One of the most powerful families in Spain, a number of whose members held important positions in government during the fifteenth and sixteenth centuries.

In war Ferdinand was to display personal bravery and a capacity for inspiring those who fought under him. Although he was pious, he was not as extreme in religious matters as his wife Isabella. As well as being pious, she was determined and energetic. A critical writer of the time, Alfonso de Palencia, described her as the 'mistress of dissimulations and deceits'. Perhaps, though, it was these aspects of her personality that enabled her to become ruler of Castile and succeed as its queen. She also worked closely with the historians of her reign, such as Hernando del Pulgar, to ensure that her subjects had a positive image of her character and achievements. Isabella inspired loyalty and respect, both at the time and in historians looking back at her reign.

The marriage partnership of Ferdinand and Isabella

The two monarchs were king and queen of Aragon and Castile, not of Spain. The union was a personal one. As we have seen above, their marriage contract made it clear that Isabella alone was the 'rightful heir to these kingdoms of Castile and León'. Ferdinand was given little personal power in Castile, apart from that allowed him by Isabella. All appointments had to have Isabella's agreement, and Ferdinand had to respect the traditions of Castile. Any children of the marriage had to be educated in Castile. Isabella in her turn was given little say in the running of the kingdom of Aragon.

In practice, the partnership seems to have been successful. Ferdinand and Isabella in general worked closely and in harmony. The heads of both appeared on seals and coins. The arms of both kingdoms appeared together on banners. The initials of both monarchs were engraved on their furniture and personal possessions. Both monarchs signed royal decrees and both were responsible for ecclesiastical and administrative appointments. Isabella also made sure that Ferdinand played an active part in the governing of Castile and much of the conduct of the foreign policy of both Aragon and Castile was left to him. So close was their working relationship that **Hernando del Pulgar** made an imaginary report that 'on such and such a day, the king and queen gave birth to a daughter'.

It was important for monarchs of the time to have children, particularly sons, to secure the succession. A daughter, Isabella, was born in 1470 and a son, John, was born in 1478, and then three more girls: Joanna 1479, Maria 1482 and Catherine 1485. Their births cemented Ferdinand's and Isabella's positions on their thrones. The children were also to prove useful in marriage treaties with foreign countries (see Figure 1.2, page 9).

It was clear from the start that each kingdom was still to be administered independently. Each was to retain its own form of government, keep its own language (mainly Castilian in Castile and Catalan in the Crown of Aragon), and its own laws and customs. Moreover, virtually nothing was done to bring the economies of the two kingdoms into closer union. Trade remained difficult

 **KEY FIGURE**

Hernando del Pulgar (1436–c.92)

A councillor of state under Isabella and historiographer-royal. His work is usually considered to be propaganda on behalf of Isabella and Ferdinand although it is also critical of some of their policies.

with the continuance of internal customs barriers between the two realms. If a merchant wished to bring his goods across the frontier between Aragon and Castile, he would have to pay duties on them. Even more divisive was the fact that, once exploration of the New World opened up new markets for goods to and from America, only those who lived in Castile were allowed to participate – much to the annoyance of the experienced Catalan merchants. By contrast, the economic unity brought about by improvements to the roads which went across both realms was of little significance.

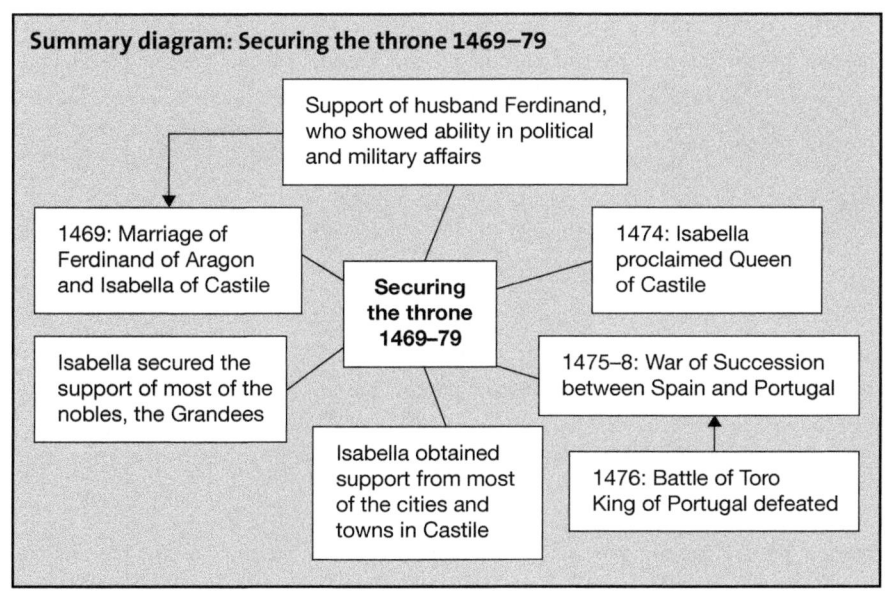

2 The Granada War 1482–92

▶ *What were the effects of Isabella and Ferdinand's victory in the Granada War?*

The marriage of Isabella and Ferdinand at least brought an end to possible conflict between the kingdoms of Aragon and Castile. The monarchs could now give attention to the last non-Christian kingdom in the Iberian Peninsula, Granada (see Figure 1.1, page 5).

Ferdinand and Isabella decide to conquer Granada

Border warfare had taken place on the frontier between Castile and Granada for many years. Raids and counter-raids continued even during periods of truce. In 1481, the capture by Moors of a frontier town in Andalusia gave the two monarchs an excuse for a military campaign against Granada.

Ferdinand and Isabella stressed the importance of the crusading aspect of the war. It was a chance to complete the Reconquest and bring the whole of the Iberian Peninsula under Christian rule, although this idea took shape only as the war progressed. In 1481 the monarchs were talking of making war 'on the Moors from every direction'. Contemporary letters refer to the Granada War as a crusade and the monarchs as taking 'on the holy expedition with the intention rather to spread abroad the religion of Christ than to increase their earthly empire'. To finance the war effort, the pope allowed the monarchs to keep the *cruzada* and granted **indulgences** to allow them to raise more money. His gift of a large silver cross was carried by the army throughout the war. The chains of Christian captives freed during the war were hung up in churches 'to be revered by successive generations as the trophies of Christian warfare'. It is likely, though, that other factors were involved, especially on Ferdinand's part. Conquest of Granada would improve national security for Castile; there would be additional land and trade available for Castilians, and the two monarchs would have ensured that the whole of Spain was under Christian rule.

KEY TERMS

Cruzada A tax, or money offering, which was earmarked for the Christian crusades against Muslims.

Indulgences The remission granted by the Church of the temporal punishment due to sins already forgiven, for example, penitents who had been given a great number of prayers to recite as their (earthly) punishment could have this reduced by receiving an indulgence.

Hermandad A local peace-keeping force (plural *Hermandades*).

Mudéjars Muslims living under Christian rule.

The war lasted ten years. Men came to join the army from all over the Spanish lands. It was an expensive struggle as supplies and troops had to be paid for. In addition to funding from the Church, Ferdinand and Isabella had to increase taxation on the towns and ***Hermandad*** (which also supplied troops) and take out loans. Many of the nobility supplied forces. In 1489 Cardinal Mendoza, for example, supplied 1000 horse and 1000 foot soldiers. The armed conflict ended with the capture of the city of Granada in 1492.

Reasons for the victory

A number of factors contributed to this eventual victory. Conquest was made easier by the fact that the rulers of Granada were divided among themselves. In addition, little help was received from other Muslim states (particularly those in north Africa). On the Christian side, the nobles of Andalusia, the area of Castile nearest to Granada, played a significant part in the victory. They knew the area well and had experience in dealing with their Moorish opponents. The personal presence of the two monarchs helped to encourage their forces. Ferdinand was in charge of the campaign and Isabella made sure that supplies reached the armies. The use of heavy artillery by the Christian forces was crucial, as it enabled them to end sieges in weeks rather than months. One Muslim contemporary had no doubt about its importance in at least one campaign: 'the Christian disposed of cannons with which he launched firebombs. These projectiles were one of the causes for the abandonment of the places on which they fell.'

The results of the war

In spite of the length and cost of the war, the treaty which ended it was generous to the defeated. Moors, or rather ***Mudéjars*** as they were now called, were allowed to keep their own religion, dress, customs and property. Those who

SOURCE B

The Capitulation of Granada, painted in 1882 by Francisco Pradilla Ortiz.

> The painting in Source B was commissioned by the Spanish government of the time. How far is it likely to be a true representation of the event depicted? What do you think this painting is intended to show?

wished to emigrate were able, and even encouraged, to do so. Out of the original half a million Moors in Granada, 100,000 died during the fighting or were enslaved, 200,000 emigrated and about 200,000 remained.

The conquest of Granada was welcomed throughout Christendom. Other rulers in Europe sent their congratulations. The pope gave Ferdinand and Isabella the title of 'Catholic Monarchs'. 'Will there ever be an age so thankless as will not hold you in eternal gratitude?', wrote one contemporary. The victory had increased the monarchs' prestige among the other countries of Europe. It had assured them of their positions on their thrones. The use of artillery had been considerably developed during the course of the war against the Moors and was to become a fixture in future wars. The conquest of Granada had also helped to bring some feeling of unity to the peoples of Castile and Aragon. Men had come from all over the two kingdoms to fight together against their common enemy:

SOURCE C

From Peter Martyr of Anghiera, an Italian-born historian of Spain, on the Christian army, quoted in Henry Kamen, *Spain 1469–1714*, Pearson, 2005.

Who would have thought that the Galician, the proud Asturian and the rude inhabitant of the Pyrenees, would be mixing freely with Toledans, people of La Mancha, and Andalusians, living together in harmony and obedience, like members of one family, speaking the same language and subject to one common discipline?

> Why did it seem a surprise to the writer of Source C that those fighting the Moors were 'like members of one family'?

KEY FIGURE

Iñigo Lopez de Mendoza (c.1440–1515)

Second Count of Tendilla, first Marquis of Mondéjar; fought in Granada War, became papal ambassador and later governor of Granada.

Lopez de Mendoza, Count of Tendilla and later Marquis of Mondéjar, was made governor. He proved to be a successful choice. The Crown took over most of the land made available by the deaths or emigration of Muslims. There was an influx of peasants from Andalusia to settle in Granada. This enabled some continuity but the newcomers did not arrive in sufficient numbers to replace the Moors who emigrated. There was also a loss of trade to northern Africa.

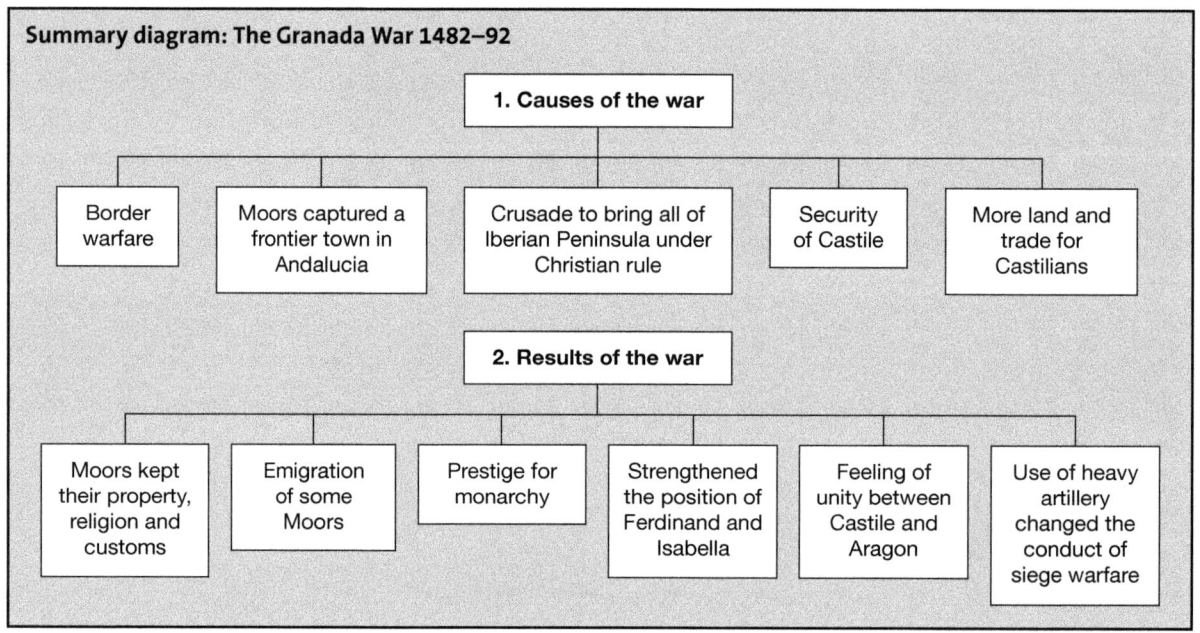

③ Government and administration under Isabella and Ferdinand

▶ *How successful were Ferdinand and Isabella in their government of Castile and Aragon?*

Efficient working of the government and administration was necessary to ensure peace within the Crowns of Castile and Aragon and to ensure that enough money was raised to meet the monarchs' expenditure.

The establishment of peace and order in Castile and Aragon

Isabella and Ferdinand ruled according to the customs already established in the kingdoms that made up Castile and Aragon. Their main aim, as stated in their own documents, seems to have been to establish a 'pre-eminent monarchy'. What this implies is that they strove to create a strong position for the Crown which would enable them to ensure justice and order in Castile and Aragon, but at the same time they were prepared to respect the rights and customs of the individual kingdoms. One of their first considerations as rulers was, therefore, the establishment of an effective system of justice and order. They put most effort into achieving this in Castile which, from early in the reign, seems to have been considered by both monarchs as the more important of their kingdoms.

Personal presence

Ferdinand and Isabella created order in part by their personal presence. This was the method by which they ensured peace in their kingdoms. In this way, they behaved like medieval rulers. As monarchs, they were constantly on the move, going from one part of their kingdoms to another. Thus, Isabella visited every part of Castile at least once, over a period of some 30 years. Ferdinand spent more time in Castile than in Aragon. Therefore, viceroys who were usually close family members were appointed to govern in Aragon in his place. There was no fixed court. The monarchs' officials and advisers travelled with them. This usually enabled them to be in any place where there might be problems. They could then arbitrate in disputes, hear lawsuits and deal personally with revolts.

Use of *Hermandades*

Another means of control was through the *Hermandades*. These were brotherhoods which had been used in several Castilian towns in the past to keep the peace.

In 1476, an *Hermandad* was set up in every place with more than 50 inhabitants. They were controlled directly by the Crown through a *Santa Hermandad* which co-ordinated the work of the individual *Hermandades*. They were meant to be a temporary measure brought in to deal with the troubles of the time. However, they remained in place until 1498. The *Hermandades* provided Ferdinand and Isabella with soldiers and regularly contributed money to finance the fighting in the civil war and the Granada War. Their main task, though, was to police the towns and villages, including the neighbouring countryside. The *Hermandades* also tried people for certain crimes such as robbery, murder and arson. The punishments they doled out were often severe and included mutilation and death. Even for the time, their brand of justice was seen as harsh; a royal physician, Lopez de Villalobos, described it in this way:

> In Source D, how does this writer justify the use of such 'rough' justice by the *Hermandades*?

SOURCE D

From Marvin Lunenfeld, *The Council of the Santa Hermandad*, University of Miami Press, 1979.

... justice was so severe that it appeared to be cruelty, but it was necessary because all the kingdoms had not been pacified, nor had the dominions of tyrants and haughty men been abased. And because of this there was much veritable butchery of men with the cutting off of feet, hands, shoulders, and heads, without sparing or disguising the rigours of justice.

By the time the *Hermandades* were disbanded in 1498, they had done much to bring the localities in Castile to law and order. However, there were limitations to their success. They could only deal with small disorders; other law officials disliked them impinging on their own jurisdiction; and their financial contributions to the Crown were seen as a burden. It was difficult therefore to introduce them into all parts of the country. The nobility in the kingdom of Aragon resented the imposition of an *Hermandad* in the cities of Aragon, and, though they were introduced here, they were very short lived.

Use of *corregidores* in Castilian towns

The Catholic Monarchs made their presence felt in many of the towns in Castile. They continued and expanded the policy, started in the fourteenth century, of sending out ***corregidores*** (or civil governors). They appointed one in every important town in Castile. The *corregidores* collected taxes, reported to the Crown on the state of affairs in the area; and tried to ensure that the councils followed royal policies and that royal jurisdiction was not interfered with by members of the Church or the nobility. Other royal officials were sent out to check on the work that the *corregidores* were doing. These were local officials whose salaries were met by the towns themselves and were, therefore, very much resented.

KEY TERM

Corregidores Crown governors appointed to Castilian towns.

Relations with the nobility

Many of the disturbances in the past had been due to the civil wars in which the nobles had played a major part. Measures were, therefore, taken to bring these nobles to heel. Troublesome ones were arrested, their castles were burned and much of their property was taken from them. The Crown also tried to recover rights and lands it had previously lost. At the *Cortes* of Toledo in 1480, almost all royal lands lost since 1464 were returned to the Crown. However, the nobles were to keep those which had been lost before that date. The Crown gave compensation for the ones it reclaimed in the conquests of the Granada War. The important coastal cities of Cartagena and Cádiz, which helped to protect the southern coast, were taken under royal control, and the nobles who had previously held these cities were granted other towns as compensation. In addition, nobles were forbidden to make private war or to build new castles. Those nobles who had the right to collect the royal tax of **alcabala** within their jurisdictions were allowed to continue to be able to collect this lucrative tax.

However, such measures were limited. As we have seen above (page 17), to secure the support of the majority of nobles to her side in the War of Succession, Isabella had had to make concessions to the nobility. Security in Spain meant working with the nobles rather than against them. Steps were, therefore, taken to try to ensure the support of the nobles. Ferdinand and Isabella encouraged the titled nobility to spend time at their court. Opportunities were given to nobles to serve in foreign wars. Support for the Crown led to rewards, and many new titles were created. The Crown also supported the efforts of nobles to remain economically viable. The nobles were encouraged to use the **mayorazgo**, which forbade sales or division of land. This meant that property and land could descend from one generation to another without being divided into smaller pieces and this helped to prevent disputes within families.

The Crown extended its hold over the military orders in Castile. These were orders of chivalry made up of knights bound by religious vows. The three in Castile – Santiago, Calatrava and Alcantara – were a group of importance. They owned large estates and received much wealth which made them extremely powerful. Isabella was determined, therefore, that they should come under the control of the Crown. This was achieved when Ferdinand became grand master of each of the orders. The Crown thus increased its income considerably. In 1489 a council was set up specifically for the administration of the orders.

The nobles, particularly those in Castile, were prepared to accept the rule of the two monarchs. One contemporary view indicates why this might be:

SOURCE E

A contemporary view of the court of Ferdinand and Isabella.

They kept a great household and court, accompanied by Grandees and leading barons, whom they honoured and elevated according to the quality of their degree, keeping them occupied in ways wherein they could be of service, and when occasion arose, mindful to serve in the government of the kingdom and the Royal Council. The monarchs were most careful to place men of prudence and ability to serve, even though such were of the middling sort rather than great men from the noblest houses.

> **KEY TERMS**
>
> **Alcabala** A sales tax, usually ten per cent.
>
> **Mayorazgo** The inheritance of an estate by a single person.

> How does Source E show that Ferdinand and Isabella tried to secure the support of the nobles in Castile?

Administration

Ferdinand and Isabella ruled the kingdoms of Castile and Aragon through royal councils.

The conciliar system

Many of the 'middling sort' referred to in Source E (page 25) were to sit on the various councils which made up the central administration of the government. The main council was the Royal Council of Castile. It consisted of five parts or chambers, dealing separately with:

- foreign policy
- justice
- the *Hermandades* (which were disbanded in 1498)
- finance
- the group of nobles and **letrados**, 'people mid-way between the great and the small whose profession was to study law', from Aragon, Catalonia, Majorca, Valencia and Sicily. In 1494, this last became a council in its own right – the Council of Aragon.

Further, new councils were formed: in 1483 that of the Supreme Inquisition (often referred to as the *Suprema*) and in 1489 that of the Council of Orders (to deal with the military orders). A group met from at least 1509 to discuss matters relating to the new lands claimed by Castile in the Americas; this 'Council of the Indies' was formally established in 1524.

There was nothing essentially new about this system. The conciliar system had been established early in the century in Castile. What the two monarchs did was to increase the number of councils to meet their growing responsibilities. The use of *letrados* can also be traced to the time before the reign of Isabella, although their numbers increased during her reign. By 1493 all members of the royal council had to be *letrados*, with at least ten years' study of law at university.

KEY TERMS

Letrados Lawyers, usually with two academic degrees and ten years' legal experience.

Ordinances Decrees issued by the monarchs.

Pragmaticas Laws which the two monarchs had issued without going through the *Cortes* of Castile but which still had to be obeyed by the inhabitants of Castile.

Audiencia A court of appeal.

Law and order

Attempts were also made by Ferdinand and Isabella to increase their control over justice. This was difficult even in Castile because of the local rights and powers of the nobles and the Church. In 1489 **ordinances** were issued establishing a permanent court at Valladolid. Further permanent courts were later established in Granada, Santiago de Compostela and Seville. The first two were considered the most important and appeals from these went to the Council of Castile, the highest court. Both criminal and civil cases were tried by the courts. Attempts were made to ensure that similar laws were in operation throughout Castile. Collections of all the late medieval law codes and the *pragmaticas* of the Catholic Monarchs were published. A different system operated in the Crown of Aragon. Here, each of the kingdoms that made up Aragon had its own *audiencia* to try cases. In the kingdom of Aragon a *justicia* was independent of the Crown and his court was, therefore, usually considered to be the protector of the *fueros* and liberties of Aragon.

The *Cortes*

Each of the Spanish kingdoms had its own *Cortes* (see page 6). These were usually called by Ferdinand and Isabella when they needed money and to confirm royal legislation. They also provided the monarchs with another means of hearing any potential grievances from the representatives who attended the *Cortes*. Looking back at the reign of Isabella and Ferdinand in 1520, representatives in the Castilian *Cortes* were able to say 'The Catholic Monarchs did and ordered in their *Cortes* many excellent things for the welfare of these realms.'

The *Cortes* in Castile generally consisted of only seventeen towns (plus Granada after 1492), each of which could send two representatives to a meeting. Neither the nobility nor the clergy usually attended, although they had the right to do so. As the main business of the *Cortes* was to vote for taxes, and these two groups were exempt from taxes, they would not have seen much need to attend. The Castilian *Cortes* did not meet at all between 1482 and 1498. This was probably because Isabella was able to obtain soldiers and money from the *Hermandad* and so did not need to ask the *Cortes* for funds. After 1498, until the end of the reign, the Cortes met twelve times (out of a total of sixteen times during the reign).

In the three *Cortes* of Aragon, it was expected that grievances would be discussed before any money was granted. This gave them considerable power. These powers were shown in 1488 when strong opposition to the *Hermandad* in the kingdom of Aragon led to the suspension of the *Hermandad* there and its final suppression in the 1495 *Cortes*.

Finances

Ferdinand and Isabella had to have money in order to secure their position. At the beginning of the reign obtaining finance was a considerable problem. Not only was Spain a poor country but the civil wars of the 1470s had made the normal income from taxes difficult to collect. In 1477 this income stood at 27 million **maravedís**. Most of it was raised from the *alcabala*, and the rest from such sources as customs. Instead of having official tax collectors, Ferdinand and Isabella accepted lump sum payments from tax farmers, who paid for the right to collect the taxes.

 **KEY TERM**

Maravedís A copper coin which was the lowest measure of Castilian money and the most used.

Money was needed mainly for the court, the army and the ambassadors who were a vital part of the monarchy's foreign policy. Ferdinand and Isabella did not pay out lavish sums on a fixed court and did not spend excessively on themselves. However, a certain amount of expenditure was necessary if the monarchs were to be seen as greater in status than their subjects. In addition, large sums had to be spent on the upkeep of royal residences and on foreign ambassadors. In the last ten years of Isabella's reign, in Castile 75 million *maravedís* were spent on ambassadors. From 1482 onwards there was also much more involvement in warfare. The cost of the royal militia and ordnance (military equipment) consequently rose from 20 million in that year to 80 million in 1504. The wars fought against France in Italy and in Roussillon (see Figure 1.1, page 5) cost an exorbitant amount. Ferdinand's foreign policy also involved expensive royal marriage alliances.

The methods used by Ferdinand and Isabella to raise money

Financing the regime's administration required more than ordinary income. Aragon was able to contribute only a small amount. This meant that the burden for raising money fell on Castile. The finance for the war in Granada had been largely met from Church sources, but other methods still had to be found for the rest. Attempts were made to make the collection of taxes more efficient. These were only partially successful. Revenue from customs duties increased as trade improved. However, it was in the extraordinary sources of income that the real change came. These increased by 66 per cent compared with earlier reigns. The military orders, the *Hermandad*, papal grants and loans all contributed much. Most of the money came from the large sums voted by the Castilian *Cortes* in special taxes, amounting to almost 300 million *maravedís* in the years 1500–4 alone. However, although income increased it was still not enough to meet the increased expenditure. Ferdinand and Isabella then had to resort to loans, many from the Spanish nobles themselves. The repayments were made at ten per cent interest in the form of ***juros***. These repayments soon became a financial burden to the Crown, not just to Ferdinand and Isabella, but also, and even more so, to their successors.

> **KEY TERM**
>
> ***Juros*** Bonds (paid as annuities) issued by the Crown to cover the costs of its military campaigns.

Summary diagram: Government and administration under Isabella and Ferdinand

Peace and order through:	Central administration through:	Justice through:	Finance		
			Expenditure	Income	
				Ordinary:	Extraordinary:
• Personal presence • Use of *Hermandades* • Use of *corregidores* • Improving relations with nobility • Control over military orders	Conciliar system: • Royal Council of Castile Councils for: • Foreign policy • Justice • *Hermandades* • Finance • Aragon • Supreme Inquisition • Orders • Indies	• Permanent courts in Castile • *Audiencia* in Aragon • Collection of all laws and *pragmatas*	• Court • Ambassadors • Militia • Wars • Armaments • Troops • Royal marriage alliances	• *Alcabala* • Custom duties	• Military orders • *Hermandades* • Castilian *Cortes* • Papal grants • Loans

4 Religion in the reigns of Isabella and Ferdinand

▶ *How successful were the religious policies of Ferdinand and Isabella?*

The former Muslim kingdom of Granada had been defeated and become part of Castile. The religious climate in Spain was changing. The old ***convivencia*** whereby Christians, Muslims and Jews had lived and worked together was becoming less acceptable to many in Spain, in particular in Castile. In addition, concerns were being raised about how far the *conversos* were practising their Jewish customs and faith in secret. There were also issues on how effective the Spanish Church itself was in the way Christianity was organised and practised within the Spanish kingdoms.

The Spanish Church

Isabella and Ferdinand were dissatisfied with the condition of the Spanish Church. They wanted to improve the spiritual condition of the clergy and **laity**. To enable this to happen the monarchs needed to reform the education and training of the clergy (the bishops, ordinary clergy and members of the monastic orders).

The two monarchs gained a number of powers for the Church in Spain from the pope which, they thought, would help them to implement reforms. Ferdinand and Isabella succeeded in gaining the pope's agreement to their making all the Church appointments in Granada and the Canaries (1486). In America, they not only held this right but could also sack clergy and raise taxes from the Church. Within Spain they managed to secure some degree of nomination rights over the appointment of bishops. They also prevented most appeals going to the pope. Less successful, however, were their attempts to reduce the legal rights of the clergy. This meant that the clergy could continue to insist on being tried for any crime before a Church court, improving the chances that, if found guilty, they would receive a much lighter sentence than in a royal court.

Attempts to improve the education, training and practices of the clergy

The Crown used its ability to appoint bishops to ensure that those appointed would set a good example. Bishops were required to be resident in their sees and to encourage reform. Some of the new appointees were of non-noble origin and so less likely to engage in war than many of the bishops from noble backgrounds. New colleges were set up especially for the education of the higher clergy. A number of the bishops, such as Talavera and **Cisneros** (see also page 87), tried to ensure that measures were taken against clergy for living with women, for not residing at the post to which they were appointed (non-residence), and for wearing unsuitable dress. They also tried to improve

> **KEY TERMS**
>
> **Convivencia** The coexistence of Christians, Jews and Muslims in medieval Spain.
>
> **Laity** People who are not clergy.

> **KEY FIGURE**
>
> **Cardinal Francisco Ximénez de Cisneros (1436–1517)**
> A man of great religious zeal and personal austerity. He became Isabella's confessor in 1492, Archbishop of Toledo 1495, cardinal and Inquisitor General 1507 and was twice regent of Castile. He was a strong supporter of Isabella's drive against Islam.

the moral and spiritual condition of the laity. But the effects seem to have been limited. In 1500 Isabella wrote to one bishop pointing out that in his diocese 'the greater part of the clergy are said to be and are in concubinage publicly, and if our justice intervenes to punish them they revolt'. Clergy in another diocese had to be told 'not to gamble or fight bulls or sing or dance in public'.

Complaints were still being made in 1511 of clergy who had obtained their positions by every means apart from their own merit. The situation was not helped by the Crown expecting bishops to play an active role in the government service. This meant that many were absent from their dioceses on diplomatic and state affairs. There were similar problems with members of the three main religious orders, the Dominicans, Franciscans and Benedictines, and these also proved difficult to overcome. However, Cisneros had some success in imposing religious discipline among the Franciscans, and the Dominicans started a programme of reform of their own based on stricter observance of the rules of the order. The laity too resented and resisted change. They did not wish to lose those aspects of Christianity which often they most enjoyed: the devotion to the saints, local rituals, processions and celebrations.

The policy towards the Jews and *conversos*

At the beginning of their reign Isabella and Ferdinand did not seem particularly concerned about the Jews who lived in Castile and Aragon. They were a minority religion. They were excluded from certain positions such as town government and in the army. They worked in both town and countryside as in such jobs as farmers and tradesmen. Many did much needed work as doctors. They also had a number of jobs connected with finance, such as tax farmers or lenders. Ferdinand himself had a Jewish doctor. In 1477 Isabella declared that 'All the Jews in my realms are mine and under my care and protection and it belongs to me to defend and aid them and keep justice.' Their position changed, however, due to their concerns about the *conversos*. In contrast to the Jews, the *conversos* or 'new Christians' as they were sometimes called, had exactly the same rights as **'old' Christians**. It can be no surprise that the pious Isabella, advised by numbers of churchmen, might be susceptible to suggestions that the *conversos* were not true Christians in their beliefs and practices. The solution that Isabella decided on was to introduce an **Inquisition** into Castile.

The Spanish Inquisition

A papal inquisition had existed since the thirteenth century in Aragon but had not operated for many years. The Spanish Inquisition, however, was to be completely under the control of the monarchs and to be independent of both pope and bishops. Appointments to the Inquisition were to be made by the Crown and its accounts closely supervised. In this way, Ferdinand and Isabella were able to gain more control over the Church in Spain. The new Inquisition received papal approval in 1478 and was introduced into Castile in 1480. It was

KEY TERMS

'Old' Christians People of Catholic faith with no Jewish ancestry.

Inquisition An organisation that was responsible for finding and punishing people who did not follow Catholic beliefs and practices.

later extended, with difficulty and after much opposition, to Aragon in 1481. Thus, for the first time there was a body whose authority extended throughout the whole of Spain and was under the control of the Crown.

Reasons for the foundation of the Inquisition 1478–80

There seems little doubt that religious motives drove Isabella to establish the Inquisition in Castile. Much evidence had come to the Crown that the *conversos* were not all genuine converts in that they still secretly practised their Jewish faith and kept at least some of their Jewish customs. It was commonly held that 'hardly any are true Christians, as is well known in all Spain'. There was probably some truth in this. Many Jews had been forcibly converted in previous years in both kingdoms. In addition, most of them had been given no adequate Christian teaching. Fear of the *conversos* was often mingled with resentment and envy, for many of them were wealthy and they, or their descendants, held important positions in the two kingdoms. Some senior churchmen such as **Torquemada** began to press for the introduction of a Spanish Inquisition. He persuaded Isabella and Ferdinand of the dangers posed by *conversos* which he claimed would undermine the stability of the country. Isabella, deeply pious and totally shocked by his revelations, decided to set up the Inquisition to detect and punish heresy.

A wish to gain additional income has also been suggested as one of the reasons for the introduction of the Inquisition into Spain and for the expulsion of the Jews. The Inquisition was an institution introduced initially to deal with the *conversos*. Wealthy *conversos* might have large estates which would be confiscated if their owner was found guilty by the Inquisition 'this Inquisition is as much to take the *conversos'* estates as to exalt the faith … goods are heretics', declared one *converso*. Certainly some large sums were raised in this way but the costs of running the Inquisition were also high and it is unlikely that the Crown made much, if any, financial gain out of it. In some cities persecution of *conversos* caused serious economic damage by removing key people, especially in the financing of trade and industry, and thereby led to a decline in royal income.

Ferdinand seemed well aware of the harm that it could do to Crown income:

> **SOURCE F**
>
> **Extract from a letter sent by Ferdinand in 1484.**
>
> *Before We decided to allow this Inquisition to act in any city … We had considered all the harm that might result to our royal rights and revenues. But, since Our firm intention and zeal is to place the service of Our Lord God before Our own … We wish that this should be done, all other interests put aside.*

> **KEY FIGURE**
>
> **Tomás de Torquemada (1420–98)**
>
> Spanish Dominican friar and first Inquisitor General. He was determined to establish orthodoxy in religion. Nicknamed 'the hammer of heretics', he was confessor to Isabella.

In Source F, what reason does Ferdinand give for the introduction of the Inquisition? What might be the 'harm' he is referring to?

The work of the Inquisition

The new body was first set up to deal specifically with *conversos*. Its work later expanded to deal with wider groups and matters. The first tribunals were set up in a number of towns, including Toledo and Seville, where there was perceived to be the most need. The first two Inquisitors were Dominican monks. As the numbers of Inquisitors increased an Inquisitor General was appointed, the first of whom was Tomás de Torquemada. The Inquisition was feared by the *conversos*. Those suspected of reverting to Jewish practices were arrested, tried in secret and, usually, found guilty. The accusers were not named and there was no means of appeal. Sentences were passed and those found guilty could be fined, have their property confiscated, be imprisoned or burned at the stake in public. Many of the guilty were made to walk in a public **auto de fé** before their sentence was carried out. Those to die by burning were handed over to the secular authorities and taken outside the city to meet their deaths.

The number who died has been very much debated. Contemporaries tend to give high figures. One writer of the time describes how in Seville alone over 700 *conversos* were burned and many thousands received other punishments between 1480 and 1488. A number of studies by historians writing in the late twentieth century such as Stephen Haliczer (1987) and J.P. Dedieu (1989) tended to give lower figures. The historian Henry Kamen, writing in 2000, suggests that some 2000 may have been executed in the whole of Spain during the first 50 years of the Inquisition. What cannot be doubted is the atmosphere of fear that it generated.

The role of the Inquisition gradually extended beyond dealing with *conversos*. It came to be concerned with matters involving people's daily lives. People could find themselves brought before its courts over what they had said or written, for sexual misconduct, **usury**, **witchcraft** or **blasphemy**.

The expulsion of the Jews 1492

The Inquisition brought to light many more cases of *conversos* practising Judaism than the Crown expected. The two monarchs decided that stronger measures would have to be employed if the contagion of Judaism was to be halted and the souls of *conversos* saved. The remedy that they eventually decided on was one that had been suggested in the past: the expulsion of all the Jews from the two kingdoms.

Hatred of, and violence against, the Jews had increased during the reign of Isabella and Ferdinand. The following comment about the Jews by a contemporary Christian chronicler and curate, Andres Bernaldez, is typical: 'All their work was to multiply and increase … They never wanted to take manual work, ploughing or digging or walking the fields with the herds … but only jobs in the towns, so as to sit around making money without doing much work.' What the writer fails to mention are the problems the Jews had in being accepted into any jobs other than those involving finance. Even a generally enlightened contemporary writer considered the Jews 'obscene, detestable, vile, execrable … to be ostracized from all human contact … My sovereigns were the wisest of men to think of exterminating that despicable and infected herd.'

 **KEY TERMS**

Auto de fé A public ceremony (literally an 'act of faith') at which the Inquisition announced its sentences for those found guilty. The burning of any heretics took place after such ceremonies and was carried out by the secular authorities.

Usury The lending of money at unreasonably high rates of interest.

Witchcraft Practice and belief in magical skills. Usually such powers were considered to be evil and associated with the Devil.

Blasphemy Action or offence of speaking in an insulting or disrespectful way towards God.

The measures taken by the two monarchs had encouraged, albeit probably unintentionally, anti-Semitism among the 'old' Christians. Ferdinand and Isabella had implemented the decrees which ordered the walling off of Jewish sections of towns from Christian sections. The Jews were made to wear distinctive yellow badges in some parts of the kingdoms. Further laws made it possible for Christians to not repay their debts if those debts were owed to a Jew.

The policy of expulsion started in 1482. It became official policy in March 1492 when a decree was issued stating that Jews must become Christians or leave the two kingdoms within four months. Estimates of how many left as a result vary considerably. The historian Richard Bonney, for example, suggests there were 70,000 Castilians and 10,000 Aragonese. However, as Kamen, writing in 2005, reminds us, many of those who left later returned as *conversos*.

The economic and social impact of the expulsion on Spain

The Jews who left Spain were a very small percentage of the total population and it is unlikely that their leaving had serious repercussions on the economies of Castile and Aragon. It was the *conversos* rather than the Jews who contributed to trade and finance. More serious was the fact, as Kamen suggests (2005), that the policy had not solved the *converso* problem but had had the reverse effect and possibly doubled the number of false converts in Spain. The question arose also as to whether the Crown would now turn its attention to the **Moriscos** and *Mudéjars* who were in Spain. What the policy did mark was that *convivencia* was coming to an end.

The expulsion or conversion of the *Mudéjars* from Castile

After the Granada War, the province had been ruled effectively by the conciliatory Lopez de Mendoza. In the early sixteenth century, however, the situation changed. Isabella tended to listen to the views of men such as the intolerant Cisneros, Archbishop of Toledo, rather than to more moderate voices. As a result, policy towards the *Mudéjars* changed in Castile.

Why was this policy introduced?

Hatred by 'old' Christians for the *Mudéjars* was nowhere near as violent as that experienced by Jews and *conversos*. In Aragon there were many *Mudéjars* to be found, mainly working on the estates of the nobles. In Castile there were fewer originally, but the conquest of Granada led to many more *Mudéjars* coming under the rule of Ferdinand and Isabella. Two major problems then confronted the monarchs. The first was that of security. There were always fears that *Mudéjars* would ally with the enemies of Spain in any invasion of the country. To the northeast, beyond the Pyrenees, were the French and to the south, the Muslims of north Africa. In the Mediterranean the Turks were a power to be feared. Second, there was, at least on Isabella's part, a genuine desire to see the spread of Christianity among Muslim lands.

KEY TERM

Moriscos Name given to the Muslims who converted to Christianity. They were suspected of secretly practising their ancestral religion as they usually retained their traditional diet and dress, and used the Arabic language.

After the Reconquest of Granada, Hernando de Talavera was made Archbishop. He worked patiently and sincerely to try to convert the *Mudéjars*. However, many in Castile thought that this policy brought change too slowly. Cisneros, therefore, pressed Isabella to pursue a more determined policy to try to convert as many of the *Mudéjars* as possible. Thousands became Christians, although probably through fear and not from any real change of faith. In addition, a heavy tax was levied on *Mudéjars* in 1495 and again in 1499. These measures made the position of many *Mudéjars* intolerable and it is hardly surprising that in 1499 a revolt broke out against Castilian rule. This was the excuse Isabella needed. A force was sent into Granada, and the revolt was put down in three months of bitter fighting.

The campaign to convert all *Mudéjars* in Castile

A campaign ensued to ensure that all *Mudéjars* were now converted. Permission was given for them to emigrate if they preferred this to conversion, but difficulties were put in their way, including having to leave behind their children, so few left. Those who remained were now known as *Moriscos*. The policy was extended from Granada to the whole of Castile. And in 1502 all the *Mudéjars* in Castile were given the choice of either becoming Christians or leaving. Again, most remained. *Mudéjars* were now only to be found in the kingdom of Aragon and Ferdinand resisted any attempt to extend this policy of conversion or expulsion there.

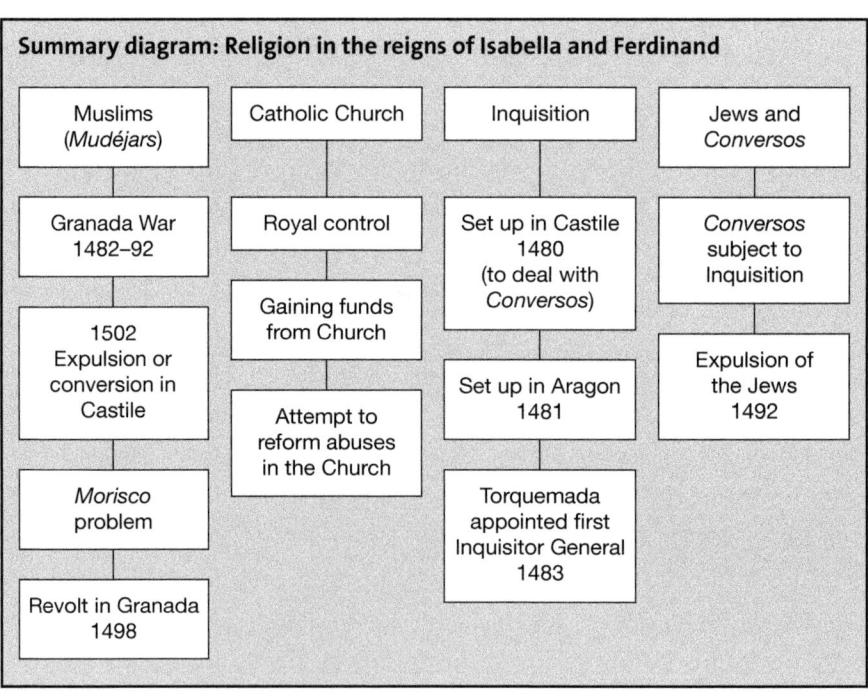

Chapter summary

It is no surprise that Ferdinand and Isabella, determined and pragmatic as they both were and working as a team, stamped their mark on Castile and Aragon. Even allowing for the propaganda that they were so adept at using, they achieved much in their domestic policies. They made their positions on the throne secure. They introduced reforms in their administration and government. They tried to ensure the spiritual welfare of their people, though these efforts were largely unsuccessful. They also tried to secure the position of Christianity in Spain. They achieved success in the Granada War against the Moors, introduced the Inquisition in both Castile and Aragon, and expelled the Jews from all their kingdoms. One must not, however, overdo the praise as so many of their contemporaries did and some historians into the twentieth century have done. Their policies at home had important negative sides. In particular, their reign saw the end of the *convivencia* which had so characterised the heritage of Castile (although it partially continued in Aragon). Their decisions in the area of religious policy planted the seeds of problems to come. Finally, in finance, their use of loans to pursue their policies would lead to the continued indebtedness of the monarchy.

Refresher questions

Use these questions to remind yourself of the key material covered in this chapter.

1. Why was the marriage contract between Ferdinand and Isabella important?
2. What problems were there in Aragon and Castile in 1469?
3. How far did the marriage of Isabella and Ferdinand lead to the uniting of Castile and Aragon?
4. What personal qualities did Ferdinand and Isabella each have which would help them as rulers?
5. Why did the Granada War take place?
6. How successful were Ferdinand and Isabella in establishing peace in Spain in the years 1474–1505?
7. How well did Ferdinand and Isabella deal with the problems caused by the nobility in the years 1474–1505?
8. What improvements did the two monarchs make to the administration?
9. What measures did Ferdinand and Isabella take to increase income for their kingdoms? How successful were they in their financial policies?
10. How successful were Isabella and Ferdinand's religious policies in regard to the Catholic Church?
11. Why was the Inquisition introduced into Spain? Why were the Jews forced to convert to Christianity or expelled from Castile and Aragon? What consequences did this have?
12. Why were the *Mudéjars* expelled from Castile or forced to convert to Christianity, but not in Aragon?

Question practice

ESSAY QUESTIONS

1. How successful were the Catholic Monarchs in enforcing royal authority within Aragon and Castile in the years 1474–1505?
2. 'The Inquisition was the most successful religious policy of Ferdinand and Isabella.' How far do you agree?
3. 'The most successful domestic policy of Ferdinand and Isabella was improving the royal finances.' Assess the validity of this view.
4. 'Dealing with the problems posed by the nobles was the most important achievement of Ferdinand and Isabella in establishing peace in Spain in the years 1474 to 1505.' How far do you agree?
5. Which of the following was more responsible for enabling Isabella to secure the throne of Castile by 1479? i) Isabella's personal character and role. ii) The failures of the King of Portugal in his support for Joanna, daughter of Henry IV. Explain your answer with reference to both i) and ii).
6. Which of the following was of greater importance in considering whether Ferdinand and Isabella deserved their title of 'Most Catholic Monarchs'? i) The conquest of Granada. ii) The establishment of the Inquisition. Explain you answer with reference to both i) and ii).
7. How far were Isabella's concerns about Jewish *conversos* responsible for the foundation of the Inquisition in the years 1478–80?
8. How accurate is it to say that it was the religious conviction of Isabella and Ferdinand that accounts for the intensification of persecution of Spanish Jews in the period 1478–92?

INTERPRETATION QUESTIONS

1. 'The government of Castile under Ferdinand and Isabella had more to do with the vigorous reassertion of royal authority than with the centralization of power.' (From S. Barton, *A History of Spain*, 2004.) Evaluate the strengths and limitations of this interpretation, making reference to other interpretations that you have studied.
2. 'The Spanish church formed another instrument for forging Spanish unity and creating a strong monarchy.' (From V.H.H. Green, *Renaissance and Reformation*, 1964.) Evaluate the strengths and limitations of this interpretation, making reference to other interpretations that you have studied.
3. Using your understanding of the historical context, assess how convincing the arguments in Extracts 1–3 (below and page 37) are in relation to the expulsion of the Jews from Spain during the reign of Ferdinand and Isabella.

> #### EXTRACT 1
>
> **From J.H. Elliott, *Imperial Spain 1469–1716*, Edward Arnold, 1963, p. 99.**
>
> *The departure of the Jews from Spain would remove temptation from all those New Christians who still looked back uneasily to their abandoned faith … [Among those leaving] included some influential but half-hearted* conversos *– men of standing in the church, the administration, and the world of finance … [The new policy of expulsion or conversion] meant that a new group of dubious converts was now added to the* converso *ranks … The expulsion of the Jews had laid the foundations for a unitary state in the only sense in which that was possible in the circumstances of the late fifteenth century. … The gains*

seemed great – but so also was the cost … The year 1492 saw the disappearance from Spain of a dynamic community, whose capital and skill had helped enrich Castile. The gap left by the Jews was not easily filled, and many of them were replaced not by native Castilians, but by colonies of foreign immigrants – Flemings, Germans, Genoese – who would use their new opportunity to exploit rather than to enrich the resources of Spain.

EXTRACT 2

From John Lynch, *Spain under the Habsburgs*, volume 1: *Empire and Absolutism*, Basil Blackwell, 1981, p. 15.

… it was precisely under the Catholic Monarchs that [Spain] lost perhaps the most enterprising of their number. In the interests of religious uniformity the Jews were expelled from the country … In the economic and urban life of Spain the Jews had occupied key positions; as financiers, artisans, and officials they dominated productive enterprises except in agriculture. Granted their number, prosperity, and influence, it is not surprising that they should arouse envy and hatred … therefore, the monarchs had no hesitation in damaging the economy of the country to secure their objectives … out of an estimated 200,000 at the beginning of the reign about 150,000 refused baptism and were forced to leave Spain in 1492, taking with them their skill and their wealth. These measures, in conjunction with the pro-aristocratic bias that was already deeply embedded in society, were a powerful deterrent to the growth of a middle class in Spain.

EXTRACT 3

From Henry Kamen, *Spain 1469–1714*, Pearson, 2005, pp. 44–5.

Out of a likely total Jewish population in Castile of 70,000 and in Aragon of 10,000, many accepted baptism and others left the country only to return again, so that the final figure for those who left permanently could not have been more than about 50,000. … The Jews … were a tiny disadvantaged minority, excluded from the major professions and public posts, and in many areas discriminated against by the law; they took no part in large-scale trade, and limited themselves to a handful of professions and to farming. They paid their taxes mainly to the crown (which ironically stood to lose most by expelling them) but were in no way either a wealthy or a successful minority, and the expulsion of 1492 accordingly seems to have had no serious negative consequences for the country. Moreover, the many who converted in 1492 carried on … all the professional roles formerly fulfilled by Jews, for example in medicine. If its motive had been religious, … the expulsion was a total failure, for [it] possibly doubled the number of false converts in the realm.

SOURCE ANALYSIS QUESTION

1. Study Source 1. Assess the value of the source for revealing why Ferdinand and Isabella introduced the Spanish Inquisition into Spain and why the Inquisition in Spain was feared.

> **SOURCE 1**
>
> **From a contemporary account of how heresy was dealt with in Seville, *c*.1480, quoted in Helen Rawlings, *The Spanish Inquisition*, Wiley, 2005, pp. 57–8.**
>
> *And he [King Ferdinand] gave principal charge of this Inquisition to a friar of upright life who had great zeal in the Faith, who was called Fray Tomas de Torquemada, confessor to the king and prior of the monastery of Santa Cruz of Segovia of the Order of St Dominic. This prior, who was the chief inquisitor, put other inquisitors in his place in all the other cities and towns of the kingdom of Castile, and Aragon, and Valencia, and Catalonia. These made inquisitions on the matter of heretical iniquity in every land and district where they were assigned; and in these places they set their charters and edicts, founded upon law, so that those who had engaged in Jewish practices or who were not in accord with the Faith, within a certain time might come to confess their faults and be reconciled with Holy Mother Church. And by these charters and edicts many persons of lineage appeared before the inquisitors and confessed their faults and the errors that they had committed in this crime of heresy. And these were given penances according to the degree of the crime that each one had incurred. These were more than fifteen thousand persons. And if some were guilty of that crime and did not come to be reconciled within the period of time that had been decreed, once there was information from witnesses of the error they had committed, then they were taken prisoner and trial was instituted against them, by means of which they were condemned as heretics and apostates and turned over to secular justice.*
>
> *Up to two thousand men and women were burned on various occasions in different cities and towns; and others were condemned to perpetual imprisonment, and to others was given as a penance that for all the days of their lives they should go marked with great red crosses placed on their clothing. And they as well as their children were declared unfit for all public office or responsibility …*
>
> *Some relatives of the prisoners and the condemned protested, saying that the inquisition and procedure was rigorous beyond what it ought to be and that in the manner in which the trials were conducted and in the execution of the sentences the ministers and executors showed that they had hatred for those people.*

CHAPTER 3

Ferdinand and Isabella 1479–1516: Europe, the wider world and the end of the reign

Through their achievements in foreign policy, Ferdinand and Isabella made their mark and added to the prestige in which Spain was viewed by other European countries. Their support of Columbus, which led to the discovery of the New World in the Americas, was to further enhance that prestige and their own reputations. This chapter focuses on the questions of how far the foundations of Spain's military power and prestige in foreign policy began during this period, and how Spain became involved in the discovery, exploration and early settlement of the New World. It concludes with the situation of Spain at the end of the reign, following the death of Isabella in 1504. These themes are developed under the following headings:

★ Foreign policy
★ The New World: discovery and settlement
★ The closing years of the reign 1504–16

The key debate on *page 59* asks the question: Was there a 'New Monarchy' in Spain between 1492 and 1516?

Key dates

1479	Treaty of Alcaçovas	1504	Death of Queen Isabella of Spain
1482–92	The Granada War		Joanna and her husband, Archduke Philip of Austria, succeeded Isabella as rulers of Castile. Castile and Aragon became two separate kingdoms once again
1492	Columbus's first voyage to the New World		
1493	Treaty of Barcelona between France and the Crown of Aragon	1504	Reconquest of the kingdom of Naples
	Papal bull confirming Spanish rights to new lands in South America	1505–10	Capture of several towns along the north African coast
1494	Treaties of Tordesillas	1506	Agreement of Villafafila between Philip and Joanna and Ferdinand
1495	Holy League set up between Spain, Austria, the Papal States, Milan, Venice and the Holy Roman Empire against the French king, Charles VIII		Marriage of Ferdinand to King of France's niece, Germaine de Foix
			Death of Philip of Austria
1496	Joanna, daughter of Isabella and Ferdinand, married Philip, son and heir of the Holy Roman Emperor	1507	Ferdinand returned to Castile and became regent
1497	John, son of Isabella and Ferdinand, married Margaret, daughter of the Holy Roman Emperor	1512	Acquisition of Navarre
			Laws of Burgos issued
		1516	Death of Ferdinand

39

Foreign policy

> ▶ By 1556, Spain had become the undisputed great military power of Europe. How far had the reign of Isabella and Ferdinand laid the basis for this power?

In foreign policy, a close partnership could be found between the two kingdoms. Here it was Aragon's lead which was in general followed, with the finances and resources coming mainly from Castile.

The aims of Isabella's and Ferdinand's foreign policy

Before the accession of Isabella and Ferdinand to the thrones of Castile and Aragon, respectively, the priorities of the two kingdoms had differed.

Traditionally, the foreign policy of Aragon had been concerned with French ambitions on its northern frontier. Looking at the map on page 5, it is clear why Ferdinand would wish to regain Roussillon and Cerdagne and challenge France over its interests in Navarre. Furthermore, Aragon needed to protect Sicily and Sardinia, its possessions in the Mediterranean, particularly against attacks by the Turks.

In contrast, Castile had followed a friendly policy towards France. Its main concern had been the kingdom of Granada on its eastern frontier. Around 500,000 Moors lived in Granada, in what was the last part of the Iberian Peninsula that remained in the hands of the followers of Islam. For many Christians in Castile this represented a challenge to be conquered. In addition, Castile had always been concerned about its relationship with Portugal on its southern frontier.

The marriage of Ferdinand and Isabella changed matters to a certain extent. Ferdinand now tended to take the lead in directing policy for both Castile and Aragon. His knowledge and interests were more extensive than Isabella's as a result of his experience with Aragon's possessions around the Mediterranean. This had given him more contact with other European countries and, therefore, more experience in foreign affairs. However, he was not in a position to carry out what were then Aragonese priorities, particularly on the borders with France, as he lacked the financial resources and manpower that Castile could supply. This meant that Isabella's views in regard to the direction of foreign policy were of crucial importance. And for her, it was the conquest of Granada which was the priority at the beginning of her reign. Consequently, for the ten years that the monarchs were involved in the Granada War, Ferdinand was able to achieve little on Aragon's northern border or in the Mediterranean. It was only after the conquest of Granada that he was able to turn his attention to those matters which had been mainly the concerns of Aragon.

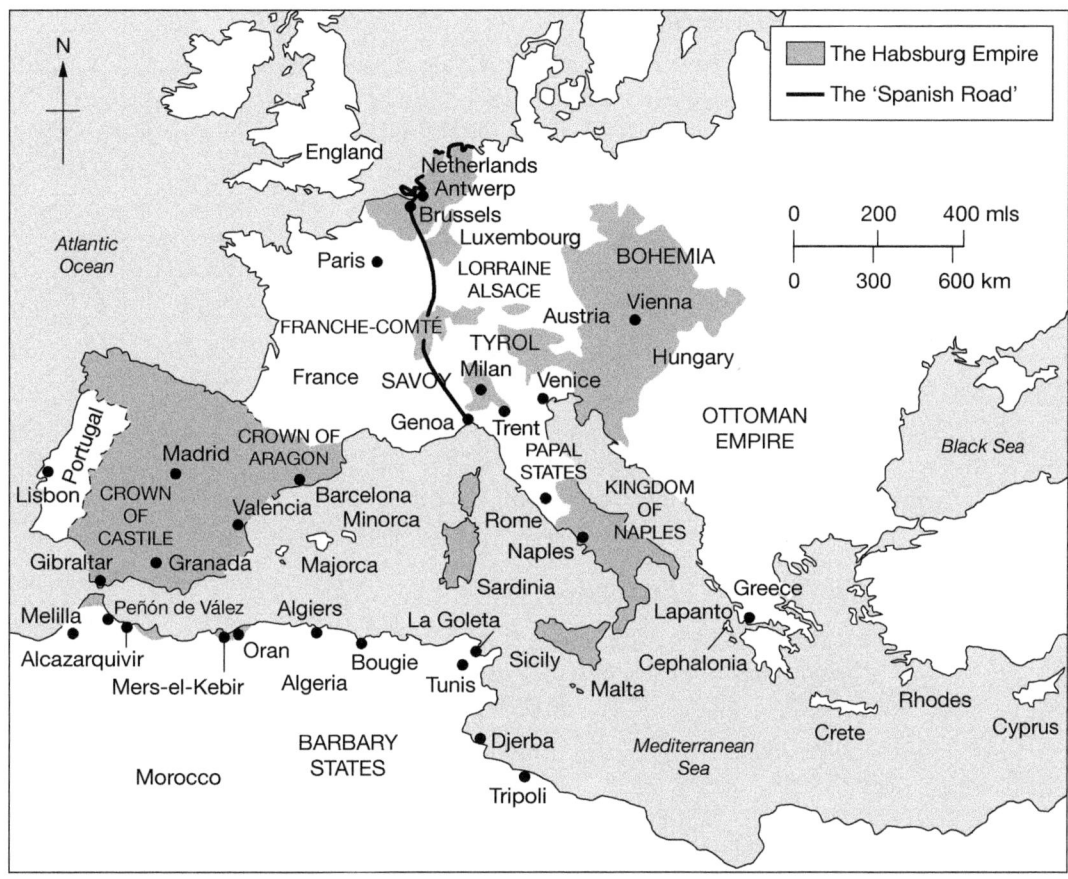

Figure 3.1 Map of the Iberian Peninsula and the western Mediterranean in the late fifteenth and early sixteenth century. Persia lies to the east of the Ottoman Empire.

However, religion was an issue for both monarchs. Both were concerned about the advance in the Mediterranean and north Africa of the followers of Islam. In the Mediterranean, Aragon's possessions were at risk of attack. For Castile, after the conquest of Granada, only the narrow Strait of Gibraltar separated its territories from the followers of Islam in north Africa. And, of course, there were the continuing concerns about Spain's frontiers with Portugal and France.

The Iberian Peninsula

From the beginning of their reign, therefore, Ferdinand and Isabella wished to safeguard Spain from the possibility of outside threats. This had involved the conquest of Granada (see pages 19–22), in part to secure Spain's position in the eastern part of the Iberian Peninsula. Now Spain needed to look at securing its frontiers with both Portugal to the south and France to the north.

Relations with Portugal

The enmity between Spain and Portugal at the beginning of Ferdinand and Isabella's reign (when Portugal invaded Castile several times in support of Joanna's claim to the throne, see page 17) was to continue over ownership of the Canary Islands. Portugal gave up its claims to the islands in the Treaty of Alcaçovas (1479), and by the late 1490s, the major islands had been conquered and made part of the Crown of Castile. These islands in the Atlantic would prove to be an important stopping point for ships going to the New World. Relations between the two countries became friendlier after this.

Isabella, the eldest daughter of Ferdinand and Isabella, first married Prince Alfonso – heir to the King of Portugal – and, when he died, married the new king, Emanuel I. On Isabella's own death in childbirth in 1498, Emanuel married her sister, Maria. The peace cemented by these marriages was to prove long lasting. It meant that Ferdinand and Isabella could turn their attention elsewhere without fearing a possible invasion of Castile from Portugal.

The conquest of Navarre

Further conquests took place in the Iberian Peninsula itself. Although small, Navarre was important because of its geographical position between France and Spain. Control of Navarre by France could give it a base from which to invade Spain. A further difficulty was that part of Navarre lay in France and was, therefore, subject to the French king. Problems over the control of Navarre had persisted over many decades. However, it was not until 1512 that Ferdinand had the resources and the opportunity to act effectively. A disputed succession to Navarre's throne led to Ferdinand's invasion of 1512. All the fortresses surrendered within a few weeks and Navarre became part of the Crown of Castile, although still keeping its independence from both Castile and Aragon.

Relations with France

Relations with France were difficult for most of Ferdinand and Isabella's reign. France was the main political and military power in Europe in the second half of the fifteenth century. In the previous century Castile had tended to ally itself with France while Aragon and Catalonia had tended to oppose France. Under Ferdinand and Isabella both Castile and Aragon aligned on policy, which was usually led by Aragon. There had long been disputes between France and the Crown of Aragon over two of Catalonia's northern provinces, Cerdagne and Roussillon (see Figure 1.1, page 5), which had been occupied by France since 1462. However, by the early 1490s, France's attention was directed towards Italy and, wanting to make sure that their own frontiers were secure, the French were willing to give up both Cerdagne and Roussillon by the Treaty of Barcelona (1493).

Opposing French expansion in Italy

A French invasion of Italy in 1494 was to lead to renewed conflict between France and Spain. Italy at the end of the fifteenth century was made up of different states (see Figure 4.1, page 93). In the south, there were the two kingdoms of Naples (ruled by an illegitimate branch of Ferdinand's family) and Sicily (ruled by Aragon). The Papal States (Rome) lay between Naples and a number of duchies and republics in northern Italy, none of which was politically stable. The French forces quickly reached as far south as Naples, meeting little resistance on the way.

In Naples, the ruler was Ferdinand's illegitimate cousin and brother-in-law, King Ferrante. Ferrante's position was weak at the time of the invasion and he could not rely on help from either his own nobles or Ferdinand. In 1495 the French army was, therefore, able to occupy Naples.

Reasons for Ferdinand's intervention in Naples

It seems clear from Ferdinand's instructions that, by 1493, some contemporaries could already foresee that Spain would wish to take possession of Naples: 'the whole of Italy is in conspiracy against your state (Naples) ... France is on the way. Spain holds you in its hand, awaiting its time.'

This suggestion that Ferdinand might wish to take over Naples for himself seems supported by his instructions to his ambassador in France: 'the war of Naples touches only [our] own interests. Naples had previously been a part of the Crown of Aragon. Therefore, it fell to them [the rulers of Aragon] to reconquer the kingdom of Naples and that of Granada, which were both usurped from their predecessors.'

The reasons given to other states for Ferdinand's involvement in Naples were different. In January 1496, Ferdinand and Isabella wrote to their ambassador in England:

> You know already that this war we have with the King of France is not for any interest of our own but to aid the pope in order that the King of France may restore what he had taken from the Church by force; and he presumes to occupy and make war on the kingdom of Naples which is feudatory of the Church and as all Christian princes must defend the pope and the lands of the Church, we, in order to fulfil that obligation and obey the pope's commands ... opened this war with France.

In a letter to his viceroy in Sicily, Ferdinand wrote in 1495: 'We, seeing the war in all Italy, and because We have heard that the Turk has a great fleet prepared, are sending a fleet and troops.'

In the main it is likely that it was his concern about France which governed Ferdinand's actions. He would not wish France to be in control of Naples and so be a danger to Spanish policy in the central Mediterranean area.

Ferdinand did not act alone against France. All the main European powers were equally concerned about the power of France. In 1495 Ferdinand joined in a 'Holy League' with the Holy Roman Empire, represented by Maximilian of Austria, the papacy and a number of other Italian states against the French. However, The French king had overextended himself on his march south and was forced to retreat.

The Spanish forces were under the command of the 'Great Captain', Gonzalo de Córdoba. His first period in Italy during 1495–7 saw his light cavalry at a disadvantage compared with the heavily armed French cavalry, and he did not achieve as much as he had hoped. Córdoba, though, was a man able to learn from what had happened and think out new approaches. In 1501 he was sent to Naples again. As well as the artillery which had been so successful in Granada, he used new methods of fighting. This involved **pikemen** with infantry support consisting of some men carrying firearms (*arquebuses*) and others armed with short swords and javelins. This infantry was grouped into larger units than before and each group was supported by cavalry and artillery. This was the infantry formation which was to develop into the Spanish *tercio*. In 1503, using these new tactics, Córdoba secured two important victories over the French, at Cerignola, which historian John Edwards (2005) describes as being 'the first time Spain was recognized as a major military power in Europe', and at Garigliano. This was a major triumph for Ferdinand. In 1504 France recognised Spanish control over Naples, and it became part of the Crown of Aragon.

KEY TERMS

Pikemen Foot soldiers who carried pikes – long weapons (about 4.9 m) topped with a metal point.

Tercio A new type of infantry formation used by the Spanish armies from 1534.

SOURCE A

? What role did each the soldiers shown in Source A play in making the Spanish *tercio* a feared fighting force in the sixteenth century?

Infantrymen of the Spanish *tercio*.

The importance of Naples to Spain

Naples was a valuable acquisition for Spain. It was important geographically, positioned as it is in the central area of the Mediterranean. Its grain supplies were a considerable asset, as was its revenue. Naples made Spain the most important influence in Italy and gave it control of southern Europe by land and sea. However, Naples also brought further foreign policy commitments. Spain's toehold in Italy through Naples was to lead to further military and diplomatic warfare against France. It also extended the length of the Spanish frontier in the Mediterranean which would need to be defended against the Turks.

Policy in the Mediterranean

The interests of Aragon in the Mediterranean meant that Ferdinand was concerned about any expansion of the Ottoman Turks into the western Mediterranean. Considerations of defence were, therefore, uppermost in Ferdinand's mind, but he also expressed an interest in a crusade against the Turks on several occasions, 'from my youth I was always very inclined to war against infidels and it is the thing in which I receive most delight and pleasure'. Isabella's own religious views and the feelings of many Castilians who had been participants in the Reconquest (see page 4) also led to a desire to fight the Turks.

In 1479–80, Spain assisted the **Knights Hospitallers** when the island of Rhodes was besieged by the Turks. A year later Spain, along with Portugal, helped Naples against a Turkish invasion, expelling Turks from Otranto. Further success followed when in 1501 a naval and military force under Córdoba helped Venice to regain the castle of St George, capital of the island of Cephalonia (off Greece), from the Turks. However, it is clear that religious considerations were not the only reason for the support Spain gave. Spanish possessions in the Mediterranean also needed to be protected.

KEY TERMS

Knights Hospitallers
Catholic religious and military order based on Rhodes during this period.

Privateering ships
Privately owned armed ships authorised by a government to take part in war.

Policy in north Africa

The Spanish were interested in the gold, ivory and slaves to be obtained from north and west Africa. However, trade along the coasts of west Africa was in the hands of the Portuguese. During the War of Succession with Portugal, fighting had not only taken place in Castile. Isabella had sent out **privateering ships** in 1476, 1477 and again in 1478 to intercept Portuguese ships as they returned home loaded with goods. On the seas the Portuguese had mainly had the upper hand and had captured a number of the Spanish ships. As far as west Africa was concerned, Portugal was the benefactor of the Treaty of Alcaçovas. Besides ending the war in 1479, it forced Isabella to reluctantly accept a Portuguese monopoly of fishing and trade along the whole west African coast.

It was not until the late 1490s that Spanish attention was again drawn to north Africa. Chief among the reasons for this were the questions of religion, trade and security. To act against the various groups of Moors who controlled most of north Africa would also be to act against the main rival faith to Christianity and continue the Reconquest. Isabella herself had wanted a crusade against Islam in Africa. In her will she had asked her heirs 'to devote themselves unremittingly to the conquest of Africa and the war for the faith against the Muslims'. Going to war in north Africa would also help prevent support being given to the *Mudéjar* population in Spain. In addition, having bases in north Africa would create trading opportunities. Several cities along the north African coast were taken in the early years of the sixteenth century. The most important of these were Oran (to which Archbishop Cisneros personally led an army), Bougie (in present-day Algeria) and Tripoli. Algiers became a vassal city, which meant it owed allegiance to Spain. However, an attempt to take Djerba, off Tunisia, failed. Small garrisons were set up in the cities taken and some trade was able to take place but there was no attempt to set up permanent colonies. In addition, the

SOURCE B

? The artwork in Source B is a nineteenth-century bronze statue by Manuel Oms Canet. What do you think it was designed to show?

A statue of Queen Isabella marching into Granada with Córdoba and Cardinal Mendoza by her side.

Chapter 3 *Ferdinand and Isabella 1479–1516: Europe, the wider world and the end of the reign*

Gonzalo Fernandez de Córdoba

1453	Born, the younger son of the Count of Aguilar
1474	Supported Isabella in the War of Succession for Castile
1482–92	Important military commander in the Granada War
1495–7	Led the Spanish forces in Naples in the First Italian War
1501	With a Spanish–Venetian army drove the Turks out of Cephalonia
1502–4	Led the Spanish forces in the Second Italian War
1504–7	Viceroy of Naples
1507	Sent back to his estates in Spain by Ferdinand
1515	Died

Gonzalo, the 'Great Captain', made his reputation during the war for Granada as one of Ferdinand's Andalusian commanders. Chosen as commander of the Spanish forces during the First Italian War, he was not at first as successful as he had hoped. However, it was during this war that he had the idea of a new type of infantry formation which was to develop into the Spanish *tertio*. These ideas he had on tactics helped to establish Spain as a major military power. During the Second Italian War 1502–4, he secured major victories at Cerignola and Gargeliliano. In 1507, however, he was recalled to Spain, probably because Ferdinand felt that he was acting too independently.

Gonzalo was responsible for training a number of the future generals of Charles V and Philip II. Others of the men who fought with him would also fight in the New World with the *conquistadores*.

conquests made were only held with difficulty for the rest of Ferdinand's reign, particularly after his interest turned towards Italy (see pages 43–5).

Political and military strategies for a successful foreign policy

Much of what Ferdinand and Isabella achieved in foreign policy was the result of the various strategies which they employed to ensure that they could call on support from other countries, as well as the methods they used to improve the fighting capacity of Spain.

Improvements in military organisation

Ferdinand and Isabella had gained considerable experience of military administration during the Granada War. They had had to make sure they could pay, feed, arm and move large groups of men, control their behaviour and divide them into operational units. Crown incomes had been used to pay the armed forces. This meant that they controlled their armies directly and did not have to rely totally on members of the nobility to supply fighting forces. After the Granada War, private armies, often used by members of the nobility for their own purposes, ceased to be as important. Royal regulations of 1495–1503 laid down how military units in the service of Ferdinand and Isabella should be organised and controlled by the central administration. Within the armed forces, officers and soldiers became accustomed to understanding that they needed to be present at musters and inspection, that they needed to obey orders, and that weapons and equipment had to be kept in good order. Soldiers were recruited to the army who would be expected to serve for longer terms in military units.

KEY TERMS

Artillery Large military weapons built to fire projectiles far beyond the range of an infantry's small arms.

Trebuchet A type of catapult used as a siege engine.

Habsburgs Rulers of Austria and the Netherlands (including modern-day Belgium and Netherlands), they also held the elected position of Holy Roman Emperor, with control over a large number of states of various sizes which made up the Holy Roman Empire.

New weaponry

The fifteenth century saw developments in **artillery** and infantry armed with gunpowder weapons. Improvements were made to the quality of the weapons. Ferdinand was responsible for setting up a number of armament works and employing specialists from Germany and France who brought state-of-the-art knowledge with them. However, it must not be thought that new weapons suddenly took over. More traditional arms, such as **trebuchets**, continued to be used alongside the latest weaponry. Field armies were better trained, heavy guns became more efficient and siege artillery could be used to destroy most fortifications. Instead of heavy cavalry, infantry formations using pikes and missile weapons were used.

Marriage alliances

Ferdinand's foreign policy was aided and supported by the marriage alliances made by members of his family (see Figure 1.2, page 9). Apart from the marriage of his daughter Isabella with the ruler of Portugal, close links were also formed with the **Habsburgs**.

In 1496 the son and heir of the Holy Roman Emperor, Philip, married Ferdinand's daughter Joanna. It was from this marriage that the future Emperor Charles V (Charles I of Spain) would be born. The following year, Ferdinand's son and heir, John, married Margaret, daughter of the Holy Roman Emperor. Alliances with England were cemented in 1489, in the Treaty of Medina del Campo, by the proposed marriage of another of Ferdinand's daughters, Catherine, to the English heir to the throne, Arthur. The marriage took place in 1501, and when Arthur died, it was proposed that Catherine should marry the new heir, the future King Henry VIII. That marriage took place in 1509. Ferdinand's own second marriage, to the King of France's niece, Germaine de Foix, occurred in 1506.

The use of ambassadors

Another arm to Ferdinand's foreign policy was the use of ambassadors. Here new methods were introduced. Ferdinand was the first European monarch, apart from the rulers of the Italian states, regularly to use resident ambassadors. Before then, ambassadors and agents had been used on a temporary basis, always for a specific purpose. By the 1490s Spain had resident ambassadors in England, the Papal States (Rome), Burgundy, Germany and Venice, the states usually allied to Spain. The ambassador could negotiate on behalf of the Spanish Crown, discover relevant information about the country in which he was stationed, and present the Spanish position on any issue to the ruler of that country. There was, of course, always the possibility of such information going astray when it was sent to Spain as the court had no permanent capital and was frequently on the move. However, on balance, having such information gave Ferdinand a clear advantage over the other rulers he was dealing with.

Achievements in foreign policy

By the end of his reign, Ferdinand had considerable foreign policy achievements to his name. His official historian, Antonio de Nebrya, writing in 1496, gives us an overview of what were then seen as the monarch's achievements:

SOURCE C

From R.M. Pidal, 'The significance of the Reign of Isabella the Catholic', quoted in R. Highfield, *Spain In the Fifteenth Century*, Macmillan, 1972, pp. 401–2.

For now, who does not see, that, although the title of the empire is in Germany, its real power is held by the Spanish Kings, who, lords of a great part of Italy and of the islands of the Mediterranean, carry war to Africa and send their fleets, following the course of the stars, to the islands of the Indians and the New World, joining the east to the western limit of Spain and Africa?

What does Source C reveal about the extent of Spain's interest in foreign affairs by 1496? How accurate do you consider the source to be?

There were good reasons for Ferdinand to congratulate himself. Spain's ambassadors were skilful and adroit at achieving success by diplomacy, as in the recovery of Roussillon and Cerdagne from France. Ferdinand's army and its equipment was on its way to becoming the most feared fighting force in western Europe. The territories held by Castile and Aragon had increased considerably to include Granada, Naples, Navarre, towns along the north African coast, the Canaries and America.

Much of Ferdinand's success was also due to his personal abilities. In foreign policy he was astute and usually showed good timing and judgement on when to act and when to negotiate. Machiavelli, in *The Prince*, is usually assumed to be referring to Ferdinand when he writes 'a certain prince of the present time never preaches anything except peace and loyalty, and is the greatest enemy of both; and both of those things, had he practised them, would on many occasions have deprived him of either his reputation or his state'. As we have already seen, Ferdinand was quite capable of saying one thing to one audience and another to other audiences (see page 43).

But as early as the late 1490s, signs of future problems were apparent. There was difficulty in finding enough money to maintain the new conquests, and it was becoming obvious that in having so many interests outside Spain, it was impossible to concentrate on any one of them properly.

This is not to minimise what, in effect, were Spain's achievements in foreign policy during the reigns of Ferdinand and Isabella. The historian Jan Glete, writing in 2002, sums them up by saying 'Spain was able to form a widespread empire in the western Mediterranean, facing the growing Ottoman Empire and at the same time carry out a major transoceanic colonising adventure in the Americas. This was the most spectacular change from weak to strong royal power in a few decades in any part of Europe.'

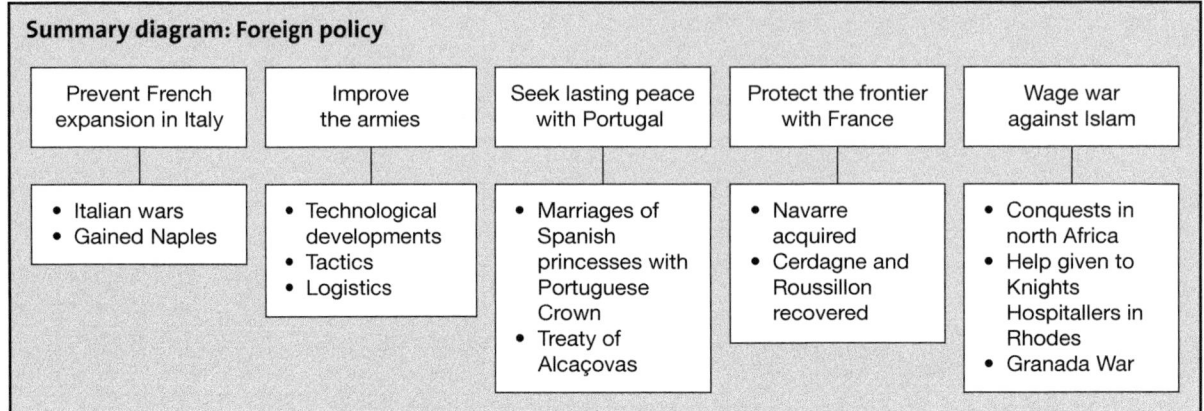

The New World: discovery and settlement

▶ *Why did Ferdinand and Isabella decide to support Columbus?*

▶ *What had been achieved in terms of discovery and settlement in the New World by 1516?*

Viewed in hindsight, the 'discovery' of America was an event of global significance. At the time, however, it was considered as the least of Ferdinand and Isabella's achievements. By the end of the reign little had been found apart from a small amount of gold and the natives who lived there.

Columbus's early attempts to gain support for a voyage west

Spanish involvement in the New World had started with the first voyage of the Genovese sailor Christopher Columbus. Rejected by the major seafaring nation of the time, Portugal, and by France and England, he had turned to Spain in 1486 in an effort to persuade Isabella to support him in his venture to find a route west across the Atlantic to the Spice Islands of the East Indies. At that time he had been unsuccessful. Ferdinand and Isabella were still involved in the war in Granada. Their advisers were sceptical about the venture. There was also the question of costs. In addition, Columbus was probably asking for too much in the form of titles, positions and privileges. However, he did spark the monarchs' interest. They gave him a small retainer and Columbus worked to build up further support for a voyage.

Ferdinand and Isabella give Columbus their support in 1492

In 1492 Ferdinand and, in particular, Isabella decided to support Columbus. There were a number of reasons why they had a change of heart.

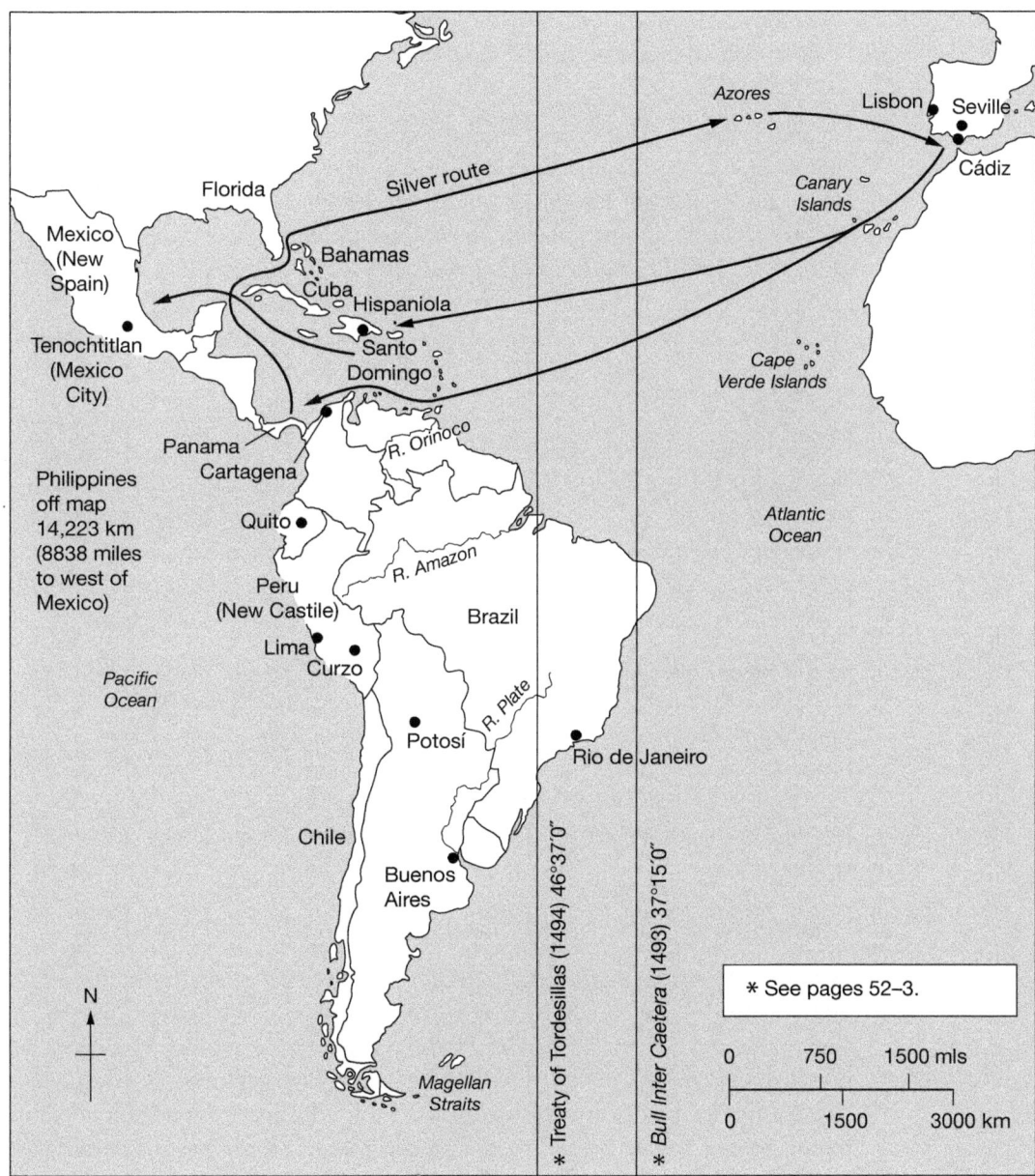

Figure 3.2 The Spanish Empire in the New World.

The war in Granada had been successfully ended and the two monarchs could now turn to other matters, particularly those that might raise their prestige in the eyes of other European countries. Trading reasons would also have been an important consideration in the wish to find a route westwards to the East Indies, India and China at this time. Travel to India and China had become difficult by the late fifteenth century. The Ottoman Empire and other Islamic states had closed the land route by which goods had travelled in the past, and their ships' control of the open waters in the east made the sea route difficult and unsafe.

Columbus maintained that a sea route west would be faster and safer. And as Spain now had control of the Canary Islands, it possessed a perfect base for such a voyage.

Columbus had used his time in Spain well, building up a number of important supporters at court. These included the treasurer of the *Hermandad*. As well as supplying funds, such supporters would have stressed to the two monarchs the prospect of acquiring treasure for the Castilian treasury, as well as the prestige that would come to Spain if the voyage was a success. This would also enable Ferdinand and Isabella to show that the Spanish could compete with the Portuguese on the seas. The Portuguese were already well established along the west coast of Africa. Might the Spanish now become masters of a route west to the Indies?

Religious issues were also possibly involved. Isabella, if not Ferdinand himself, may have had some thoughts of the conversion of souls to Christ. However, that was certainly not a major consideration in regard to the first voyage. Nothing, for example, was said in the agreement made with Columbus (the Sante Fe agreement) about religious matters. It was only with the second voyage (1493–6) that twelve missionary priests were sent out to convert the island natives.

Cost is likely to have been the deciding factor. In comparison to expenditure elsewhere, the financial cost of the venture to the monarchs was low. The historian Hugh Thomas (2003) compares the 2 million *maravedís* that the monarchs contributed to the voyage to the 60 million that was spent on the marriage of their daughter Catherine to Prince Arthur, heir to the throne of England at that time. For the monarchs there was little to lose and, potentially, much to gain.

Achievements of the voyages 1492–1516

In 1492, sailing from Palos with three ships, Columbus reached the Bahamas and from there went on to Hispaniola. Columbus thought he had reached the East Indies and the valuable Spice Islands on his voyage west. This was the exciting news he took back to Spain. Three further voyages were undertaken by Columbus, who discovered more of the West Indian Islands and part of the mainland of South America. Gradually it became clear that what had been found were new lands to the Europeans. Columbus had discovered the sea route to and from the continent which came to be known as America. From 1499 onwards, not only Columbus, but other explorers as well made voyages of exploration, including along the coast of South America. Although the Indies in the form of China and Japan had not been reached nor the sought for wealth found, it seemed that the new lands did offer opportunities – a 'new world'.

Establishing Spanish claims to the new seas and lands

Ferdinand and Isabella wished to ensure ownership of their new possessions, particularly as they feared that the Portuguese, the major seafaring nation in Europe at the time, might put in their own claims. Pope Alexander VI, a Spaniard himself and, therefore, likely to be sympathetic to the Spanish cause, issued a number of **papal bulls**. The most important was the *Inter Caetara* of 1493 which confirmed the Spanish rights to the new lands in South America. In the Treaty of Tordesillas, made with the Portuguese the following year, Spain agreed to move the line which marked Spanish territory further west. This change was thought to be relatively unimportant at the time but it meant that when Brazil was later explored and settled in the early sixteenth century, it became part of the Portuguese rather than the Spanish Empire.

Early settlements

The earliest settlements were located mainly in what is now referred to as the West Indies, in particular, Hispaniola. Here the first Spanish city, Santo Domingo, was founded in 1496. Some small settlements were also established on the mainland. Life in these settlements was tough both for the settlers and for the natives, whom the Spanish coerced to labour on the land and in the mines. Large numbers of natives died, and so did a large number of the settlers who suffered from the climate and malnutrition.

For Spain, one of the main appeals of the new discoveries was land. This meant the need for labour to work the land. Grants of *encomiendas* were given by the Crown to settlers. Under this system, the natives had to work for, or produce goods for, the *encomenderos* (the recipients of *encomiendas*). In return, the *encomenderos* were supposed to protect and educate the native workers and instruct them in the Christian faith.

The question of how the natives should be treated arose early. Columbus, along with his two brothers, seems to have been more concerned with acquiring personal wealth and meeting the financial demands of Castile. They and other early settlers failed to treat the natives as fellow humans and felt that they had the right to enslave the native population. This was completely unacceptable to the Dominicans and Franciscans who had come to the New World to convert the natives to Christianity. Their attitude is summed up in a sermon given by one Dominican, Fray Montesinos, in 1511:

SOURCE D

Part of a 1511 sermon by Fray Montesinos, criticising the colonists of the New World for how they treated the natives.

Tell me, by what right, or by what interpretation of justice, do you keep these Indians in such a cruel and horrible servitude? … Why do you keep those who survive so oppressed and weary, not giving them enough to eat, not caring for them in their illnesses? For, with the excessive work which you demand of them, they fall ill and die, or, rather you kill them with your desire to extract and acquire more gold every day … Are these not men? Have they not rational souls? Are you not bound to love them as you love yourselves?

KEY TERMS

Papal bull A document issued by a pope. It is named after the metal seal (*bulla*) which it bears as a mark of authenticity.

Encomienda A land grant given to an individual in return for his services to the Crown. Settlers receiving these grants also received a specified number of natives from a particular community.

Why does the author of Source D say that Indians should not be kept in conditions of slavery?

Spain 1469–1598

Christopher Columbus

1451	Born, probably in Genoa
1477–85	Based in Lisbon before moving to Castile
1492	First voyage west to find the Indies: three ships, the *Santa Maria*, the *Pinta* and the *Niña*, set sail from Palos, near Cádiz
	Landed in the Bahamas and went on to Cuba and Hispaniola
1493	Made Admiral of the Seven Seas and viceroy of the Indies on his return to Spain
1493–6	Second voyage with seventeen ships and 1200 men, including twelve missionary priests to settle Hispaniola
1498–1500	Third voyage: explored the Orinoco River. Columbus sent back to Spain in chains as a result of serious disputes among the settlers of Hispaniola
1502–4	Fourth voyage: went along the coast of modern-day Honduras
1506	Died a rich man with a number of titles and honours

Columbus has aroused much controversy. Most historians agree that his main abilities were as an explorer and that he was much less successful in his administrative skills. His wide knowledge of astronomy, geography and seamanship do not seem to be in doubt. As a teenager he had sailed to such places as Iceland, Ireland and down the coast of Africa, eventually settling in Portugal. This had given him extensive knowledge about sailing.

In particular, Columbus had knowledge of trade winds, without the help of which an Atlantic crossing from Europe would take too long and it would not be possible to carry enough water and food for the sailors. By making use of the brisk trade winds from the east, the voyage could be made in around five weeks. He would then, for a return voyage, need to ride the westerly winds.

Columbus's idea had been to sail west to reach the eastern lands of China and Japan. However, he thought that the westward distance from Europe to Asia was shorter than it in fact is and that Japan lay further to the east from China than it does. At the time, this was a matter of dispute and went against other more realistic estimates of the distance. To the end of his life Columbus seems to have convinced himself that he had found outer lying islands of Japan. What he did find was far more important; it would lead to the development of an entire new world for Europeans.

Such views by members of the religious orders had already reached the ears of Ferdinand and Isabella. In 1500, they forbade slavery and decreed that the natives were 'free vassals of the Crown'. This was reaffirmed in 1512 by the 'Laws of Burgos', which set a code of behaviour for Spaniards in their handling of the natives. Exceptions were made for those who attacked Spain or practised such habits as cannibalism; exceptions of course which the settlers could use to their advantage.

Establishing government in the new possessions

Gradually the Crown established government institutions in the new lands. The new discoveries belonged to Castile, not Aragon, and it was Castilian laws and customs which Isabella wished to see implemented. It was only after her death that a few Aragonese were allowed to emigrate to these new lands. In 1503, a central trading office had been set up in the Castilian port of Seville. All trade between Europe and the new lands had to go through it. A council, which came to be known as the Council of the Indies, was set up in Spain to oversee governance. However, one of the major problems was the difficulty of ensuring good government from so far away and in conditions different from Spain itself. Consequently, royal orders, particularly those in favour of the natives, such as the Laws of Burgos mentioned above, were often ignored.

Contemporary view of the discoveries by 1516

The significance of the early discoveries was slow to be recognised. What little information was available about the New World did stimulate curiosity among those who heard about it. There was also some interest in the novelties that Columbus brought back, such as the pineapple. But there was no rush of people wishing to go to the new lands. The journey was long and dangerous and conditions of life were difficult for the early settlers. It was only from about 1509 onwards, when the mainland began to be explored, that evidence of precious metals was found. To many contemporaries the discoveries ranked among the least of Ferdinand's achievements. The possibilities of the world empire to come were as yet unseen by most.

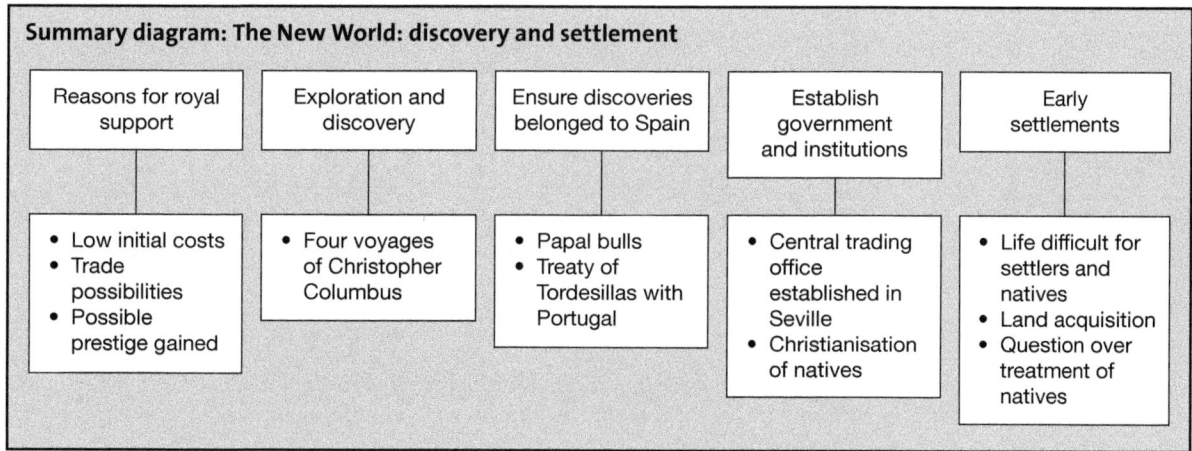

3 The closing years of the reign 1504–16

▶ *What were the consequences for Spain of the death of Isabella?*

The years 1504–16 had been a period of achievement in regard to foreign policy and the discovery and settlement of the New World. However, in Spain itself, difficulties arose, partly as a result of the death of Queen Isabella.

The succession to the Crown of Castile 1504

Isabella died in 1504, worn out by the exertions of her travels and the loss of a number of her children and grandchildren, in particular, her only son John, and her favourite daughter, Isabella, Queen of Portugal (see page 9). The fragile links that bound Aragon and Castile together were now threatened. Isabella's will left Castile to her eldest surviving daughter, Joanna. However, Joanna had already shown signs of mental instability and it was laid down in the will that 'in her absence, or if she proved unwilling or unable to govern' Ferdinand was to act as **regent**. In this way, it was hoped that Ferdinand would keep some control over Castile and that too much power would not fall into the hands of Joanna's husband, Philip of Austria. Philip resented this. In addition, many of the Castilian nobles did not wish Ferdinand to have any further say in matters relating to their country. Even in the final years of Isabella's life there had been complaints about Aragonese officials in Castile. Some of the Castilian nobility were also keen to regain the power they had lost in previous years.

When Philip and Joanna arrived in Castile from Burgundy in 1506, Ferdinand went to meet them. After a hostile discussion, he agreed, in the Treaty of Villafafila, to give up the government of Castile to Philip and Joanna, or to Philip in the event of Joanna's death, and promised not to play any part in the affairs of Castile. Ferdinand then returned to Aragon. He must by then have concluded that he would not be accepted by the Castilians and that his future was in his Aragonese kingdoms.

In the same year, 1506, Ferdinand took Germaine de Foix for his second wife, probably hoping for an heir, which would prevent Aragon as well as Castile coming under the rule of Joanna. It seemed that the two kingdoms would again separate, the one to be ruled by Joanna, the other by the heir of Ferdinand and Germaine.

The death of Philip and its consequences

Chance was to decree otherwise. Only a few months later, Philip died unexpectedly and Joanna's mind went completely. She refused to let his coffin be buried and took it with her to the fortress of Tordesillas. Cardinal Cisneros became regent briefly, and in accordance with Isabella's will, invited Ferdinand to return to Castile. Cisneros was concerned about the unrest in Castile, with some of the nobles trying to increase their own powers again.

Ferdinand spent most of his remaining years in Castile, working closely with Cisneros to govern the country. On his return to Castile, in 1507, Ferdinand dealt with any troublesome nobles. And in 1510 he was sworn in as regent of Castile. It was during this period that he accomplished much in foreign affairs and the New World. His own hopes of a male heir to Aragon were, however, unrealised. A son was indeed born to Germaine in 1509, but only survived for a few hours.

> **KEY TERM**
>
> **Regent** Ruler of a kingdom during the absence, childhood or illness of the king or queen.

Ferdinand himself died in 1516 and Cisneros became regent again, but this time on behalf of the sixteen-year-old Charles, son of Joanna and Philip.

Castile and Aragon in 1516: the question of unity

To what extent would Charles I, the successor to the kingdoms of Castile and Aragon, take over a united Spain in 1516? Several questions can be asked in approaching this issue: was there some formal agreement between the two kingdoms which made them one? Were there institutions or organisations which were common to all the kingdoms? Or was there a tacit form of unity, a feeling of oneness that was shared by the people of Castile and Aragon?

A formal agreement?

One can quickly dismiss the first question. At no time was there any agreement that Ferdinand and Isabella were rulers over a kingdom of Spain. In fact, the monarchs of Castile and Aragon would not start referring to themselves as 'Kings of the Spains' until the end of the seventeenth century, and even then, there was no legal basis for the title. The marriage contract between Ferdinand and Isabella also showed the determination of the two kingdoms, particularly Castile, to maintain their separate identities.

Signs of unification

Looking for signs of unification between the two kingdoms requires detailed investigation, but here again, there is scant evidence of even an intention on the part of Ferdinand and Isabella to bring about a full union.

In religious matters there was certainly some coincidence of policy. Both monarchs wished to be in charge of the Church in their respective kingdoms. The Jews were expelled from both. However, it was only in Castile that the Muslims were forced into a choice between conversion and expulsion. The Inquisition was introduced into Castile and Aragon, and the Council of the Inquisition was answerable to the two Crowns.

Other than the Inquisition, however, there was no important joint council which looked at affairs in both Castile and Aragon:

- As Ferdinand spent most of his time in Castile, he had to decide how Aragon should be governed in his absence. The solution was to set up not a joint council for the two kingdoms, but rather, a separate council to advise solely on the affairs of Aragon.
- Administratively, the *Cortes* of the kingdoms remained separate, as did their laws and coinage. *Corregidores* were only introduced into Castile, and the *Hermandades* were very short lived in Aragon compared to Castile.
- Almost nothing was done to bring economic union. Merchants and traders still had to pay customs duties at several points across the kingdoms.

- No central body was formed to deal with foreign policy. When additional territory was acquired, it was assigned to either Castile or Aragon. Thus, Castile obtained the New World – from which the Aragonese were excluded – and to Aragon went the kingdom of Naples.

Signs of informal unity

More evidence exists to support the idea of informal unity:

- Ferdinand and Isabella certainly worked closely together on a personal level. The two monarchs acted together over foreign policy, in which Castilian troops and money supported generally traditional Aragonese aims. People from many parts of the two realms fought together, as in the Granada War.
- Castilian gradually became the dominant language.

But one must not overstate the situation, and there are clear signs that there would be resistance to the prospect of a union:

- Many in the non-Castilian kingdoms feared that union with Castile meant losing their distinct identities and tried to ensure that it did not happen.
- Many resented the Castilians, who received the majority of the rewards and offices that the union of the two crowns brought about.

Finally, it must be remembered that on the death of Isabella, Castile and Aragon separated again for a short time, with Joanna and her husband ruling Castile and Ferdinand returning to his Aragonese kingdoms. There was then a real possibility that this split would remain permanent.

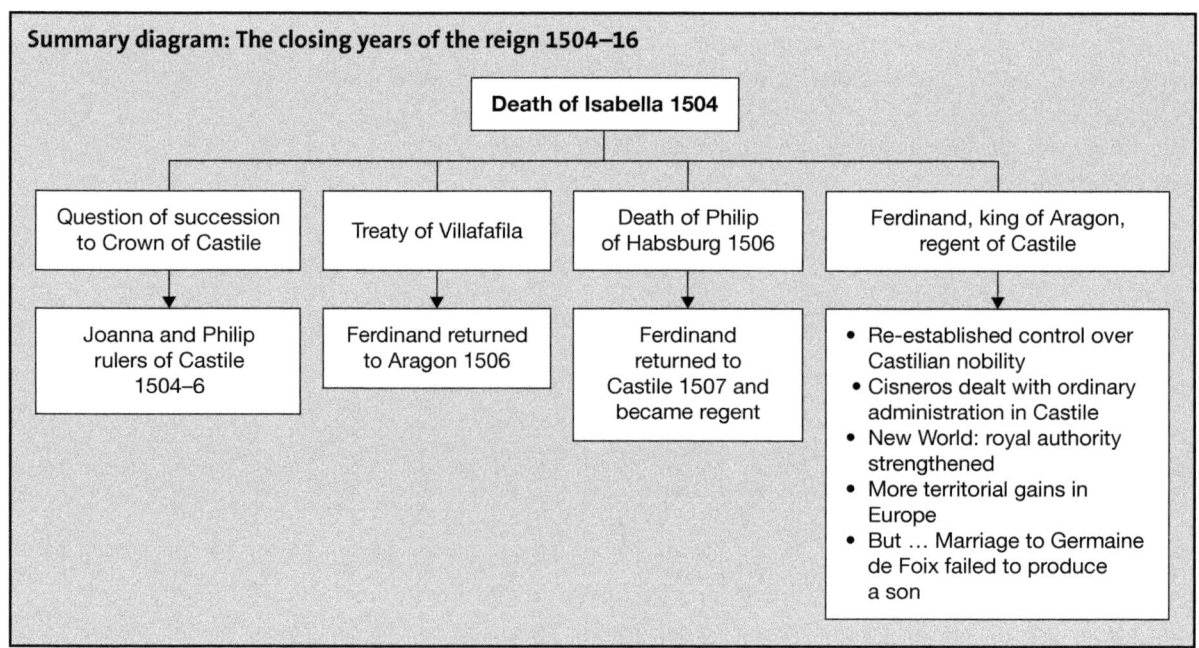

Chapter 3 Ferdinand and Isabella 1479–1516: Europe, the wider world and the end of the reign

Key debate

▶ *Was there a 'New Monarchy' in Spain between 1492 and 1516?*

This debate centres around how far Ferdinand and Isabella consolidated the power of the monarchy in Spain. Did they create a unified and centralised state under royal control? Was this state innovative and effective in what it did?

Prescott, writing in 1837, certainly thought so.

EXTRACT 1

From William H. Prescott, *History of the Reign of Ferdinand and Isabella the Catholic*, edited and abridged by C. Harvey Gardiner, George Allen & Unwin, 1962, p. 296.

Spain, under the glorious rule of Ferdinand and Isabella, we beheld emerging from chaos into a new existence … Ferdinand and Isabella, on their accession, saw at once that the chief source of the distractions of the country lay in the overgrown powers and factious spirit of the nobility. Their first efforts, therefore, were directed to abate these as far as possible. Another practice steadily pursued by the sovereigns was to raise men of humble station to offices of the highest trust … The queen's government was equally vigilant in resisting ecclesiastical encroachment … She took more effectual means to circumscribe the temporal powers of the clergy. Towards the Roman See she maintained the same independent attitude … she succeeded in restoring the ancient discipline of the church … Persons and property were alike protected under the fearless and impartial administration of the law … the crown absorbed the power, in whatever form, retrieved from the privileged orders.

In Extract 1, Prescott refers to the monarchs as bringing Spain into a 'new existence' by increasing their powers and control. For him, Ferdinand and Isabella did this by dealing with the power of the nobility and employing men of 'humble station' – the *letrados*. In regard to the Church, Prescott also refers to the controls over the Church in Spain which Isabella made.

J.H. Elliot also sees their government as 'new', but not for the same reasons as Prescott.

EXTRACT 2

From J.H. Elliott, *Imperial Spain 1469–1716*, Edward Arnold, 1963, p. 74.

Inevitably their exalted sense of their own office – of their obligation as rulers to restore order and impose justice – tended to cut through many of the legal limitations by which they were surrounded. The unity of their persons transcended the disunity of their dominions, and gave reality to a Spain that was something more than merely Castile and Aragon. [They] strengthened the upper tier of their own royal power, but also tightened the whole governmental structure, subtly transforming it in the process, so that, in Castile at least, they left behind them a state far more subordinate at every level to royal authority than the one they had found ... They laid the foundations of a new state, not by introducing new institutions but by revivifying old ones, and by bending them to serve their own ends and to assert their own authority over the entire body politic. The 'new monarchy' in Spain, as elsewhere in Europe, was in the first instance the old monarchy restored – but restored with a sense of royal authority and national purpose capable of launching it on a radically different course.

For Elliott, the 'new' came in the form of perfecting the state institutions to assert the powers of the Crown. To him it was 'new' too in the sense that, by unifying Castile and Aragon, the joint rulers had created a much stronger state than would otherwise have been possible.

Henry Kamen, in contrast to Prescott and Elliot, is completely clear – Isabella and Ferdinand are medieval monarchs, not 'new' monarchs.

EXTRACT 3

From Henry Kamen, *Spain 1469–1714*, Pearson, 2005, p. 64.

Ferdinand and Isabella were still mediaeval rulers, not 'new monarchs': for them good government did not mean the imposition of the apparatus of a modern state. Indeed, under the Catholic Monarchs there was no nation state, no new bureaucratic apparatus, no absolute monarchy. Ferdinand wished if anything to strengthen local communities so as to allow them to achieve viable self-government under the tutelage of the crown, and encouraged the view that cooperation with the crown was liberty from oppression ... Ferdinand realised that without strong, homogeneous, government below there was little hope of control from above. It was accepted, in any case, that the crown had limited powers ... Even when they were most high-handed in their political actions, the sovereigns ruled with consent, a fundamental component of their style of government.

> **?** Which of the Extracts 1, 2 and 3 makes the strongest case that Ferdinand and Isabella introduced a new monarchy into Spain?

With debates such as this, it is important to think through the meaning attached to words. Prescott and Elliott particularly emphasise the effectiveness of the monarchs' control over their respective countries. But how effective was that control in all the areas that they dealt with: was it complete, partial or perhaps even lacking? How far was the personal bond that united Castile and Aragon helpful in achieving effective government? How successful were the monarchs in taming the nobility? Looking at their methods of government – the personal rule, the systems they put in place such as the *letrados*, *corregidores* and the royal councils – how far were these simply trying to improve on existing methods to firmly assert the Crown authority? In what sense were their religious policies new and/or effective?

Chapter 3 Ferdinand and Isabella 1479–1516: Europe, the wider world and the end of the reign

Chapter summary

By 1516 much had been achieved to enhance Spain's prestige and standing in international affairs. The northern frontiers of Spain had been secured by gaining Roussillon, Cerdagne and Navarre from France. The peace with Portugal had been cemented by marriage ties. Granada had been reconquered. The kingdom of Naples was now part of Aragon. A foothold had been established in north Africa and Castile had gained the Canaries. Castile was also the main beneficiary of the New World discoveries. In the years between 1504 (Isabella's death) and 1516, however, it seemed a strong possibility that Castile and Aragon would again become two separate countries. The key debate considers the question of whether what Ferdinand and Isabella achieved was a 'New Monarchy'.

 Refresher questions

Use these questions to remind yourself of the key material covered in this chapter.

1 How important was religion as a factor in Ferdinand and Isabella's foreign policy?
2 How far did defence of their lands factor in Ferdinand and Isabella's foreign policy?
3 Why was peace with Portugal so important to Ferdinand and Isabella?
4 What new fighting methods and armaments did the Spanish army introduce during this period?
5 What was the importance of securing Naples for Spain?
6 Why did Spain engage in fighting with France so often during the reign of Ferdinand and Isabella?
7 How successful was Spain in fighting the forces of Islam during the years 1479–1516?
8 How important were marriage alliances to the conduct of Ferdinand and Isabella's their foreign policy?
9 What were Spain's foreign policy achievements during this period?
10 By the time of Ferdinand's death, what problems were apparent in the foreign policies pursued by Spain?
11 Why did Ferdinand and, in particular, Isabella, decide to support Columbus in 1492?
12 What did Columbus achieve during his four voyages to the Americas?
13 How were the New World discoveries viewed in 1516?
14 Why did the death of Isabella create difficulties for the government of Castile?
15 Did Ferdinand and Isabella create a united Spain?

Question practice

ESSAY QUESTIONS

1 To what extent was Spain's foreign policy during the years 1474–1516 driven by fear of the advance of Islam?
2 How successful was Spain's foreign policy during the period 1474–1516?
3 'Ferdinand I of Aragon's only concern in foreign policy was to secure Aragon's possessions in the western Mediterranean.' How far do you agree?

INTERPRETATION QUESTIONS

1 With reference to Extracts 1 and 2 (below), and your understanding of the historical context, which of these two extracts provides the more convincing interpretation of the foreign policy of Spain between 1474 and 1516?
2 Using Extracts 1–3 (below and page 63) and your understanding of the historical context, assess how convincing the arguments are in relation to the foreign policy of Spain between 1474 and 1516.

EXTRACT 1

From Henry Kamen, *Spain 1469–1716*, Pearson, 2005, pp. 8–9.

Ferdinand committed Spain to a foreign policy that it pursued throughout the sixteenth century: containment of French interests, domination of the western Mediterranean, repulsion of the Turkish advance … The foreign policy of the Catholic Monarchs was undeniably aggressive. Though the direction and decisions were largely those of Ferdinand, the resources used were principally those of Castile. It was, therefore, in effect a joint foreign policy, drawing on the one hand from Castile's Reconquest traditions and superiority in men and money, on the other from the active Mediterranean aspirations of the old Aragonese Empire. To further their policy the sovereigns made highly effective use of dynastic alliances and diplomatic missions.

EXTRACT 2

From Geoffrey Woodward, *Spain in the Reigns of Isabella and Ferdinand, 1474–1516*, Hodder & Stoughton, 1997, pp. 92–3.

In theory, peace was always preferable to war but, if necessary, Ferdinand was prepared to fight and in the 1490s, the Spanish army came of age. Techniques in the use of artillery had been learned in the Granada war and were applied to good effect in the Italian campaigns by Gonzalo Fernandez de Córdoba … From 1492 to 1504, Castile and Aragon made spectacular gains. Victory over Granada raised the idea of further expansion into the heart of Africa, and the discovery of America opened up new horizons beyond the Canaries. Both ideas appealed to Castilians. Aragon, on the other hand, gained the fruits of Ferdinand's diplomatic labours, by recovering its lost Pyrenean counties and snatching Naples from the jaws of France.

> **EXTRACT 3**
>
> **From J.H. Elliott, *Imperial Spain 1469–1716*, Edward Arnold, 1963, pp. 43–4.**
>
> *The most obvious reason for Spain's failure to establish itself effectively in North Africa lay in the extent of its commitments elsewhere. Ferdinand … was too preoccupied with other pressing problems to devote more than fitful attention to the African front. The cost of failure was very high in terms of the growth of piracy in the western Mediterranean, but it is arguable that the nature of the land and the insufficiency of Spanish troops in any event made effective occupation impossible. It is conceivable, however, that the formidable natural difficulties would not have been insuperable if the Castilians had adopted a different approach to the war in North Africa. … they thought principally in terms of marauding expeditions, of the capture of booty and the establishment of … frontier garrisons. There was no plan for total conquest, no project for colonizations … Africa offered few attractions to the individual warrior, more concerned to obtain material rewards for his hardships than the spiritual recompense … Consequently, enthusiasm for service in Africa quickly flagged, with entirely predictable military consequences …*

CHAPTER 4

Charles I: 1516–56

Isabella and Ferdinand were the last Spanish monarchs of Castile and Aragon. In 1516 their thrones would fall to Charles I, the sixteen-year-old Habsburg. To many Castilians, Aragonese, Catalans and Valencians, he was a 'foreigner' who had grown up away from Spain, and was not the Spanish ruler they desired. This chapter examines how the approach that Charles and his advisers took on arrival in Spain would set the scene for events in 1516–22, his early years as king. It then covers the period from 1522 to 1529, when Charles returned from the Netherlands and established himself as King of Spain, and analyses his administrative reforms, his relationship with the *Cortes* of his kingdom, his financial position and religious matters. It goes on to detail the main points of Charles's foreign policy – an area of mixed success which was costly in financial terms. Finally, it presents an assessment of the position of Spain in 1556. The material is covered under the following headings:

★ The succession to the Crowns of Aragon and Castile
★ Revolts in Spain 1519–21
★ Charles's return to Spain 1522
★ The government of Spain
★ Finance
★ Religion and the Church in Spain
★ Foreign policy
★ The New World
★ Spain in 1556

The key debate on *page 73* asks the question: What was the significance of the defeat of the *comuneros* revolt?

Key dates

1500	Charles born in Ghent in the Netherlands	1520	Charles left Spain for the Netherlands
1516	Charles proclaimed joint ruler of Castile and Aragon with his mother	1522	Charles returned to Spain
		1526	Charles married his cousin Isabella, daughter of the King of Portugal
1517	Charles arrived in Castile to take up the Crown of Spain	1527	Birth of Charles's son Philip
1519	Charles succeeded Maximilian as Holy Roman Emperor	1543–56	Charles remained mainly out of Spain. Philip acted as regent
1519–22	*Germania* revolt in Spain	1556	Charles abdicated in favour of his brother Ferdinand and his son, Philip
1520–1	*Comuneros* revolt in Spain. Rebels defeated at Battle of Villalar	1558	Death of Charles I

Chapter 4 Charles I: 1516–56

The succession to the Crowns of Aragon and Castile

 Why were Spaniards reluctant to accept Charles as king?

Following the death of his grandfather Ferdinand in March 1516, Charles was proclaimed King of Aragon, and King of Castile jointly with his mother, Joanna. At the time, Charles was still in the Netherlands and Archbishop Cisneros continued to act as regent in Castile and Aragon.

Awaiting the arrival of Charles

The period until Charles arrived in Spain was one of unrest and uncertainty. Ferdinand had left the regency of Aragon, Catalonia and Valencia to his illegitimate son. Castile was in the hands of Cardinal Cisneros, who had already been responsible for Castile during the time that Ferdinand had been appointed as regent. The great nobles (the grandees) saw this as an opportunity to make trouble. A number of Spaniards had previously travelled to Charles's court in Brussels to criticise Cisneros's regency in Castile and ingratiate themselves with the king. The death of Ferdinand led others from the Aragonese kingdoms to journey to Brussels and lobby Charles for positions and power. In Castile local factions vied for control. Cisneros tried to introduce a citizen militia which would have made the Crown independent of the great nobles. Resistance and risings against this by the Castilian towns and nobility led Cisneros to abandon his plans. Some writers, such as Stewart MacDonald, writing in 2000, see this as a time when royal authority under Cisneros all but collapsed. In contrast, the historian John Lynch (1981) writes that Cisneros 'saw Spain safely through the critical months that followed, suppressing incipient disorder, preserving the royal power intact, and transmitting to Charles his Spanish inheritance as it had been left by the Catholic Monarchs'.

Charles's early life

After his father's death, Charles's mother, Joanna, remained in Spain, along with his younger brother Ferdinand and one of his sisters, so Charles was brought up with three of his sisters in the loving care of his aunt, the archduchess Margaret of Austria. His education was that of a Burgundian prince. His chief tutor was **Adrian of Utrecht**, later to be a regent and one of his most important advisers in Spain in the early years of his rule. Adrian had a great deal of influence on Charles, instilling in him a genuine devotion to the Church and both regular attendance at mass and making confession. As Charles was heir to the Netherlands, Adrian was likely to have emphasised the history of his family to him, and to have instilled in him the dream of reclaiming the original heart of the Burgundian lands, the duchy of Burgundy, which had been lost to France in the previous century. Even his name must have reminded him of his brave

 KEY FIGURE

Adrian of Utrecht (1459–1523)

Appointed Charles's tutor in 1507. He served with Cisneros as co-regent of Spain when Charles was a minor and became regent of Spain in Charles's absence in 1520. He became a cardinal in 1517 and was elected pope in 1522.

Charles I

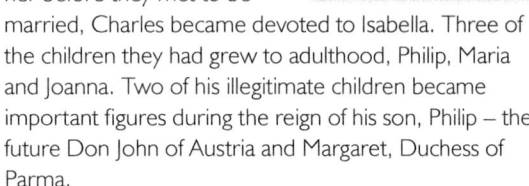

1500	Born in Ghent in the Netherlands
1517	Arrived in Castile to take up the Crown of Spain
1526	Married his cousin Isabella, daughter of the King of Portugal
1527	Birth of Charles's son Philip; left Spain
1529–56	Irregular visits to Spain; ruled Spain through regents
1530	Crowned emperor as Charles V
1556	Abdicated and returned to Spain
1558	Died at Yuste monastery in rural Spain

Charles had, along with his three sisters, been brought up in the Netherlands by his aunt, Margaret of Austria. His mother, Joanna, lived in Spain and Charles did not see her until he was seventeen years old when he went to Spain to become King of Castile. Charles seems to have been a lonely boy. His appearance, in particular his Habsburg jaw, led some at the time to consider him to be mentally defective. What all his contemporaries agreed on, though, was his religious piety, attending mass and confession regularly. This piousness was to remain with him for the rest of his life.

Charles's marriage to his cousin Isabella of Portugal seems to have been a success. She was an extremely competent young woman, able to act as regent in Charles's absences from Spain. Although he had never seen her before they met to be married, Charles became devoted to Isabella. Three of the children they had grew to adulthood, Philip, Maria and Joanna. Two of his illegitimate children became important figures during the reign of his son, Philip – the future Don John of Austria and Margaret, Duchess of Parma.

Charles's life was spent almost continuously in warfare. He rarely stayed for long in any of the lands over which he ruled. The longest he stayed in any of the countries over which he ruled was the seven years he spent in Spain between 1522 and 1529. In his youth he had enjoyed the joust and other knightly activities. In manhood he was an experienced leader of his armies.

It can be no surprise that, worn out and disillusioned by what he perceived as his failures, particularly in regard to the fight to secure Catholicism against Lutheranism and in relations with the German princes of the Holy Roman Empire, he should decide to abdicate in 1556 and retire to a spacious house at the monastery at Yuste, surrounded by luxurious tapestries, furniture and works of art, including paintings by Titian. Here he was to die in 1558.

Key figures in the Habsburg family

- *Margaret of Austria* (1480–1530): the daughter of Maximilian of Austria and Mary of Burgundy, sister of Philip I of Castile. She became the guardian of her nephew Charles I, supervising his upbringing in the Netherlands. Margaret was well educated and a patroness of the arts. Between 1507–15 and 1519–30 she acted as governor general of the Netherlands. Her presence there for so long ensured continuity in the administration, while she also proved to be a valuable source of advice to Charles on wider imperial matters.
- *Ferdinand I* (1503–64): Charles's younger brother was born and brought up in Spain. Sent to the Netherlands, he was made ruler of the Habsburgs' Austrian lands and heir to the Holy Roman Empire. By his marriage, Ferdinand became King of Bohemia and Hungary from 1526.
- *Mary of Hungary* (1505–58): Charles I was fortunate that when Margaret of Austria died his sister Mary, the widowed Queen of Hungary, was available to replace her in 1530 as governor of the Netherlands. Mary had been widowed since 1515 when her husband, the King of Hungary, had died. She became one of Charles's most trusted advisers on foreign and imperial affairs. She always tried to prevent any disagreements that arose within the Habsburg family becoming too serious.

and warlike great-grandfather, Charles the Bold, Duke of Burgundy, who was killed in battle in 1477. The life Charles would have grown used to was one of luxury, of expensive clothes and works of art, of hunting and jousting, banquets and music – all the culture and festivities which were such an important feature of the Burgundian court. Charles had also been carefully instructed in public affairs. A Burgundian nobleman, **Chièvres de Croÿ**, was appointed when he was nine years old to instruct him in affairs of state.

Charles arrives in Spain 1517

It was not until September 1517 that Charles left for Spain to receive oaths of allegiance from his new kingdoms. Charles could not afford to be away from the Netherlands while there was a possibility that the French might invade. Before he set out, therefore, better relations had to be established with France, which was done in the Treaty of Noyon in August 1516. He was then free to travel to Spain.

In some ways Spain was very similar to the Netherlands. Both consisted of a collection of lands which were united by their ruler in name only, each retaining its different laws and institutions. In other ways they were different. The lack of festivities and ceremony, such as Charles had known in the Netherlands, must have made Spain seem a less welcoming country than the one he had left. Spain's past history was very different from that of the Netherlands. In Spain there were recent memories of fighting the forces of Islam. For Castilians, in particular, their interest and concern had been in the *Reconquista*, of pushing forward the frontier of Christian Spain, as many of their fellow countrymen were now doing in the New World (America). They felt a great pride in their achievements and much dislike and distrust of foreigners, among whom they included people from other parts of Spain. It was in this country that Charles's brother, Ferdinand, had been born and brought up and many Spaniards would have preferred him to be king.

A king with everything to prove

To the Spanish, their new king was a foreigner. A contemporary writer tells us that 'among Spaniards no foreigner is accounted of importance'. Any Spaniards who witnessed his arrival in Spain probably doubted his ability to rule. What the Spaniards most wanted was a king who would support Spanish interests and concerns; not those of other lands. Charles did not speak any Spanish language and had never visited Spain. Nor did he have much knowledge of Spain and Spanish affairs. At sixteen years of age, with a large nose and outsized lower jaw, along with a slight build, Charles probably did not project the image of a king to those who met him. With him were his advisers and others of his household. Few were Spanish. His chief adviser was his former tutor, the Burgundian, Lord of Chièvres, William de Croÿ.

In addition, Charles's early actions as king seemed designed to lead to resentment among the Spaniards rather than to reconcile them to his rule. Ximénez de Cisneros, the regent in Spain during the period between

KEY FIGURE

William II de Croÿ (1458–1521)
Lord of Chièvres, was the chief tutor and later counsellor of Charles I. He was a member of one of the most important families of Brabant.

? How far does this portrait help to explain why Charles' first visit to Spain proved to be so difficult?

SOURCE A

This portrait was painted between 1514 and 1516 and shows Charles I wearing the Order of the Golden Fleece and a hat with the badge of the Virgin Mary. In his left hand, Charles holds a sprig of rosemary symbolising love and friendship.

Ferdinand's death and Charles's arrival, was dismissed in spite of the way he had maintained control over Spain during Charles's absence. Favours and important Spanish offices were given away to Charles's Burgundian supporters. Chièvres himself gained an important post in the government of Castile.

Adrian of Utrecht received the bishopric of Tortosa; but most anger was aroused by the granting of the main archbishopric in Castile, that of Toledo, to Chièvres' nephew, Guillaume Jacques de Croÿ, who was only sixteen years old. Further complaints were made about Spanish money being sent out of Spain to the Burgundian court. An additional cause for dissatisfaction was Charles's own election as Holy Roman Emperor on 28 June 1519. Most Spaniards saw this as a means of drawing Charles's attention away from his new kingdoms in Spain.

Charles's acceptance by the *Cortes*

To be fully accepted, Charles had first to be acknowledged as king by the various *Cortes* of his new kingdoms. The *Cortes* of Castile held in Valladolid in 1518 started badly. Charles had been so ill-advised as to choose a Burgundian councillor, Jean le Sauvage, as president of the *Cortes*. The representatives of the towns immediately expressed their resentment and protested against the inclusion of a foreigner at a meeting of their *Cortes*. They requested further that Charles respect the laws and privileges of Castile, administer justice, remove foreigners from his service, and learn to speak Castilian. But the *Cortes* had little power to force acceptance of their will. Charles did, however, swear to respect the traditional laws of Castile as was customary, and in return was granted a *servicio* of 600,000 **ducats** without conditions.

In Aragon, Charles needed to receive the acceptance of each of the three separate *Cortes*. The *Cortes* of Aragon was more able to resist royal power than

 **KEY TERMS**

Servicio A sum of money to be raised by taxation.

Ducat A variety of gold and silver coins that became widely used in western Europe. One ducat was worth 375 *maravedís*.

that of Castile and was even more reluctant to recognise Charles as king, particularly while his mother, Joanna, was still alive. It was not until January 1519 that they did so, and voted him a grant of 200,000 ducats. Acceptance by the *Cortes* of Catalonia, which met at Barcelona, took over a year to be agreed. Again there were objections to his Burgundian advisers, and it was only with reluctance that 250,000 ducats were granted to him. The delays, therefore, meant that Charles had no time to visit Valencia, the third main kingdom which made up the Crown of Aragon, for it was while at Barcelona that Charles received news, on 28 June 1519, that he had been elected Holy Roman Emperor.

The *Cortes* at Santiago (and later Corunna) 1520

Charles needed to obtain money to pay the expenses incurred in becoming Holy Roman Emperor. He, therefore, called another *Cortes* in Castile in an attempt to acquire the necessary funds. It was at this *Cortes* that many of the concerns and fears of the Spanish were expressed. The *Cortes* was called to meet at Santiago in March 1520. This choice of meeting place created great annoyance. It had been chosen because of its convenience for Charles and his retinue leaving the country. No *Cortes* had ever met in such a remote place before, and Santiago did not even have the right to send representatives to a *Cortes*. Further resentment was caused by the fact that the previous subsidy had been granted less than three years before. The representatives of many of the towns present tried to obtain discussion of their grievances before they would grant any money. It is hardly surprisingly that this did not suit Charles. Some of the representatives were bribed, and eventually a majority voted to approve the grant. Although Charles had made some concessions, the incident further increased the growing hostility to him. This was to find expression in the revolts which broke out almost immediately. To make matters worse, on leaving Spain in May, Charles broke earlier promises not to appoint foreigners. He appointed Adrian of Utrecht as regent in his absence.

Summary diagram: The succession to the Crowns of Aragon and Castile

Awaiting Charles's arrival	Charles I, the 'foreigner'	Resentment over Charles's early actions as king
• Cisneros, regent of Castile • Spanish lobbying of Charles in the Netherlands • Unrest in Spain	• Brought up in the Netherlands • Not fluent in Castilian Spanish • No first-hand knowledge of Spain	• Royal favours and important offices awarded to Burgundians • Protest from the *Cortes* of Aragon and Castile • Election as Holy Roman Emperor would take Charles out of Spain

Revolts in Spain 1519–21

▶ *Why did revolts break out in Spain in the 1520s?*

The revolts of the 1520s in Spain mark a significant turning point in the reign, and their suppression was to help secure Charles's position. The most important one broke out in Castile in May 1520.

The revolt of the *comuneros*

Discontent had been growing for some months, not only in Castile, but elsewhere in the Spanish peninsula. There had already been a number of outbursts of violence, particularly in Aragon, before Charles left Spain for his coronation as Holy Roman Emperor in Germany. The major threat to his position, however, was the revolt which began in Castile as he was departing for Germany. This revolt is usually referred to as the revolt of the *comuneros*.

Reasons for the revolt

The majority of those involved seem to have been resentful of Charles's leaving Spain, and to have hated the foreigners who filled important positions and offices, and were seen as taking the wealth of Spain out of the country. There were fears that their country would lose its separate identity as part of the empire and that Charles would not return. There was also resentment that Charles had asked for money, not once but twice in three years. Rumours even circulated that there would be taxes on the baptism of infants, on air and on water!

Some of these points are reflected in the demands made by the ***Junta*** of Tordesillas in 1520, when it petitioned Charles to:

- live in Castile
- bring no 'Flemings, Frenchmen, nor natives of any other country' to fill the positions in his household
- follow the customs of the 'Catholic Sovereigns Don Fernando and Dona Isabel, his grandparents'.

For the historian J.H. Elliott, writing in the 1960s, it was not, however, in the years when Charles became King of Spain that the seeds of the movement were sown but before, in the time of Ferdinand and Isabella and Cisneros's regency. It was felt that many of the traditional powers and prerogatives of the Castilian towns and cities had been eroded under the rule of the two monarchs. In support of this view, he cites the demand of the *Junta* of Tordesillas that no *corregidor* should be appointed in the future, except at the request of the town concerned. The *corregidores*, particularly in the 1490s, had become disliked as an inefficient and even corrupt body, for which the towns had to pay. Moreover, it was not just the *corregidores* that aroused the concern of the towns. The historian Stephen Halicazer, writing in 1981, argues that a wealthy and growing urban middle class in Castile was becoming resentful of the political dominance of the

> **KEY TERMS**
>
> ***Comuneros*** The city dwellers who organised themselves to defend the rights of their communities against the government. The term is often associated with a rebellion or revolt. (Spanish for members of a community.)
>
> ***Junta*** A council.

Castilian nobility, who were being favoured by the Crown at the expense of the towns. However, it was probably the actions of Charles which brought the revolt to a head and gave the movement wide appeal.

The course of the revolt

Although many areas of Castile were affected, most of the action took place in urban centres. The rebellion started in Toledo. Here, a member of the nobility, **Juan de Padilla**, took command and a government was set up in the name of the king, the queen (Joanna) and of the *comunidad*, indicating that this was not a revolution aimed at overthrowing the king. Toledo's lead was followed by other towns such as Segovia, Salamanca and Valladolid, the residence of Charles's regent, the unpopular Burgundian, Adrian of Utrecht. Supporters of the rebellion came mostly from the lower nobility and town dwellers. The most important nobles, however, tended to stand aside and wait to see how matters developed.

KEY TERM

Comunidad Many of the towns in Castile joined together in a league to rebel against the imposition of Habsburg authority.

An attempt was made to gain the support of Queen Joanna when Tordesillas, where she was staying, was taken. Although she was prepared to show her support when meeting with some of the *comuneros*, she would not commit herself to the rebellion on paper. This refusal left the leaders of the revolt with no claim to legality. Had they been able to say that they were attempting to restore the rightful monarch they would have had a purpose. As it was, they had no clear aim in view.

The situation started to turn in favour of the king. Charles made some concessions. The collection of the *servicio* voted by the *Cortes* of Santiago was stopped; no more foreigners were to be appointed to offices in Castile; and two Castilians, the two most important grandees, the admiral and the constable of Castile, joined Adrian as regents. These concessions came at the right time.

KEY FIGURES

Juan de Padilla (c.1490–1521)

A member of a noble family of Toledo. He became a popular captain-general of the *comuneros* forces, capturing Tordesillas on their behalf. He was defeated and captured at Villalar and executed.

Juan Bravo (c.1483–1521)

From a noble background and was one of the leaders of the *comuneros* revolt.

During the same time, the character of the rebellion changed and became more extreme. There were a few attacks on property and some demands were made for economic and social reforms, such as curbs on the powers of the nobles and criticism of their exemption from taxation. Such developments would concern many of the nobles who had so far not intervened. They were also likely to have been concerned at developments in Valencia, where a social rising was taking place (see page 72).

As a result, more nobles were now prepared to support the regents in trying to put down the revolt. A royal army was formed which defeated the *comuneros* at the Battle of Villalar in 1521. The two leaders, Padilla and the Segovian *comunero* leader **Juan Bravo**, were captured and executed. This was a major defeat. The *comuneros* lost control of most of northern Castile and only Toledo was able to hold out for a little longer.

The impact and significance of the revolt

Charles, returning to Spain with an army of foreign mercenaries, was now in a position to deal firmly with the rebels. Some were executed and others received various punishments. Beyond this, Charles was willing to show leniency and issued a general pardon. The powers of the *corregidores* in the towns were increased. The eighteen towns previously represented in the *Cortes* were still able to send their representatives but there was little opposition to Crown policies and, although each king at the beginning of his reign still swore to uphold the liberties and privileges of Castile, this became only a formality. Some of the changes Charles introduced were generally welcomed. Thus, the unpopular Chièvres was replaced by **Mercurino Gattinara**, a respected counsellor of Charles's mother.

The revolt of the *Germania*

A second major revolt was also put down. This one had broken out in Valencia in 1519 and was much more of a social than a political revolt. The ***Germania*** was a Christian brotherhood of armed volunteers from the poorer classes which had been formed to defend the Valencian coast against Muslim pirates. Members of the *Germania* held grievances mainly against the local Muslims and the powers of the nobles who employed many of them. Plague had broken out in the area and this was seen by many as a punishment for tolerating the presence of Muslims in their community. There was also resentment against the privileges of the nobles and the near starvation conditions in which many members of the *Germania* lived. Further complaints were made against Charles, who had frequently postponed the meeting of the *Cortes* of Valencia and did not seem interested in remaining in Spain. Support for the rebellion was, therefore, to be found among a wide section of the middle and lower classes – the poorer craftsmen, small farmers, weavers and spinners for example – but not among the nobles or wealthier clergy.

The course of the revolt

At first the violence of the movement was directed against the Muslim peasants in the country areas around Valencia. Some were murdered and many were forcibly baptised into the Christian faith. As many of the rich had moved away from Valencia because of the plague, the supporters of the *Germania* were able to take over the city. They also experienced success against the small military forces sent against them which were led by nobles and representatives of the Crown. The movement spread beyond the city of Valencia to include most other parts of the kingdom, even taking control of the island of Majorca.

However, support was lost when a new leader, **Vicent Peris**, took over and incited his followers to more violence and radicalism, such as demanding a wider distribution of land. Many members of the middle classes, in particular, withdrew their support. As a result, the supporters of the Crown made gains. The city of Valencia was recaptured, and an army of troops loyal to the nobles and to the Crown had defeated the undisciplined and ill-equipped army of the *Germania* by the end of 1521. Shortly after this defeat, Pens himself was captured

KEY FIGURES

Mercurino Gattinara (1465–1530)

An Italian statesman, lawyer and clergyman. He became a cardinal of the Catholic Church in 1529. Gattinara served as Charles's grand chancellor and had a wider vision of empire than Charles did.

Vicent Peris (1478–1522)

An artisan and leader of the weavers' guild in Valencia. He was violently anti-nobility and anti-Muslim.

KEY TERM

Germanía 'Brotherhood'. It was a Christian brotherhood of armed volunteers formed to defend the Valerian coast against Muslim pirates.

and executed. The resistance continued with much less support until 1524, when the remaining areas in revolt surrendered. Many of the rebels were sentenced to death; others suffered fines and the confiscation of their possessions. The local nobility had, by their victories, strengthened their own position.

Summary diagram: Revolts in Spain 1519–21

	When	Where	Causes	Reasons for defeat

Comuneros	1520–1	• Started in Toledo and Segovia
		• Spread to other cities in Castile
			Various:
			• Charles's foreignness
			• Greed of Burgundians
			• Long-standing concerns over freedoms being lost
				• Failure to get support from Charles's mother
				• Radicalisation of the revolt
				• Charles made concessions:
				  – stopped collection of subsidy
				  – two Castilians became co-regents with Adrian of Utrecht
				• Nobility took firm action

Germania	1519–22	Valencia	• Dislike of privileges and nobility • Dislike of Muslims	• Nobility took firm action

3 Key debate

▶ *What was the significance of the defeat of the* comuneros *revolt?*

Historians vary in their assessment of the consequences of the *comuneros* revolt and have interpreted the events in different ways.

Some historians, such as V.H.H. Green, saw it as the defeat of 'parliamentary' government and democracy in Castile and the victory of 'royal absolutism'. Others, like John Lynch, go further, stressing that the defeat signified the 'absolutism' of Charles's rule over Castile and that, in the future, his powers there would not be checked. Henry Kamen, while agreeing that the cities did not achieve the political power they had been hoping for at the time, puts forward the view that their major demands were in fact implemented by the government. For him, Charles was indeed the 'true victor' in terms of political power, even though it was the grandees who had defeated the rebels.

EXTRACT 1

From V.H.H. Green, *Renaissance and Reformation*, Edward Arnold, 1964, p. 135.

The failure of the Comuneros *meant the end of 'parliamentary' government and the victory of royal absolutism … Although the* Cortes *did not disappear, either in Castile or in Aragon, the royal authority in future overcame all possible opposition, whether from the nobility or the towns or the Church.*

The historian John Lynch takes a similar stance:

EXTRACT 2

From John Lynch, *Spain Under the Habsburgs*, Basil Blackwell, 1981, p. 49.

The defeat of Villalar left Castile even more exposed to absolutism than it had been before. The comuneros *had been concerned not only with objectives but also with means; the revolt was not only a protest against Spain's involvement in the European and imperial policies of Charles V, it was also an attempt, no matter how vague or rudimentary, to defend the interest of Castile by imposing constitutional checks on royal power. These were now brushed aside and from this moment Castile lay completely at the mercy of its sovereign. Municipal government was already incapable of exercising independent authority ... even the elected officers of the towns had little power when face to face with the* corregidores *... Towns browbeaten by royal* corregidores *and their ally the aristocracy could hardly be expected to send independent representatives to a national* Cortes.

Henry Kamen supports the view that the defeat was 'a permanent blow to the political hopes of the cities'. However, he goes on to say:

EXTRACT 3

From Henry Kamen, *Spain 1469–1714*, Pearson, 2005, p. 83.

Ironically, over the next few years all their major demands were put into effect: the Cortes, *for example did meet regularly, to renew the* servicios; *and in 1525 and 1534 the collection of taxes was granted to the towns. But Charles made it perfectly clear that the cities were to play no part in government. Who then gained from Villalar? The grandees, whose enormous military power had helped to save the government, were confirmed amply in their social position and seigneurial privileges; but they were denied any increase in political power, which thereafter rested firmly in the hands of the crown, the true victor of Villalar.*

> **?** What are the various reasons that the historians in Extracts 1–3 use to explain the significance of the defeat of the *comuneros* revolt?

Are some of these views too extreme? No attempt was made to reduce the existing powers of the *Cortes* in either Castile or Aragon. Castile already had few means by which she could impinge on Charles's powers in the *Cortes* in any case. The role of the nobility in government, particularly in local government, continued as before Villalar. Kamen argues above that the nobility's authority and prestige were enhanced by their contribution to the victory over the *comuneros*. There were, however, complaints from some members of the nobility that they did not receive the rewards they felt entitled to after the victory. One wrote bitterly that Charles had 'not granted any *mercedes* [rewards] to those who took lance in hand with the result that Your Majesty is validating the proposition of those who say that the conflict was with the nobles and not with Your Majesty'. A generally accepted view put forward by historians such as Elliott is that the failure of the *comuneros* meant a failure of purely Spanish interests. The defeat at Villalar signified the end of attempts to prevent Spain from playing a major role in the events of Europe – a role which Charles was determined to pursue and which was to have dramatic consequences for Spain's future.

Charles's return to Spain 1522

▶ *Why were the Spanish more prepared to accept Charles as king when he returned to Spain in 1522?*

The *comuneros* revolt had been dealt with by the time Charles returned to Spain by Charles's government and the nobility working together. The *Germania* revolt was put down by the nobility of Valencia. Charles's return heralded a new stability in the kingdoms that made up Castile and Aragon. For the rest of his reign there were no further revolts against his rule. His return marked a clear difference from how he had been received when he first arrived in Spain.

Reasons for stability

When Charles had left Spain to succeed Maximilian as Holy Roman Emperor, he was still a youth. The 22-year-old who returned three years later looked and acted more like a self-confident king. A description by an English statesman of the time calls him 'very wise and well understanding his affairs, right cold and temperate in speech with assured manner couching his words right well and to good purpose when he doth speak'.

There was now a period of calm in the reign of Charles in Spain. There was growing acceptance of him as king. The lack of major events in the internal history of Spain after the two major revolts has often been remarked on. It must, to some extent at least, be related to Charles's tactfulness and wisdom in his handling of the Spanish. It could also mean that he had learnt from previous mistakes. In a speech he made in 1529, he referred to the time when he left Spain in 1520 to become Holy Roman Emperor:

SOURCE B

From J. Sanchez Montes, 'Actitudes del español en la época de Carlos V', *Estudios Americanos* **iii, 1951, p. 193 (translated).**

I was managed and governed by M. de Chièvres, and I was not old enough to know these kingdoms or experienced enough to govern them. And as I left immediately for Flanders, having spent very little time here, and what is more, being still unmarried and without an heir, it is not surprising that there was scandal and disturbance.

In Source B, how accurate do you think is Charles's description of his first visit to Spain?

Perhaps lessons had also been learnt from the demands made during the *comuneros* revolt. Charles was certainly prepared to be more 'Spanish' on his return in 1522. Now he spoke Spanish, or rather Castilian, at court. Charles, like his grandparents, had no fixed royal capital during his residence in Spain. Like them he travelled through his various Spanish lands to meet and listen to his subjects. He made a popular marriage when, in 1526, he wedded his cousin Isabella, sister of the King of Portugal. There had been traditional links between Spain and Portugal, particularly during the reign of Isabella and Ferdinand, and Charles was to leave his wife to act as his regent during any absences he might have, knowing that, because of her Portuguese origins, her rule would probably be acceptable to his Spanish subjects. The following year, to great rejoicing, his first child and heir, Philip, was born in Castile.

During the *comuneros* revolt the nobility had proved their value to the Crown and this created a strong partnership for the future. Spaniards, particularly Castilians, began to play a more important role in government. More and more Spaniards took offices in the administration, not only in Spain but also in other parts of the empire. The conquest of Mexico in 1521 by Cortés and that of Peru in 1525 by Pizarro led to the development of a New World empire which gave opportunities to many Castilians (see pages 97–8).

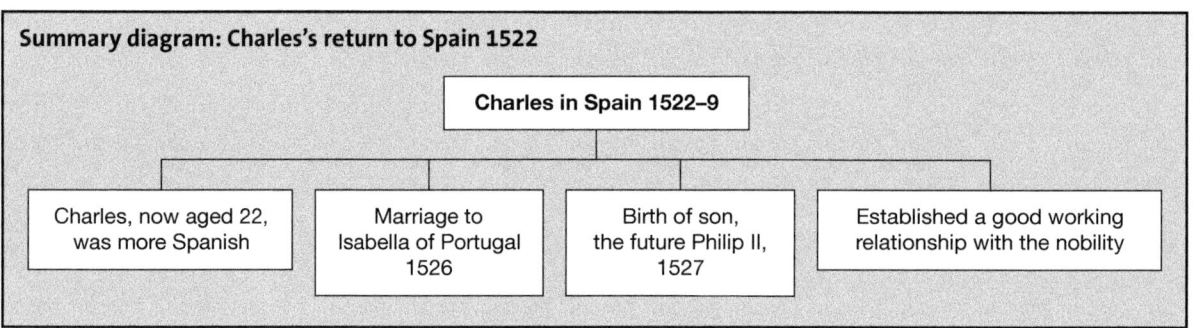

5 The government of Spain

▶ *How effective were the methods Charles employed to govern Spain?*

Charles's aims in government

The New World and Spain were only a part of Charles's personal empire. Figure 3.1 (see page 41) gives some idea of the extent of the lands that Charles ruled. Opinions among historians differ as to how Charles saw his role in governing this empire. To some historians, his dream was of a universal monarchy. This is reflected in a letter that Gattinara, the Italian who had become Charles's main adviser, wrote to him in 1519:

SOURCE C

Extract from a letter written by Gattinara to Charles I.

… now that God in His prodigious grace has elevated Your Majesty above all Kings and Princes of Christendom, to a pinnacle of power occupied before by none except your mighty predecessor Charlemagne, you are on the road towards Universal Monarchy and on the point of uniting Christendom under a single shepherd.

> How does Source C reflect the concerns that many had in other European countries about Charles's ambitions in Europe?

It seemed possible to his contemporaries that Charles, with the amount of lands over which he ruled, could become the sole ruler over all Christian countries. One wrote, after the 'Sack of Rome' (see page 92) in 1527, that 'Christ has granted an extra-ordinary opportunity to the men of our age to realize this ideal, thanks to the great victory of the Emperor and the captivity of the Pope.'

But there is little in Charles's own writings to support this view. He continually refers to his House and his dynasty, indicating that these were his major concerns. In fact, when speaking to the pope and cardinals in 1536, he denied that he had any idea of gathering a universal empire under his rule, 'There are those who say that I wish to rule the world, but both my thoughts and my deeds demonstrate the contrary.'

It was probably not one of Charles's aims to bring all the lands over which he did rule under central control with common institutions. In any case, each of his lands would have resented any such attempt and he must have known this. It was concern for his dynasty and the need to protect his lands which led him into fighting wars almost continuously until his abdication. In addition, his commitment to Catholicism involved him in fighting wars to defend Catholicism against the growing Protestant threat within his own empire and against the Muslims from without. This involvement in so many areas of Europe meant that Charles was rarely in a position to concentrate on dealing with any one problem before he was called to deal with another. His Spanish subjects, though never completely reconciled to those responsibilities which took him out of Spain so much, did in general come to sympathise with him. And, it was Spanish, particularly Castilian, wealth and arms which supported him in many of his endeavours.

Charles remained in Spain after his return in 1522 until 1529. This was the longest time he spent in any one of his territories and he used the opportunity to try to establish his authority over the government of his kingdoms there. As with the other sections of his empire, Charles did not envisage joining the separate kingdoms of Spain into one or introducing a single institution through which he could govern the whole of Spain. Charles was King of Castile and King of Aragon, not King of Spain. On the other hand, if he was to have control over Spain, and in particular obtain the money he needed for his various enterprises, it was vital that he ensure his hold over the administration, especially that of the richest of his Spanish kingdoms, Castile.

The councils

Charles continued the reforms in conciliar government already begun by Ferdinand and Isabella. Councils were still the most important feature of the administrative system, composed not of the most important nobles but mainly of *letrados* (see page 26). At the same time, additions and changes needed to be made to the system for Charles to establish his control and for it to be able to meet the demands of running an empire as widespread as his.

The councils can be divided into two main types. The first was mainly advisory, and the second mainly administrative.

Advisory councils

The new Council of State set up in 1526 fell within the first category. In theory, its purpose was to advise Charles on the most important matters concerning the government of Spain, and to deal with the decisions of the other councils. In practice, its existence under Charles was probably designed to give social distinction to its members, who constantly attended the emperor. It had little political influence and little administrative importance during Charles's reign.

A second advisory council was that of war. This was also newly formed. It came into existence in 1522 and usually had the same membership as the Council of State, with the addition of military experts. Its responsibility was to co-ordinate all the military matters concerning the Crown.

Administrative councils

The second main type of council was made up of those concerned with administration. Some of these dealt with the administration of geographical areas of Charles's empire, some with particular functions. The Royal Council of Castile was probably the most important of these – the one Charles referred to as 'the support of my realms'. It dealt with most of the internal affairs of Castile; acted as a court of law, hearing appeals from the lower courts; and advised the king on many matters, especially relations with Portugal, with which there were traditional links. Charles reduced the size of the council and included fewer nobles. Typical members were ecclesiastics and *letrados*, men who were thoroughly reliable but who tended to show little sense of independence.

The administrative role of the Council of Aragon was more limited than that of The Royal Council of Castile. It dealt mainly with the administration of justice, acting as the court of highest appeal, and had some internal administrative functions. Its officials were usually not from the nobility but were *letrados*. Charles generally respected the tradition that they should come from the three kingdoms of Aragon. This was useful in keeping Charles informed about the opinions of the people of Aragon. An exception, however, was the treasurer, who throughout Charles's lifetime was a Castilian. Another new council was the Council of the Indies, formed in 1524 and given extensive control over all matters concerning the running of Castile's American possessions.

There were also general administrative councils which were not linked specifically to geographical areas. One of the most important of these was the Council of Finance. This was originally created in 1522 for the management of Castile's finances, but it gradually assumed responsibility for all Charles's finances. As such, it can probably be considered the most innovative and important of the councils. The Council of the Supreme and General Inquisition was one of the few elements which linked all the kingdoms of Spain together, for it dealt with all matters of heresy not only in Castile but in all the kingdoms of Spain.

The effectiveness of the conciliar system

The system of councils became more efficient during Charles's reign. There were now fewer representatives of the nobility and more professional administrators in the form of the *letrados*. The new councils helped to meet the increasing demands of administering an extended empire. However, the councils were in existence mainly to advise Charles. They were not responsible for making sure that decisions were implemented, and they had no officials with which to do this. Nor did Charles make any attempt to unite the various institutions of his empire into one co-ordinated unit. Those of Aragon, Naples, Sicily, the Netherlands and Germany remained separate from those of Castile. As a writer of the time wrote, 'Charles's individual realms continued to be ruled as if the king who keeps them together were only the king of each.'

The importance of Charles's secretaries

The effectiveness of government depended very much on Charles and his secretaries making the system work. The organisation of the secretariat was based in each kingdom, the most important one in Spain being in Castile. Aragon already had a highly organised secretariat – the Chancellery – which Charles retained. In Castile it was different. The secretaries here were responsible for preparing the agendas for council meetings; all royal documents had to be countersigned by them; when correspondence arrived it was they who decided whether it should go to Charles or to one of the councils. They could also issue royal decrees without the agreement of the council. Much patronage was at their command. Their powers, therefore, often caused resentment, particularly from the members of the councils themselves. However, because of the speed with which they were able to act, more use was made of them by Charles. Consequently, their powers increased during his reign.

Francisco de los Cobos

The most important secretary for much of Charles's reign was **Francisco de los Cobos**. His office dealt with the affairs of Castile, Portugal, the Indies and, from 1530, Italy. Cobos improved the quality of those working in the secretariat. He usually chose men from the minor gentry who had had administrative training and experience and came from the smaller towns. They were not the younger sons of nobles, nor necessarily men of learning or those with university training. Those chosen by Cobos looked to him for their rewards and advancement. So he was able to rely on them to support him in his policies.

However, there were drawbacks as well as advantages to this. As the most important means of access to the king, Cobos received many gifts from those seeking to see or gain favours from Charles and, like other secretaries, he was able to acquire a large fortune and estate. Charles was prepared to accept this for he had no doubt of Cobos's personal loyalty and efficiency. These mattered more to Charles than concerns about the way in which Cobos had built up his fortune. Charles showed his opinion of Cobos in a letter he wrote to his son:

> **SOURCE D**
>
> **From a letter Charles sent in 1543 to his son, the future Philip II.**
>
> *Cobos is growing older and easier to manage, but he is true. The danger with him is his ambitious wife. No one knows so much of all my affairs as he, and you will always have reason to be glad of his service. But do not give him more influence than I have sanctioned in my instructions. And above all do not yield to any temptations he may throw in your path; … Cobos is a very rich man, for he draws a great deal from the dues for smelting bullion from the Indies, as also from the salt-mines and other sources. He looks on these things as his own particular privilege, but do not let them become heritable in his family. When I die, perhaps, it would be a good moment to resume these rights to the Crown. He has great gifts in the management of finances; circumstances not he is to blame for the deplorable condition of our revenues.*

To prevent excessive corruption it was important that Charles did not depend completely on his secretaries. He tried never to leave any matter entirely in the hands of those who were his servants but aimed to play at least some personal part in dealing with every issue. Sometimes too he wrote to his ministers and ambassadors himself, rather than relying on his secretaries to do so, and letters survive annotated in his own handwriting.

The *Cortes*

After a difficult beginning (see pages 68–9), Charles established a sound working relationship with the *Cortes* of his kingdoms. The *Cortes* could not make laws. They could only present petitions to the king who might or might not listen to them. The one important weapon they had was their ability to vote or to refuse money in the form of a *servicio* and to allow new taxes.

KEY FIGURE

Francisco de los Cobos (c.1472–1547)

Born into a noble family and was an important patron of the arts. He played an important role in advising Charles for much of the reign, particularly in financial matters.

? Why do you think Charles I was advising Philip in Source D to treat his relationship with Cobos cautiously?

The three *Cortes* of Aragon

The three *Cortes* of Aragon had a long tradition of independence and of rights over taxation (see page 6). Charles called a General *Cortes* of the representatives of the three kingdoms to meet six times during his reign, but, although they met at the same place, Monzón, they each sat separately and had to be dealt with separately. In addition, the individual *Cortes* met twice in Catalonia and once each in Aragon and Valencia. But for Charles, it was hardly worth the effort to persuade the representatives to grant him money, for, even when they agreed a *servicio*, it amounted to little and a third of it had to be spent on internal purposes. This meant that relatively little was available for the main reason for which Charles required it: the financing of his wars. Therefore, it is not surprising that the *Cortes* were not summoned very often.

Charles's relations with the *Cortes* of Castile

More funds were obtainable, and more easily, from elsewhere, especially from Castile. The Castilian *Cortes* traditionally had fewer powers than those of Aragon and voted grants of money for Charles before discussing other matters. It usually consisted only of the representatives of the eighteen towns who had a right to meet there, not of the nobles or clergy. During Charles's reign, the *Cortes* met fifteen times, mainly to vote on the money that Charles so often desperately needed. An attempt was made, early in Charles's reign, at the 1523 meeting at Valladolid, to discuss general political matters before granting taxes but this was firmly dealt with by Charles:

SOURCE E

Charles asserts his rights at the 1523 *Cortes* at Valladolid.

Yesterday I asked you for funds; today I want your advice. Which seems to you better, that you should grant me the servicio *at once, on my promise not to dismiss you until I have replied to, and provided for, everything that you justly ask me, and that I should do so of my own free will; or that I should first reply to the petition which you bring me, and have it said that I do so in order to get the* servicio? *You know that the custom has been to grant this first; thus it was done under my royal predecessors … Why try to establish an innovation with me? And since many evils have brought me to this necessity, you, like good and loyal subjects, will remedy them by doing your duty as I expect you to do.*

> What does Source E show about the powers of the *Cortes* of Castile? Why do you think that Charles was so keen to assert his rights here?

Charles was making it quite clear that taxes must be granted by the *Cortes* first, and that only then would the *Cortes* be free to discuss other matters.

The reasons why the Castilian *Cortes* had only limited power

Part of the reason for the lack of power of the Castilian *Cortes* was that only eighteen towns were able to send representatives (two each), and these did not represent all areas of the kingdom. In addition, the nobles and clergy were not usually called. However, in 1527, Charles was in desperate need of money for the campaign against the Turks in eastern Europe and wanted the nobles and clergy to agree to a special grant. To this end he called a General *Cortes*. But both nobles and clergy feared that such a precedent would mean a loss of their right to freedom from taxation, so Charles obtained nothing except some private donations from members of the clergy. Nobles and clergy were also called to a *Cortes* at Toledo in 1538, when Charles was again in need of money. This time it was not only because of the campaigns fought in Germany, north Africa and France, and that proposed against the Turks, but also to help meet the ordinary expenses of government. Charles now asked for a new tax, the *sisa*. Such a tax would clearly have to be paid by all in Castile, nobles and clergy as well as the rest of the population. Again the nobility refused. Charles realised that there was no point in continuing and dismissed this *Cortes*.

Although Charles had failed to gain contributions from the richer elements in Castile, he was able to gain the agreement of the representatives of the towns to raise most of the money he requested. That they had little power to deny Charles is partly shown by the way the 1544 *Cortes* requested that they should not be summoned more frequently than once every three years 'on account of the great costs and expense'. They seem to be implying here that they knew they could do little more than agree to what Charles wanted.

The importance of the evolution of government during Charles's reign

There has been some debate as to whether or not there was a revolution in the development of government under Charles. Certainly, administrative machinery had to evolve to meet the increasing demands of government. But, of course, the conciliar system itself already existed in Spain; Charles merely added to it and adapted it to meet his needs. The Councils of State and War were both new creations, but other councils were more clearly linked with what had gone before. With the expansion of lands under Charles's rule, the number of territorial councils consequently increased. These too looked back to previous reigns, being organised on the lines of the Council of Aragon already set up under Ferdinand. The administrative councils can all be traced back to earlier reigns. One major change, however, was that under Charles, secretaries such as Cobos grew in power and status.

Other instruments of government remained similar to those which had gone before. Members of Charles's family were appointed as governors or **viceroys** in important realms of the empire. When Charles was not in Spain in person members of his family led the government. In 1529 his wife, Isabella, became regent and governed with the help of the Archbishop of Toledo, **Cardinal Tavera**, until her death in 1539. In 1543 Charles appointed his son, Philip, as regent. Charles gave him instructions on what he was expected to do and also advice on how to deal with the powerful ministers and advisers he had appointed for him. There continued to be no fixed capital, although much

KEY TERM

Sisa A tax on food.

Viceroy An official who runs a country or state in the name of, and as a representative of, a king or queen.

KEY FIGURE

Juan Pardo de Tavera (1472–1545)

Held a number of important government and religious posts under Charles I. He was Archbishop of Toledo 1534–45, Grand Inquisitor of Spain 1539–45 and became a Cardinal of the Church. He was president of the royal council 1524–39 and regent of Spain 1539–41.

administration was done in Valladolid. Like his grandparents, Isabella and Ferdinand, Charles was constantly on the move, accompanied by his secretaries and advisers. The powers of the *Cortes* in both Castile and the three kingdoms of Aragon remained unchanged. In local administration the Crown still had to rely on the nobles and others who were respected in the localities. The changes that did occur were important but in no real sense did they constitute a revolution.

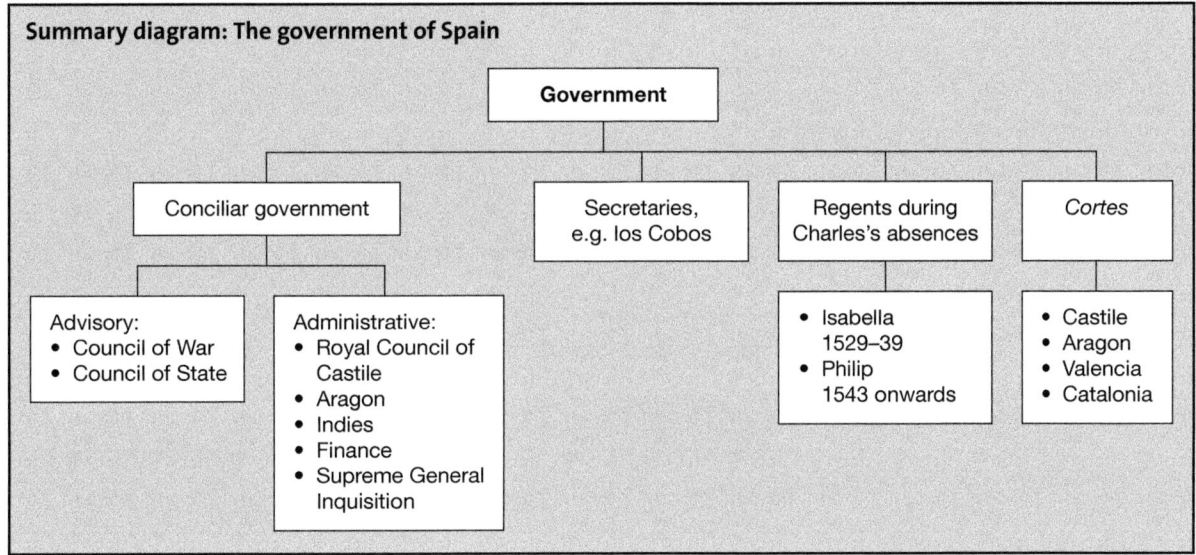

6 Finance

▶ *How successfully did Charles deal with finance during his time as king?*

Vital to Charles was the need to raise funds to pursue his ambitions, particularly those involving foreign policy.

Shortage of money was always Charles's main reason for calling a *Cortes*, and throughout his reign he had difficulties in meeting his financial needs. The Crown's financial position had not been strong when he became king. It worsened in the early years of his reign as a result of the greed of his Burgundian followers and the expenses of the imperial election. As early as 1523 he was saying that government debts in Castile 'amount to far more than I receive in revenue', at a time when all the prospective income for the following year had already been spent. His responsibilities as emperor led to an enormous demand for money: fighting wars in the sixteenth century became very expensive. In addition, there was the cost of the upkeep of his royal household.

KEY TERM

Order of the Golden Fleece An order of chivalry founded in the fifteenth century by a Duke of Burgundy and headed by the king. Members of the order had a number of privileges.

The cost of the ceremonial of the court had increased considerably compared to the cost under Isabella and Ferdinand, for Charles had made it more like the Burgundian court to which he had been accustomed. The **Order of the Golden Fleece** was introduced into Spain, with all the pageantry associated with it. Money had to be found to meet the salaries of the many new positions created, such as that of gentlemen of the household, and for the buying of jewels and works of art. All this amounted to about a tenth of the Crown's income.

Sources of income

Finance came from all parts of Charles's empire. Each area was expected to be self-supporting and, in addition, to give support to the general needs of the empire. The imperial coronation expenses were mainly paid for by Castile; at the end of his reign the Netherlands made the major contribution towards the wars against France; and payment for the armies to defend Vienna from the Turks in 1532 came from the empire. Usually, however, there was reluctance for money raised to be used for anything other than the needs of the country from which it came. It was only money raised from Castile which was regularly used for the general expenses of the empire.

Income from Castile

It was Castile, too, which contributed most of the income that came to Charles from Spain. There was little resistance from the *Cortes* to higher taxation. In any case, the majority of taxes were indirect rather than personal and could be collected without the need to refer to the *Cortes*. The most significant of these was the *alcabala*, which everyone had to pay whatever their income. In 1534 it was argued that this should be a fixed sum and, because of continuing inflation, its value in real terms gradually fell.

Of the other indirect taxes, only the customs duties made a valuable contribution. Charles did not manage to obtain any new taxes. However, he did establish the Crown's right to receive the *servicio*, granted by the Castilian *Cortes*, on a regular basis. This was the result partly of the defeat of the *comuneros* and partly because of the increase of royal power in the towns where the Crown was able to influence the selection of representatives to the *Cortes*.

To obtain more of the country's wealth, Charles needed to able to tax more fully the richer social groups of his kingdom, particularly the nobles who paid little in taxes. The direct tax burden fell only on one section of Castile, the lower and middle classes. His failure to increase the taxation of the rich meant that he had to turn to borrowing. This was done partly through the sale of *juros*, bonds paying a set rate of interest, the interest payable being assigned to a specific source of ordinary revenue. However, as more and more loans were raised, less and less of the ordinary revenue, of course, came directly to the Crown.

Income from Aragon

Apart from Castile, the Spanish Crown had three sources of income. First, there was Aragon. However, the constitution there meant that little could be raised in taxes. In any case, by Charles's reign, Aragon was not economically strong enough to be able to give him much financial help.

Income from the Church

The second source of income was the Church. Although in theory it did not have to pay taxes, in practice it gave a great deal of money. The pope allowed Charles to receive a proportion of all the income of the Spanish Church. In 1532, 372,000 ducats were raised in this way and by 1551 this had reached 500,000 ducats. A further source of income was the *cruzada*, a special contribution paid by both laity and clergy which, between 1523 and 1554, raised an average of 121,000 ducats a year. The money contributed in this way amounted to about a quarter of the royal income. The Crown had already gained control of the orders of military knighthood under Ferdinand and Isabella, and in 1523 the pope declared that they were in the Crown's ownership for ever. However, partly as a result of the loans Charles received from the German banking house of the **Fuggers** for the cost of the imperial election, the income from these military orders went there rather than to the Crown. As well as an annual income, the Church provided gifts of money from time to time. Other sources of funds which went from the Church to the Crown included the income of **sees** between the death of one bishop and the appointment of his successor.

 **KEY TERMS**

Fuggers A politically influential banking family from Germany with trading links throughout Europe. The loans they made to Charles I enabled him to become Holy Roman Emperor.

See The area of a bishop's ecclesiastical jurisdiction.

Income from the New World

The third source of income was the wealth which went into Castile, particularly from the 1540s onwards, with the discovery of the silver mines in the New World (see page 98).

This would seem to have been the solution to Spain's financial problems. Certainly, the sums were high. Between 1534 and 1540, the average annual receipts were 324,000 ducats, between 1545 and 1550 they were 382,000 ducats, and between 1551 and 1555 they were 871,000 ducats. The Crown was entitled to revenue from taxes, customs duties, Indian tribute and, most significantly, a fifth of all precious metals mined. There can be no doubt that income from America made a vital contribution to Charles's finances, but it did not provide the solution to all his financial problems. Even without any repayment of loans, a million ducats per year were needed for ordinary revenue. In addition to this were the expenses that Charles's foreign policy involved him in; the Metz campaign of 1552 alone cost over 2 million ducats (see page 95).

Other methods

Such were Charles's problems over finance that in 1552 he started to resort to other measures to try to raise money, measures which were to make it even more difficult to manage the country's finances efficiently. Sales of public offices took place, which prevented the advancement of people according to their ability. There was also the sale of certificates of nobility, which further decreased the size of the tax-paying population and increased the burden falling on those who did still pay taxes.

The only way in which Charles could have improved his financial position was to cease fighting expensive wars. And this he felt unable to do.

Summary diagram: Finance

Expenditure	Sources of income

• Greed of Burgundian followers
• Imperial election expenses
• Increased cost of royal court
• Cost of paying officials
• Royal household items (e.g. works of art)
• War
	• Individual parts of empire expected to be self-supporting and to contribute to general needs
	• Castile was a major contributor to general needs expenses
	• *Alcabala*, main indirect tax (its value fell in real terms)
	• General right to *servicio*, on a regular basis
	• Little revenue coming from Aragon
	• Church:
	  – Income from military orders
	  – Proportion of all income of Spanish Church
	  – *Cruzada*
	  – Gifts
	• Borrowing, e.g. *juros*

 # Religion and the Church in Spain

> ▶ *How effective were the measures taken to secure Roman Catholicism as the sole faith in Spain during this period?*

During this period little progress was made in reforming the Church in Spain. The same concerns that were apparent in Ferdinand and Isabella's reign over the poor levels of clerical training, absenteeism, lack of proper teaching of the Catholic religion and low levels of morality among the clergy persisted into Charles's reign. The years spent by Charles away from Spain meant that reform of the Church in Spain could not take priority.

Individual reformers of the Church

Some reforms did take place and a number of key individuals were active in trying to introduce improvements in the religious life of the Spanish people.

John of Avila was a popular preacher, writer and clerical reformer, called the 'Apostle of Andalusia' for his extensive ministry in southern Spain where he preached, helped the poor and promoted religious education among the laity. His views and actions led to his arrest in 1531 by the Inquisition (he was released in 1533). **Ignatius Loyola**, a hermit, spent his time in prayer and looking after the sick and poor . He was also questioned by the Inquisition for suspected **Illuminist** ideas. As a result, he fled to Paris where he was to found the Society of Jesus (see page 132). **Teresa of Jesus** was an important Spanish mystic who emphasised meditation and private prayer, and who reformed the Carmelite order.

The effects of the work of Cardinal Francisco Ximénez de Cisneros

The work of Cisneros, started during the reign of Ferdinand and Isabella, continued into the reign of Charles I. However, most ordinary clergy still did not have the education or training to carry out changes either to their lives or to their ability to teach the Christian doctrine and preach the gospel. The improvements among the Franciscans and Dominicans were more successful, however, and it was missionaries from the Dominican order in particular who were the most active in the New World.

Cisneros had founded the University of Alcalá, which opened in 1508 during the reign of Ferdinand and Isabella for the training of clergy. This became an important centre of learning by the time of Charles's reign, producing some of the most important spiritual leaders of the day. A printing press was set up there which became responsible for the reproduction of a number of spiritual texts. It was here that the **Polyglot Bible** was printed in 1522. This was the name given to the first printed polyglot of the whole Bible in its four original languages. It had been started and financed by Cisneros in 1502 with the purpose of reviving study of the scripture. The improvements in the intellectual standards of the bishops as a result of these developments meant that many of them were able to take an important role in the councils of the Church, particularly the Council of Trent.

Suppression of heretical views

The wars that Charles was fighting included those against Protestants in Europe. He had little success in defending the Catholic faith against Protestantism in the Holy Roman Empire, but within Spain the situation was very different. Charles was determined to suppress any signs of heretical ideas, particularly those associated with Protestantism.

Two groups accused of holding heretical views became associated with Protestantism during the 1520s: the Illuminists and the **Erasmists**.

KEY FIGURES

St John of Avila (c.1499–1569)

A priest in the Catholic Church who advocated reforms of priests and of religious education.

St Iganatius Loyola (1491–1556)

A Spanish knight who founded the Society of Jesus and believed in absolute obedience to the pope.

St Teresa of Jesus (1515–82)

A Carmelite nun who came under the suspicion of the Inquisition in 1576.

KEY TERMS

Illuminist Someone who believed in direct communion with God.

Polyglot Bible A version of the Bible that contains side-by-side versions of the same text in a number of different languages.

Erasmist Follower of Erasmus and his doctrine.

- Illuminism began among a group of friars. The Illuminists believed that they could put themselves in direct, personal communication with God through meditation and prayer, and many, like the Protestants, believed that good works were useless. This group was easily dealt with by the Inquisition, who persecuted members of any group found and condemned their ideas as heretical.
- The philosopher **Desiderius Erasmus** started a movement which would become even more important. Erasmianism promoted the idea of a reformed Church which incorporated learning, private prayer and meditation. At first his ideas were well received in Spain and he gained many influential supporters, both at court and in the universities. Charles himself showed interest in his work.

Despite the king's good disposition, his tolerance would not last. By the end of the 1520s, the first steps were taken to eradicate anything, however minor, which was not clearly Catholic in doctrine and practice. There were a number of reasons for this change:

- Charles had left Spain in 1529, taking with him many of the most powerful supporters of Erasmianism.
- At the same time, in Germany, a number of the German princes had pledged support for Lutheranism. This led Charles to be concerned about any signs of Protestantism being found in Spain.

To many in Spain, Erasmianism was associated with Protestantism, although Erasmus himself was firmly Catholic in his views. The Inquisitor General **Alonso Manrique**, who had supported the ideas of Erasmus, also fell from favour and in 1529 was confined to his see of Seville. This led to supporters of Erasmianism being persecuted by the Inquisition in Spain and a number fled the country. It became dangerous to even own copies of the writings of Erasmus or quote from them. The only acceptable route to God in Spain was being seen to follow the traditional methods and doctrine of the Catholic Church.

Charles's policy towards the *Moriscos*

By 1502 all the *Mudéjars* in Castile had had to become Christians or leave the country (see pages 33–4). Now known as *Moriscos*, they were mainly to be found in Granada. In Aragon, many *Mudéjars* had been forcibly converted to Christianity during the *Germania* revolt (see page 72). In 1525 those still not converted here were given the same choice as those in Castile: convert or leave the country. In neither Castile nor Aragon were any effective measures taken to ensure that they became genuine converts, and it is not surprising that people forcibly converted should try to retain their traditional ways as much as possible.

On a visit to Granada in 1526 Charles V was informed that 'the *Moriscos* are truly Moors; it is twenty-seven years since their conversion and there are not twenty-seven or even seven of them who are Christians'. In the same

 KEY FIGURES

Desiderius Erasmus (c.1467–1536)

A distinguished Dutch scholar who was influential across Europe during the first half of the sixteenth century. He wrote and published extensively and wanted to see reforms of clerical abuses in the Church.

Alonso Manrique de Lara (1476–1538)

A Spanish churchman who became Archbishop of Seville from 1523 and Inquisitor General from 1525.

year attempts were made to remove completely all existing traces of Moorish civilisation in Granada such as the use of Arabic, the wearing of traditional Moorish dress and the performance of a traditional dance, the *zambra*. There were attempts to get the local clergy to improve the Christian education of the *Moriscos*. Neither policy had much success. Charles, however, suspended the legislation against Moorish customs in return for a large subsidy paid by the *Moriscos* in Granada.

Relations with the pope

Relations between Charles and the papacy were generally poor for the majority of his reign. The popes of the time feared either Charles or the French king becoming too powerful in Italy, thus leading to the diminution of their own political power there. Sometimes, therefore, the popes allied with Charles and sometimes they allied with France to try to stop either country becoming too powerful in Italy. A particularly low point was when Charles's troops sacked Rome in 1527 (see page 92).

Difficulties with the papacy were not just over Italy. Although it does not concern our study of Spain, conflict also arose over how to deal with the Protestant challenge in Germany.

Finally, a third major area of conflict arose over the question of reforms to the Catholic Church throughout Europe. Charles was keen that a General Council of the Church be held to introduce needed reforms into the Church. However, he was unable to persuade the papacy of the urgency of the matter and it was not until 1545 that the first meeting of what was to be the Council of Trent to discuss reform was held.

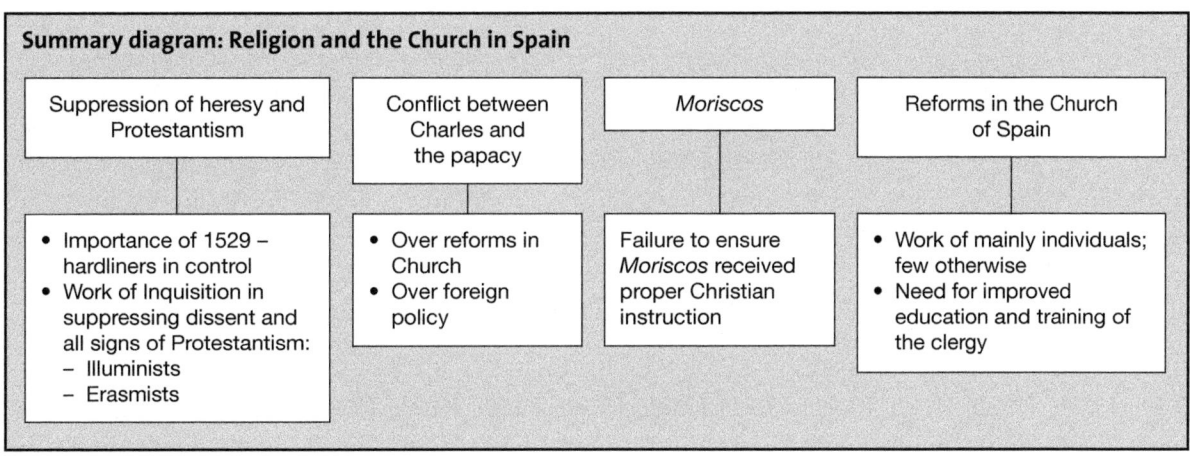

Summary diagram: Religion and the Church in Spain

8 Foreign policy

▶ What were Charles I's main aims?
▶ How successful was Charles in the foreign policies he pursued?

Charles I's aims

Charles, by birth, had come into possession of a vast array of lands:

- the Habsburg lands, which included Austria and the Tyrol in central Europe
- the Burgundian lands, mainly made up of the Netherlands, but also including Franche-Comté in eastern France
- Castile and the discoveries of the New World
- Aragon and the lands that made up the Aragonese Empire: the Balearic Islands, Sardinia, Sicily and Naples (see Figure 3.1, page 41).

In addition to these territories, Charles became Holy Roman Emperor (see page 11), responsible for the states which made up the Holy Roman Empire.

Charles did not feel any need to centralise his lands and make them one. Rather, it was a collection of individual states which owed him allegiance. His role as Holy Roman Emperor meant that he had to defend the Catholic faith, bring peace to the Christian countries of Europe and lead a crusade against Islam. He also wished to protect and extend the lands ruled by his family, particularly by regaining the Burgundian lands which had been lost to France.

A key part of his strategy was making alliances through the marriages of members of his family.

Rivalry between France and Spain

Spain and France had already been at war in Italy in the time of Ferdinand and Isabella. By 1516, the kingdom of Naples was in Spanish hands. It needed constant protection, particularly as a result of the persistent ambitions of France, which held Milan. War between Spain and France was to continue for most of Charles's reign.

Reasons for the rivalry

There was personal rivalry between Charles and the King of France, Francis I, who had succeeded to the French throne in 1515 at the age of 21. This rivalry intensified in 1519 when Charles defeated Francis in the contest to become Holy Roman Emperor. Once Charles had become Holy Roman Emperor (as Charles V), Francis became even more concerned. France was now encircled by Habsburg territories: Spain in the south, the Netherlands and Germany in the north and east. In Italy Francis had inherited claims to Naples, which was under Charles's control, and Milan which was under French control. Milan was important to both. For Charles it was an important strategic point enabling good communications between the lands of the Holy Roman Empire and the kingdom of Naples. Milan also helped communications between the Habsburg lands in Austria and Spain itself. In addition, Charles was also keen to regain the parts of the former family territories of Burgundy which had been lost to the family in the previous century.

Charles, as ruler of the Netherlands, had already made friendship overtures to France at the Treaty of Noyon (1516). By this, he had promised to return Navarre to France. He had, however, postponed carrying this out because of Navarre's position on his Spanish borders. This was clearly an area of concern to Spain. The French had taken advantage of the *comuneros* revolt to enter Navarre. Once this revolt had been dealt with Charles used his army to drive the French out of Navarre.

Conflict in Italy

From 1521 to 1529, the major area of conflict between Spain and France was in Italy. In those years, Italy was a collection of divided and weak states. French and Spanish interests were focused mainly on Naples and Milan. The Papal States lay between the kingdom of Naples to the south and the northern Italian states (see Figure 4.1, page 93). The popes during this period did not wish to see either Spain or France gaining further control in Italy. They feared that it would put their own positions in jeopardy.

A change of Charles's advisers helped to lead to a revised policy towards Italy. In 1521, Charles's closest adviser, Chièvres de Croÿ, who had supported a policy of peaceful relations with France, died. His replacement, Mercurio Gattinara, supported the idea of removing French influence from Italy. This was the policy Charles determined to pursue.

A joint Habsburg and papal army drove the French out of Milan in 1521. Charles now had control of northern Italy. A new pope, Clement VII, became concerned about Charles's rising power in Italy and formed an alliance with France and two of the important cities in Italy: Venice and Florence. This enabled France to retake Milan. However, on 24 February 1525, Charles's twenty-fifth birthday, his army, under Lannoy, inflicted a crushing defeat on the French outside Milan in the Battle of Pavia. This was a key development in the conflict between Francis and Charles. During the battle, the Habsburg army had made effective use of the **arquebuse** against the French cavalry. This expensive piece of weaponry was to become more widely used in future battles. Francis I himself, found trapped under his horse, was taken captive. Milan was again in Charles's control. But he failed to make the most of his great victory. In the Treaty of Madrid, Francis renounced his claims in Italy and the Netherlands and agreed to give up the Burgundian lands. However, no firm measures were taken to force him to keep to the conditions. Charles relied on Francis's word. Although his two sons were held in Spain as hostages, as soon as Francis returned home he renounced the terms.

KEY TERM

Arquebuse An early musket.

In 1526, fear of Charles's power led to the formation of another alliance, the League of Cognac, consisting of Pope Clement VII, France, England and some Italian states. Its aim was to free Italy from Charles and Habsburg domination. The next key event took place in 1527. Charles's army, made up mainly of German mercenaries under the Duke of Bourbon, marched on Rome from Milan to lend support to one of Charles's allies. In a successful attack on Rome, Bourbon himself was killed. The army, unpaid and out of control, entered and sacked Rome. This event inspired horror all over Christian Europe. Charles was deeply shocked by what had happened, but he tried to find scapegoats, blaming the pope and the French king for having instigated the events which led to this 'Sack of Rome'.

The following year, Francis I led his forces again into Italy. He entered the kingdom of Naples and laid siege to the city of Naples. At the same time, the Genoese fleet commanded by Andrea Doria blockaded the city from the sea. Still, events would unfold in Charles's favour. Francis's treatment of the Genoese led Doria to switch sides and he threw his support behind Charles. This was a major coup for Charles:

- From now on the important Genoese fleet was on Charles's side in the Mediterranean.
- Communications would be easier between Spain and Naples.
- He would be able to have easy access to loans from Genoese bankers.

The French were now in a very weak position. They no longer had the support of Doria and the plague hit their army. They were forced to break off their siege of Naples and retreated north. The following year, 1529, their army was defeated decisively at the Battle of Landriano. By then, both the Spanish and French

Men at arms

- *Charles de Lannoy* (c.1487–1527) was a soldier and statesman from the Netherlands in the service of Charles I. He had a reputation for bravery and military and political leadership. In 1522 he was made viceroy of Naples, and in 1523 commander-in-chief of Charles's imperial armies in Italy.
- *The Duke of Bourbon* (1490–1527) was a French military leader who had distinguished himself in war. He was made constable of France in 1515 and governor of Milan. However, Francis I recalled him from Milan and, in addition, confiscated parts of his lands in France. Bourbon, angered by Francis's actions, joined Charles I. He fought at Pavia and was killed outside Rome in 1527.

- *Andrea Doria* (1466–1560) was a Genoese statesman, mercenary commander and admiral with outstanding tactical and strategic talents. He was considered the greatest naval leader of his time. He was active in fighting the Ottoman Turks and Barbary corsairs at sea. In 1522 he entered the service of Francis I of France and helped him to capture Genoa (1527) from the imperial forces of Charles. However, he became concerned about French policies towards Genoa and transferred his services to Charles. In 1528, he and his forces drove the French out of Genoa. Charles made him grand admiral of the imperial fleet, which he commanded in several naval expeditions against the Turks.

Chapter 4 Charles I: 1516–56

Figure 4.1 Italy in the late fifteenth century.

sides had exhausted their resources in further fighting and were prepared to make peace.

The Peace of Cambrai was signed in 1529. In this, Charles achieved most of what he wanted. He gave up his claims to the duchy of Burgundy. But the French gave up their claims to Naples, Artois, Flanders and Milan. This secured Habsburg control in Italy. The treaty was cemented by the marriage of Francis I to Charles's sister Eleanor and a large sum of money was paid for the release of Francis's two sons from Spain.

Although there was further fighting in the years that followed, the situation for Charles and the French changed little. In the 1530s many of the cities in Italy were more strongly fortified by the building of ramparts and fortresses. This made them less likely to be taken by direct assault. Fewer of the Italian cities were prepared to support France. To ensure the continuing support of Milan, Charles married off his niece, the eleven-year-old Christina of Denmark, to the ruler of Milan, Francesco Sforza. Conflict between Habsburg and Valois still continued but it was mainly now further north in the Holy Roman Empire and the Netherlands where Charles was more vulnerable.

Waging war against Islam

This was a traditional policy for Charles to wage. Here the Burgundian traditions of war against Islam joined with the Spanish crusading drive. As Charles declared to the pope in 1536, he wished to wage 'not war against Christians but war against the infidel'. Charles's personal emblem, the Pillars of Hercules, bore the words *Plus Oultre* ('Still Further'). The motif of the Pillars was chosen in 1516 to suggest the Herculean task facing the king in fighting Islam, particularly in north Africa. In 1532 Charles had joined with his brother Ferdinand in marching east to relieve Vienna, which was being besieged by the Turks. However, fighting did not take place as the Turks withdrew and peace was made.

A war against the Turks far away in central Europe would not have commended itself to the Spanish people. Far more acceptable to them were the measures he took to try to deal with the supporters of Islam in north Africa. Commitments elsewhere meant that Charles was not able to do this until after 1529, when the north African ruler, **Barbarossa**, took from Spain the island fortress of Peñón, off Algiers, and a small Spanish fleet was defeated near Ibiza. By this time, Charles had the support of a regular naval force under Doria to help him. In 1532–3 a naval expedition including Spanish troops took Coron and Patras in Greece. This did not, however, affect Barbarossa's power in the western Mediterranean. Charles, therefore, organised an expedition against Tunis (1535) which proved far more successful. A large fleet of 82 galleys and about 300 transport ships with around 30,000 troops under the leadership of Charles and Doria attacked and captured the fortress of La Goleta and the city of Tunis. Most of the Turkish fleet was captured but Barbarossa managed to escape.

However, this major success could not be followed up, mainly due to Charles's commitments in northern Europe. Further attempts to stop first Barbarossa and then the pirate Dragut failed. An attempt on Algiers in 1541 came to a disastrous end when a storm wrecked the fleet and forced Charles's navy to withdraw. From then on, the Turks had the upper hand. They took Tripoli in 1551, the Peñón in 1554 and Bougie in 1555. By the end of the reign Spain was left in possession of just Melilla, Orán, Mers-el-Kebir and La Goleta.

> **KEY FIGURE**
>
> **Hayreddin Barbarossa (c.1478–1546)**
>
> A pirate and later admiral of the Ottoman fleet. He secured Ottoman power in the eastern Mediterranean and made Algeria and Tunisia part of the Ottoman Empire.

SOURCE F

Source F shows Charles with his troops as they are about to embark from Barcelona, to go to Tunis. Why was it important to Charles to mark that victory in this way?

The first of a series of cartoons (preparatory drawings for a piece of art such as a tapestry) showing the story of Charles I capturing Tunis.

Events in the Holy Roman Empire (Germany)

For most of his reign Charles was absent from Spain fighting wars and usually leading his armies himself. The early years of his reign saw most of the action in Italy. He was then able to give some time to trying to fight the forces of Islam. However, from the 1530s onwards he became increasingly embroiled in the German states that made up the Holy Roman Empire. It had been made clear to Charles when he became emperor that the German princes would not tolerate any interference in their affairs. Still, difficulties in the Holy Roman Empire were compounded by the spread of Lutheranism, which had led to a split between Catholic and Lutheran princes and cities. Charles was not able to follow up his military victory over Lutheran forces in Germany at the Battle of Mühlberg in 1547. A failure to retake Metz from the French in 1552 left Charles feeling unable to carry on and he fled from Germany to return to the Netherlands. Ill and disillusioned, he gave up his imperial authority to his brother Ferdinand. Ferdinand was able to negotiate a settlement in the empire which was acceptable to the German princes. This he concluded in the Treaty of Augsburg in 1555. It left the German princes independent and confirmed the role of the emperor as a figurehead only.

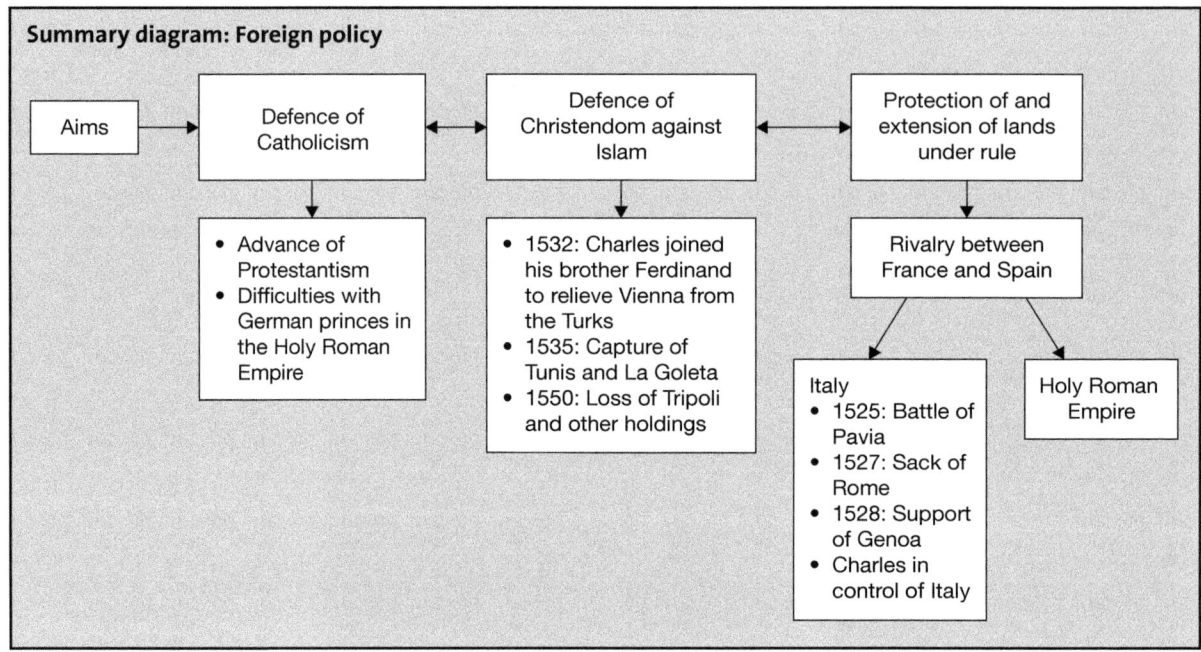

Summary diagram: Foreign policy

9 The New World

> How might developments in the New World during the reign of Charles I be considered successful?

Ferdinand and Isabella had set in motion the early stages of the discoveries and settlement of the New World. Under Charles much greater expansion took place, first to New Spain (Mexico) and then to New Castile (Peru) (see Figure 3.2, page 51).

The *conquistadors*

The exploits of the ***conquistadors*** still have the power to stir the imagination.

In 1519 Hernán Cortés led an expedition to Vera Cruz in Mexico, with about 600 men, sixteen horses and six pieces of artillery. Two years later he had conquered Tenochtitlan, capital of the powerful Aztec empire. Despite their small numbers, the Spanish were able to take Emperor Montezuma prisoner, and completely overwhelm the Aztec forces in the capital.

In 1532 Francisco Pizarro, with about 160 men, defeated the Incas in the Andes of Peru. That so few were able to conquer so many was due to the superiority of their steel swords and guns, as well as the horses that they introduced into the New World.

KEY TERM

Conquistador A conqueror, especially one of the Spanish conquerors of Mexico and Peru in the sixteenth century.

In addition, both the Aztecs and Incas had created discontented subjects or enemies who were only too willing to join the *conquistadors*, not only adding to their numbers, but also giving them important knowledge about the geography and the inhabitants of the areas which they were invading. This meant more effective fighting. The *conquistadors* were also determined; these were men who were often former soldiers and sailors who had fought in the wars in Granada and Italy. Some, like Cortés, were minor nobles; others might be illiterate labourers like Pizarro. They were usually motivated by hope of easy riches in the form of gold to be found in the New World. As the chronicler of Cortés's expedition writes 'We came to serve God and His Majesty … and to get rich.' The role of religion though was clearly also an important additional motivator. Every expedition that took place had at least one priest, determined to convert the natives to the Christian faith. However, there was also the attraction of personal gain.

Establishing royal government in the New World

Once conquest had taken place, just as in the Caribbean, settlements were established and land was cultivated. With the settlements came the need for effective royal government. Here Charles was presented almost with a 'blank canvas'. There were no noble families to placate and no representative assemblies. Charles first had to deal with the powers of the *conquistadors* themselves. He was not prepared to see them set themselves up as powerful, virtually independent nobility as had been the case in the past in Spain. In 1524 a Council of the Indies was established. It was made up of *letrados*, many of whom had lived in the Indies for at least a period of time. The council became the main authority over all affairs in the New World. It acted as the supreme court of appeal and drew up all the laws necessary. Spanish viceroys were appointed for Mexico and Peru. These were the representatives of, and answerable directly to, the king. In addition, various safeguards were brought in to prevent a viceroy becoming too powerful. These included the *audiencia*, a council of state made up of a number of judges and the viceroy. It oversaw the implementation of the Crown's policies and acted as a court of law. The viceroys were also subject to a review of their conduct at the end of their term of office. There were difficulties, especially the problems associated with communication between Spain and the Indies and within the Indies itself. On the whole, however, the system seems to have been effective.

Religious policies in the New World

Charles was also able to control Church appointments, and oversee the activities of the Church in the New World, without papal interference. Of great importance to him, as it had been for his grandparents, was the conversion of the native Indians to Christianity. To enable this to happen was the presence of large numbers of Franciscans, Dominicans and Jesuits, men who were determined to see to the spiritual needs of the natives and encourage them to accept

Christianity. Their dedicated work led to much success, for example, between 1524 and 1536 about 4 million conversions were recorded in Mexico alone.

Treatment of the native Indians

> **KEY FIGURE**
>
> **Bartolomé Las Casas (1484–1566)**
>
> A sixteenth-century Spanish historian, social reformer and Dominican friar. He became the first officially appointed 'Protector of the Indians'.

There is no doubt that the Spanish Crown, administrators and Church for the most part wished to see a just system introduced for the treatment of the native Indians. The most influential of the supporters of Indian rights was **Las Casas**. He attacked the system of *encomiendas* as unjust and tyrannical. His actions led to the New Laws of 1542, which forbade all forms of Indian slavery and granting of any new *encomiendas*. Colonists found guilty of mistreating their Indians were ordered to lose their *encomienda*. These laws caused such outcry among the colonists that they had to be rewritten. The view of many colonists was that the Indians were naturally inferior and, therefore, they could treat them as they wished. In spite of all the efforts of the Spanish administrators, large numbers of the natives died. In central Mexico, for example, the Indian population declined from a possible 25.2 million in 1518 to 2.65 million in 1568. Overwork played a part. Of more significance, though, were the diseases, especially smallpox, brought by the Europeans to the Indies.

Economic and social impact on Spain of the Indies

Charles wanted to exploit the economic potential of the Indies in the interests of the Crown and Spain. The Indies provided a market for Castilian products such as cloth, oil and wine. It received new products such as chocolate, pineapple, tomato, rubber and many kinds of wood. Most important was the silver and gold which were transported over to Spain. Large increases in the amount of silver sent followed the discovery of the great silver mines of Potosí in 1545. The Crown benefited financially. The colonists paid taxes, the Crown took one-fifth (the *quinto real*) of the value of silver and gold imported into Spain and it was able to borrow from European bankers on the security of its gold and silver imports. The implications of this are dealt with in more detail in Chapter 5. There were other more indirect benefits. The increased wealth led to more social mobility. Cortés, for example, became a marquis and gained enormous territory in Mexico. The New World generated new ideas and thinking. Those made rich built new houses and invested in the arts.

Summary diagram: The New World

Greater expansion of empire	Establishment of royal government	Impact on Spain	Treatment of native Indians
• 1521: Mexico, Hernán Cortés • 1525: Peru, Francisco Pizarro	• Council of Indies 1524 • Spanish viceroys • King's control over the Church in the New World	• Export markets for products • Imports of silver and gold • Social mobility • New ideas	• Work of Las Casas • Settlers' attitudes • Charles made concessions • New Laws 1542

10 Spain in 1556

▶ *What were the strengths and weaknesses of Spain in 1556?*

On 25 October 1555, worn out and extremely ill, Charles entered the ducal palace in Brussels. Surrounded by family and officials he announced his decision to abdicate. To his son Philip he abdicated the Netherlands with immediate effect; in early 1556 he would also abdicate to Philip all the Spanish realms, both in Europe and in the Indies. His brother Ferdinand had already ruled the Holy Roman Empire since 1553. Officially Charles was only allowed to abdicate as emperor in 1558 when Ferdinand was elected in his place. In September 1556, Charles sailed home to Spain and entered Yuste, a monastery where he had chosen to spend the remaining years of his life; he died there in September 1558.

The condition of Spain in 1556

Charles ensured that there would be a smooth transition from one king to the other. He left an adult son, Philip, who had already proved his capabilities in ruling Spain as regent from 1543. Unlike himself, Philip had been born and brought up in Spain. There would be no questioning his acceptability as king.

Peace and order in Spain

Charles left a secure country to his son. Charles's subjects, although some grievances remained, had generally become reconciled to his rule and by 1556 there were few signs of any opposition to the Crown. In Castile, the most influential nobles continued to play an important part in government and at the royal court – even though there were grumbles about the growing cost of the latter. In the non-Castilian kingdoms there was satisfaction that Charles had been prepared to respect their particular laws and privileges, although there was some resentment at the number of positions and rewards which were reserved for Castilians. The most discontent registered among Castilian taxpayers, especially in the poorer agricultural areas, as they were expected to contribute ever-increasing sums of money in taxes. But after the revolts of the 1520s, any signs of discontent were kept under control by the tax-exempt nobles and clergy.

The size of the empire

The division of his inheritance between his son Philip and his brother Ferdinand made the rule of the Spanish kingdoms more manageable. There was a vast overseas empire in the Indies which gave Spain income and prestige. The Netherlands were also wealthy – although here, with the growth of Protestantism, there were potential signs of unrest. Changes in the administration had been made to drive improvements and efficiencies in the government of the Spanish kingdoms.

Religion

The position of Roman Catholicism in Spain in 1556 was secure. 'Exterminate heresy, lest it take root and overturn the state and the social order', was Charles's order to the regents he left to govern Spain during his many absences. Any possible threat of Protestantism in Spain had been swiftly and completely dealt with, although the *Moriscos* who, in effect, had been forced to convert to Christianity continued to be seen as a problem.

Finance

The major area of concern was finance. Although none of Charles's wars was fought in Spain itself, the kingdoms, particularly Castile, had to supply much of the money needed for the waging of these wars. The cost was so high that Charles's son, Philip, had to declare a bankruptcy at the start of his reign in 1556. Charles's need for money also led to him obtaining loans from foreign bankers and using future Castilian revenues as security. This resulted in foreign bankers having an increasing hold over the royal income from Castile. Charles was mortgaging the future for the sake of the present.

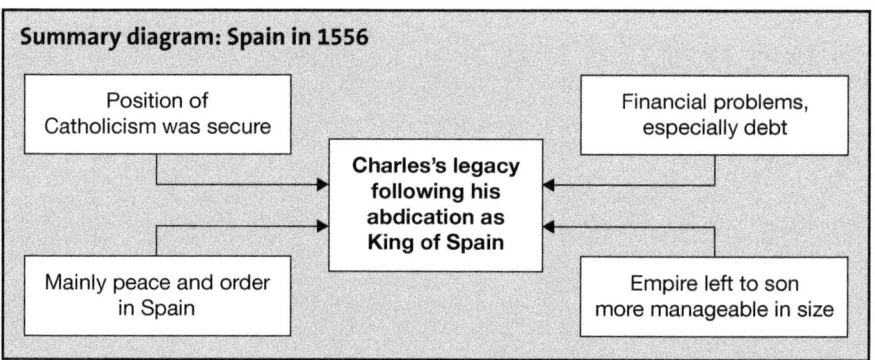

Chapter summary

This chapter has examined Charles I as King of Spain, as well as other aspects of his rule which impinged on his performance as a monarch. Should he, could he, have done more for Spain and his legacy there? There is little doubt that the costs of his empire were a drain on Spain, and particularly on Castile. However, his religious policies maintained and ensured the place of Catholicism in Spain; there were no revolts against his rule there after 1522 and he protected its frontiers from possible invasion. The wars in which he was virtually continuously engaged all took place outside Spain. In addition, he had extended for Spaniards, particularly Castilians, opportunities in a growing empire in the New World. How far what Charles accomplished was beneficial for the future of Spain continues to be debated as more and more of the archival material held in Spain is researched by historians.

Refresher questions

Use these questions to remind yourself of the key material covered in this chapter.

1 What was the attitude of Spaniards towards Charles when he first became king?
2 What features of Charles's early life and upbringing would impact on the way he approached becoming King of Spain?
3 Why did the *comuneros* revolt break out and why did it fail?
4 Why did Spaniards view Charles differently in the years when he returned to Spain 1522–9?
5 What were Charles's relationships with the nobility?
6 What were Charles's relationships with the various *Cortes* in Spain?
7 Was there a revolution in government during Charles's reign?
8 Why did expenditure increase so much during Charles's reign?
9 What was Charles's attitude to the *Moriscos* in Spain?
10 How far were any reforms made to the Church in Spain?
11 What were Charles's aims in foreign policy?
12 Why did conflict between Spain and France take place? How successful was Charles in this conflict?
13 In what ways did Charles try to prevent the expansion of the Ottoman Empire? How successful was he in this?
14 How effectively was the New World governed?
15 What benefits did the New World bring to Spain?

Question practice

ESSAY QUESTIONS

1 How successful were Charles's domestic policies 1522–59?
2 Assess the reasons why there was unrest in Spain in the years 1519–24.
3 'Charles's major success in foreign policy was in challenging the forces of Islam.' How far do you agree?
4 Which of the following had the greater impact on Spain during the reign of Charles I? a) Charles's foreign policy. b) The development of the New World. Explain your answer with reference to both a) and b).
5 To what extent was Charles I more successful in his relations with the Spanish people between 1522–9 compared with 1517–20?
6 To what extent can Charles I be held personally responsible for the revolt of the *comuneros*?

INTERPRETATION QUESTIONS

1 With reference to Extracts 1 and 2 (page 102), and your understanding of the historical context, answer the following question. Which of the two extracts provides the more convincing interpretation of Charles's success in ruling Spain?
2 Using your understanding of the historical context, assess how convincing the arguments in Extracts 1–3 (page 102) are in relation to Charles's problems in ruling Spain.

EXTRACT 1

From Stanley G. Payne, *A History of Spain and Portugal*, University of Wisconsin Press, 1973, pp. 184–5.

The Habsburg crown was successful in Spain during the reign of Carlos V [Charles I] because it accepted the institutional status quo of the Hispanic kingdoms, and because of the increasing Hispanization of the ruler himself, who eventually lost nearly all Flemish identification and came to associate himself more and more with the base of his empire Castile. If rebel movements such as the Comunero and Germania revolts were thoroughly suppressed, the Habsburg crown in return fully accepted the pluralistic 'Aragonese' structure of the united monarchy, and even extended this system to the new domains conquered in Italy. There were no efforts whatever in the sixteenth century to unify the various Hispanic states; the existing constitutional integrity of the separate principalities was fully respected.

EXTRACT 2

From Stewart MacDonald, *Charles V: Ruler, Dynast and Defender of the Faith 1500–58*, Hodder & Stoughton, 2000, p. 36.

The Castilian nobility enjoyed substantial advantages under Charles. Their pride was flattered and their self-interest satisfied as Charles increasingly loosened his ties with his Burgundian lands and put Spain at the centre of his empire. Castilian nobles found lucrative employment in the running of Charles's empire. In addition, Charles exempted the nobility from the heaviest tax burdens. The absenteeism of the monarch also provided opportunities for the nobility to consolidate and advance their own interests. As a result, it has been argued that Charles's partnership with the Castilian nobility was one of the major pillars of his success in ruling Spain. During the Comuneros revolt the nobility had proved their value to the Crown in the maintenance of effective royal government. In its aftermath, Charles was careful to avoid offending them. But the victory of the nobility over the Comuneros rebels brought them into a longer-term alliance with a monarchy much strengthened in its own right.

EXTRACT 3

From Helen Rawlings, *Church, Religion and Society in Early Modern Spain*, Palgrave, 2002, p. xiii.

By the end of the fifteenth century the Spanish Church had become firmly associated with the authoritarian power of the monarch and the repressive arm of the Holy Office [the Spanish Inquisition]. Spain's reputation as a major bastion of religious orthodoxy and racial intolerance was reinforced in the early sixteenth century as it took a leading role under Charles V ... in checking the spread of Protestant heresy through the lands of the Holy Roman Empire in northern and central Europe and in combating the onslaught of Turkish power in central and southern Europe.

CHAPTER 5

Spain in the sixteenth century: the price revolution and its effects

Before 1500, prices in Spain and throughout Europe had remained fairly stable. There had been changes over the years, depending on the quality of the harvests and seasonal foods, but there had not been a pronounced trend. Price variations had remained within a fairly consistent range. One might compare this to an elastic band which stretches out and then contracts back to its original size. One might say that in the sixteenth century the elastic band was stretched so far that it broke. Spanish commentators of the time, like others throughout Europe, noticed that prices were reaching much higher levels than was to be expected. Although they went up and down as before, an overall upward trend was now noticeable. The technical term for this is inflation, then a newly observed phenomenon. It is usually referred to by historians as the 'price revolution' of the sixteenth century. To examine how sixteenth-century Spain was affected by this price revolution, the material is covered under the following headings:

★ Evidence for inflation in sixteenth-century Spain
★ Sixteenth-century explanations for inflation
★ Modern interpretations for inflation
★ The social impact of inflation
★ The impact of inflation on agriculture and industry

Key dates

1556	Martín de Azpilcueta published his monetary theory on the causes of inflation in Spain	1934	Earl J. Hamilton published *American Treasure and the Price Revolution in Spain*, linking the price rises to the New World treasure
1569	Tomás de Mercado published *Suma de Tratos y Contratos* linking rising prices to the New World treasure entering Spain		

1 Evidence for inflation in sixteenth-century Spain

▶ *What evidence of inflation was there in the sixteenth century in Spain?*

KEY TERM

Inflation A sustained increase in the price of goods and services, resulting in money losing value.

Prices in Spain rose at a much higher level than would normally be expected in the course of the sixteenth century. It is generally agreed that the **inflation** rate reached around 400 per cent over that period. This increase was not evenly spread throughout Spain, nor was it the same throughout the century. The historian Nadal Oller's research, published in 1959, indicates that the annual rate of inflation was 2.8 per cent in 1501–62, but only 1.3 per cent in 1562–1600. This means that inflation was highest in the first half of the sixteenth century, but slowed down in the last 30 years.

This did not mean that the prices on all goods rose by 2.8 or 1.3 per cent. Nor were the rises the same in all parts of Spain. The steepest increases affected the goods most needed by people to survive, in particular produce such as wheat. Thus, the historian Earl J. Hamilton (1934) shows that 'throughout the first three quarters of the sixteenth century agricultural prices rose considerably faster than non-agricultural [prices]'.

At the time, any price increase was seen as unusual and it led to widespread commentary. Alonso de Herrera, writing in 1513, notes that 'a pound of mutton costs as much as a whole sheep used to, a loaf as much as a sack of wheat'. Another writer, Tomás de Mercado, remarks in 1568 that 'thirty years ago a thousand pennies was something, today it is nothing'. The records of the *Cortes* of Castile throughout the century continually complain of the high cost of grain and meat. The historian Fernand Braudel cites a book containing detailed accounts pre-dating 1600 from at least 33 writers who discuss the rise in prices 'of which they were all witnesses and victims'.

Summary diagram: Evidence for inflation in sixteenth-century Spain

Contemporary accounts		Research by modern historians	
Cortes of Castile	Chroniclers and writers: • Martín de Azpilcueta • Tomás de Mercado	Nadal Oller on rates of inflation	Earl J. Hamilton tracked prices of a number of goods over the century

Chapter 5 *Spain in the sixteenth century: the price revolution and its effects*

2 Sixteenth-century explanations for inflation

▶ *What reasons did writers of the sixteenth century suggest for the price rises?*

Although the high price rises were obvious to the people of the time, why they happened was not so obvious. This led to multiple and varied interpretations. Some gave moral reasons, believing it to be the wickedness of individuals. Some blamed foreign **speculators** for the increased price of meat, horses, wool, cloth and silk. The Castilian *Cortes* of 1551 claimed that 'the principal cause of the rising prices of bread and other food is that [foreigners in Castile] speculate in all kinds of provisions'. Braudel (1966) gives an example where high prices were blamed on the poor. He writes that in 'the Basque province of Viscaya in Northern Spain an official report of 1588 attributed the rising prices to the people of the lowlands who eat and drink to excess in the taverns, where they pick up vicious and lazy habits, neglecting their fields and orchards. So it is not to be wondered at if cider is scarce and sold at exorbitant prices!'

KEY TERM

Speculator A person who makes risky investments in anticipation of prices going up in order to resell at a profit.

Linking Spanish imports of gold and silver with rising prices

In the mid-sixteenth century theologians of the University of Salamanca were the first to put forward the idea that there was a connection between Spanish imports of New World gold and silver and rising prices.

The opinion of Martín de Azpilcueta

Writing in 1556, Martín de Azpilcueta noticed the causal effect between the level of prices and the amount of gold and silver in circulation. Looking at what was happening in Spain, he saw that prices and wages had risen and attributed these increases to the imports of New World gold and silver. Embracing supply and demand theory, according to which the value of currency and the price of goods fluctuate, so that in the same way that prices fall when goods are plentiful, currency loses value when there is a large supply of it circulation, he writes:

SOURCE A

From Martín de Azpilcueta, writing in 1556, quoted in Marjorie Grice-Hutchinson, *The School of Salamanca*, Oxford University Press, 1952, pp. 94–5.

The reasons for this opinion are as follows:

First, that this concept is common to all men, good and evil …

Second, and of great importance, that all merchandise becomes dearer when it is in great demand and short supply, and that money, in so far as it may be sold, bartered, or exchanged by some other form of contract, is merchandise and therefore also becomes dearer when it is in great demand and short supply.

How does Source A help to explain why prices were increasing in Spain?

Third, that … other things being equal, in countries where there is a great scarcity of money, all other saleable goods, and even the hands and labour of men, are given for less money than where it is abundant. Thus we see by experience that in France, where money is scarcer than in Spain, bread, wine, cloth and labour are worth much less. And even in Spain, in times when money was scarcer, saleable goods and labour were given for very much less than after the discovery of the Indies, which flooded the country with gold and silver. The reason for this is that money is worth more where and when it is scarce than where and when it is abundant. What some men say, that a scarcity of money brings down other things, arises from the fact that its excessive rise [in value] makes other things seem lower, just as a short man standing beside a very tall one looks shorter than when he is beside a man of his own height.

Fourth, if there is a shortage of gold coins their value may well increase, so that more coins of silver or other metal are given in exchange for them.

Men of ideas

- *Martín de Azpilcueta Navarro* (1492–1586) was a scholar famous for his saintly life and learning. He had taught canon law at Toulouse before going to hold a professorship at the University of Salamanca. In 1538 he was chosen by Charles I as rector of the newly established University of Coimbra, where he lectured on international law. Azpilcueta spent the last years of his life in Rome, where he acted as an adviser to a number of popes. His monetary theory was published as an appendix to a 1556 edition of a manual of moral theology dedicated to his friend and protectress, Princess Joanna, sister of Philip II.

- *Tomás de Mercado* (c.1525–75) moved to Mexico when he was a young man and joined the Dominican order. In 1562–3 he journeyed to Spain where he completed his studies at the University of Salamanca and later lectured on philosophy, moral theology and law at Salamanca and Seville. Mercado's most famous and popular work, the *Suma de Tratos y Contratos (Manual of Deals and Contracts)*, was published in 1569. It was intended as a manual of commercial and financial practices for traders and clergy, essentially putting business practices into a moral context. In 1575 Mercado died aboard the ship that was taking him home to Mexico.

Tomás de Mercado on the laws of demand

Another important figure linking the rising cost of living to the imports of American treasure, was the economist and theologian Tomás de Mercado. In his *Suma de Tratos y Contratos (Manual of Deals and Contracts)* he notes the effect of demand in the New World – which he calls the 'Indies' – on Spanish prices. Part of the reason the New World trade raised prices was because, he says, it created a heavy demand for goods. He gives a helpful example of this:

SOURCE B

From Tomás de Mercado, writing in 1569, quoted in Marjorie Grice-Hutchinson, *Early Economic Thought in Spain, 1177–1740*, Routledge, 1978, p. 124.

*I saw velvets in Granada that were priced at 28 and 29 **reales**. A fool arrived … and began to treat and bargain so indiscreetly for the lading of a caravel [loading of a caravel ship] that within a fortnight he had put up prices to 35 and 36. And the velvet-merchants and weavers went on in this way, and afterwards charged the same prices to their fellow countrymen [in Spain]. So, in Seville, is the daily trend of prices, as much in the mercery [textiles] that comes from Flanders as in the cloths from Segovia and Toledo, and the wine and oil produced in the Axarafe [near Seville].*

In 1568, **Jean Bodin** published a work which became much more widely known in Europe than those of Mercado and Azpilcueta. He, too, observed the effect of New World treasure on prices. In writing about how far the price rises were due to the **debasement** of the coinage in France, he pointed out that there had been no debasement of the coinage in Spain. He, therefore, came to the same conclusion as Azpilcueta and Mercado; that it was the import of New World gold and silver which was responsible for rising prices.

> What reason does Source B give as to why prices were going up?

> **KEY TERMS**
>
> **Real** A unit of currency fixed at a value of 34 *maravedís* in 1497.
>
> **Debasement** Lowering the value of currency, particularly in connection with the reminting of coins. A coin is debased if its gold, silver, copper or nickel content is reduced.

> **KEY FIGURE**
>
> **Jean Bodin (1530–96)**
> A French philosopher, economist and professor of law. He wrote on a wide range of issues including inflation.

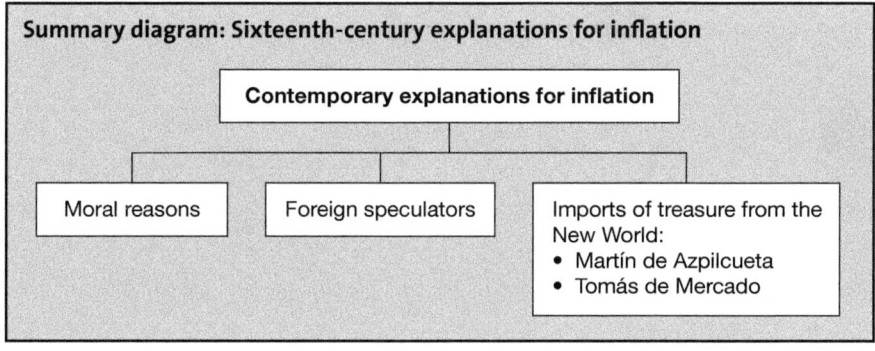

Summary diagram: Sixteenth-century explanations for inflation

Contemporary explanations for inflation
- Moral reasons
- Foreign speculators
- Imports of treasure from the New World:
  - Martín de Azpilcueta
  - Tomás de Mercado

Modern interpretations for inflation in this period

> ▶ How correct were Azpilcueta and his contemporaries in asserting that the cause of inflation in sixteenth-century Spain was the importing of gold and silver from the New World?

Modern historians have put forward similar and additional reasons for the price rises.

The work of Earl J. Hamilton

The link between the **bullion** coming from the New World, in gold and silver **pesos**, and the inflation that contemporaries observed is supported by the work of a twentieth-century historian, Earl J. Hamilton. His research on the New World treasure and Spanish prices was based on the official registers at Seville and published in 1934. Hamilton compared the fluctuations in the price of goods to the amount of bullion imported into Spain from the New World throughout the sixteenth century. He noticed how the inflation rate correlated with the amounts of gold and silver made available in Spain year on year. He therefore concluded that there was an 'extremely close correlation between the increase in the volume of treasure imports' and the increase in the prices of goods 'throughout the sixteenth century, particularly from 1535 on' and that this demonstrated 'beyond question that the "abundant mines of America" were the principal cause of the "Price Revolution in Spain".'

> **KEY TERMS**
>
> **Bullion** Amount of gold and silver valued by weight, before it is minted into coins.
>
> **Peso** New World bullion was normally reckoned in *pesos*. The New World silver *peso* was valued at 272 *maravedís* and the gold *peso* at 450 *maravedís*.

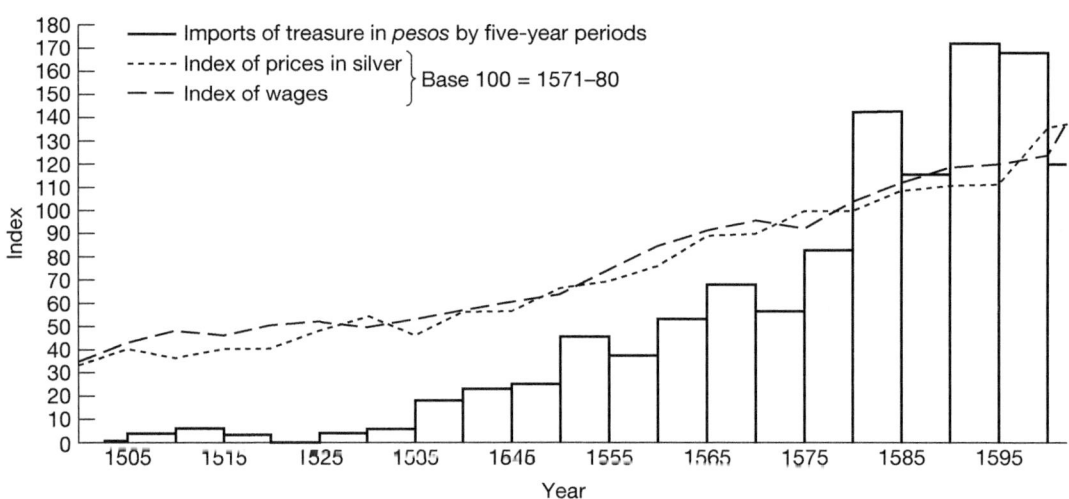

Figure 5.1 Treasure imports, prices and wages in Spain 1500–1600.

Chapter 5 Spain in the sixteenth century: the price revolution and its effects

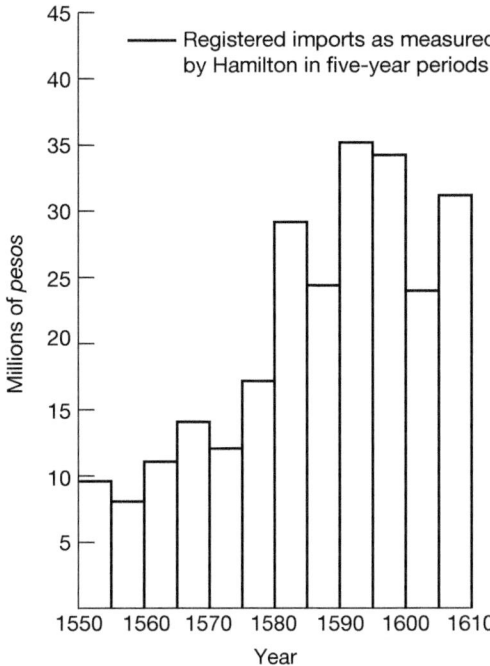

Figure 5.2 Imports of American bullion to Spain 1550–1610.

Criticisms of Hamilton's work

Hamilton's results were widely accepted when they were published in 1934 but further research has led a number of historians, such as J.H. Elliott and Henry Kamen, to criticise Hamilton's theory.

The rise in prices did not in fact closely follow the amount of gold and silver coming into the country. Prices had increased at a faster average rate in the first half of the sixteenth century than during the second half. The inflation rate was, therefore, much higher in the early sixteenth century, when little bullion was entering Spain. In contrast, inflation slowed down in the second half of the sixteenth century. However, it was at this time, the 1550s onwards, that silver, in particular, started entering the country in much larger amounts as a result of the discovery in 1545 of the silver mines at Potosí (in present-day Bolivia).

Furthermore, prices in that period did not rise evenly across all goods, which would have been the case if inflation had been purely monetary (that is, caused by the surge in imported treasure). There was a large difference between rises in agricultural products, especially grain and wool, and manufactured goods which went up by about half as much.

Questions have also been raised about whether Hamilton is accurate on the total quantity of silver entering Spain. Was the amount registered at Seville a true indication of the total quantity of silver entering Spain? It is suggested, probably rightly, that it was not. One of the reasons for this is the probability of large-scale smuggling of silver into Spain. According to Kamen (2005), this 'may have been as little as 10 per cent of registered values for the early period (as Hamilton suggests) but was certainly very much higher by the late century'. If this is correct, then even more treasure was entering the country at the end of the century when the inflation rate was at its lowest.

Further questions relate to what happened to the silver once it reached Seville. Much of the bullion did not remain in Spain. It was quickly re-exported to pay for Spanish imports, for the pay and provisions of Spanish forces abroad and to repay the loans which German and Genoese bankers had made to the Spanish government.

Another issue with the figures that Hamilton presents is that they do not allow for the wide differences in price fluctuations over the country as a whole and even within Spanish regions. The steady price rise that his summary shows did not necessarily happen in the same way all over the country.

This is not to dismiss the argument that American treasure had inflationary effects in Spain. But it was clearly not the only and perhaps not even the most important cause of rising prices. Overall there was undoubtedly a connection but exactly what that connection was remains a matter for economic historians to unravel.

Other possible causes

A number of other explanations for the rise in prices have been put forward.

The law of supply and demand

In other countries, such as France, debasement of the coinage pushed up prices but this did not happen in Spain until the seventeenth century. The historian John Lynch (1981) points out that prices are affected by supply and demand. When the total supply of money in circulation goes up without an increase in industrial and agricultural production, then the same amount of goods is 'chasing more and more money'. The result of this is that prices will rise.

The population increase in Spain

A number of studies in recent years have shed light on the population of Spain during the sixteenth century. At the time, there were no censuses in the modern sense, but households would be counted in individual towns or districts, usually for tax purposes; there would be for some places registers of land and there might be Church records, particularly after the introduction of birth, marriage and death records in parish churches. Although not completely reliable, there are, therefore, some general statements that, with caution, may be made:

- Spain's population had been steadily rising since the fifteenth century and by the 1550s was probably about 6.5 million.
- The greatest population growth took place between about 1530 and 1570 and reached its highest point in the 1580s. After that it slowly declined. In the 1590s Spain's population was probably around 7–8 million.
- There were large population increases in some of the towns, mainly in Castile. Seville, for example, tripled in size between 1534 and 1561, going from 33,000 to 95,000 inhabitants. Salamanca almost doubled, from 13,400 to 25,200.
- When the population level goes up without a corresponding increase in the amount of basic staples such as food, then shortages happen. This means that food producers can raise prices knowing that people will have to pay the higher amounts or starve.

The population boom, particularly in the towns, had two important long-term consequences. It led to a rise in demand, particularly for food. This fits in with Hamilton's figures on food prices. This meant that it was profitable to increase the amount of food produced.

However, no new techniques were introduced to increase the amount grown on existing land. Instead, the increase came from converting common and public land into **arable** land, putting less fertile or less accessible land to agricultural use, and ploughing pastureland into fields to grow crops. This meant that the cost of producing, and consequently the price, of agricultural products went up.

KEY TERM

Arable Land that can be ploughed and is suitable for growing crops.

The increasing population also led to more demand for goods such as textiles. And again there was difficulty in meeting demand from within Spain as no new technical innovations were introduced to increase production. This, as we shall see below, had important consequences for Spanish industry.

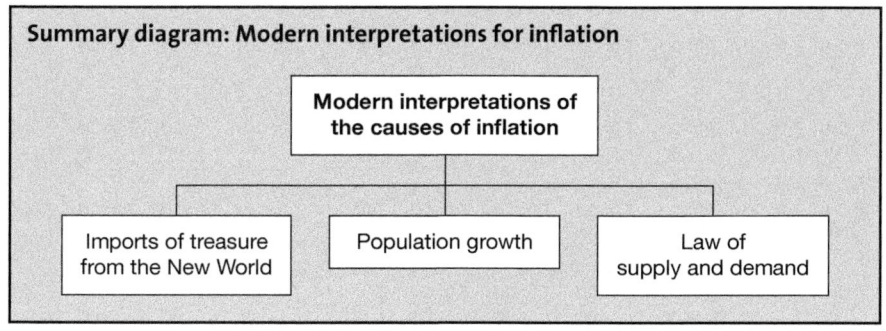

Summary diagram: Modern interpretations for inflation

Spain 1469–1598

The social impact of inflation

▶ *Who were the winners and losers during the periods of inflation in the sixteenth century?*

At a time when many workers and landowners were living on fixed incomes, the impact on living standards could be severe. Others might be able to seize the opportunities offered and do well.

The main losers

The main sufferers were the masses living on fixed incomes, or the people who received low rents or cash income in lieu of goods. These people could not increase their incomes to match rising prices. Among them were small landowners, the lower clergy on fixed incomes, government officials, as well as farm labourers and many town dwellers. For them, the impact of prices rising year after year was devastating. Each year their standard of living went down as the price of the goods they needed to buy went up. The historian Henry Kamen quotes an Italian engineer, Antonelli, who, in 1581, stated that in Spain 'the prices of goods have risen so much that nobles, gentry, commoners and clergy cannot live on their incomes'.

Unskilled labourers reliant on seasonal work fared even worse. Wages did usually rise but not enough to cope with the rising prices. The 1959 study on the wages of Valencian workers in the building trade by the historians Henry Phelps Brown and Sheila Hopkins shows clearly the problems that workers were experiencing as the century went on. Figure 5.3 shows how the cost of living for workers went up but the real value of the wages that they received went down. Thus, workers could afford to buy less and less of what they needed for their basic needs on what they earned.

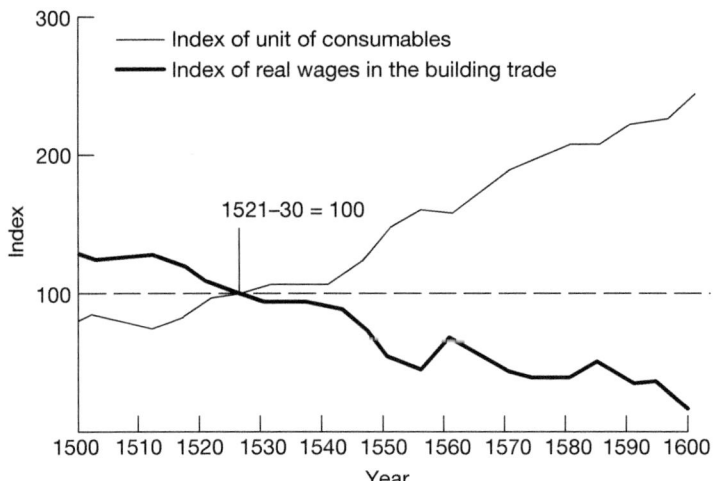

Figure 5.3 Prices and real wages at Valencia 1500–1600.

Added to this, of course, were the new taxes introduced during the century, particularly those like the ***millones*** which was levied on basic foods, which impacted on everyone, including the poorest, who also had to pay these taxes. Nor was it just the price of food which went up, so did rents. A study of land and house rents in Valladolid, for example, has shown that rents almost doubled between 1530 and 1555.

Many people struggled, therefore, to feed, clothe and house themselves and their families. No wonder the roads of Spain thronged with beggars, vagabonds and the unemployed.

KEY TERM

Millones A tax on basic foods – wine, meat, olive oil and vinegar – introduced in 1590.

The Crown

Royal income suffered from inflation as well. The costs of administration and of paying, feeding and equipping the armed forces went up. In some ways, inflation was helpful to the Crown as it meant that the cost of loans was lower in real terms. In addition, the king had the advantage of being able to increase revenue by levying more or new taxes to keep up with inflation. Overall, it does not seem that the Crown was as affected as severely as many of its subjects were.

The higher nobility (the grandees)

Like the Crown, the higher nobility generally seem to have managed to keep their income levels up in line with inflation. Many had vast estates, so the need for more land to grow crops meant that they could raise their rents at least as fast as inflation. Nor did they have to rely on the economy for income. The Crown needed their support and so there were opportunities for them to serve in the highest military and administrative positions. They were then usually well rewarded for these services.

Entrepreneurs

Anyone with something to sell or trade could benefit from inflation, as many manufacturers and merchants did, particularly until 1550. As the century went on however, inflation had an adverse effect on exporting Spanish goods, particularly to the colonies. Even then, the more powerful merchants were able to survive foreign competition and do well. Large fortunes were made in the trade with the Indies, particularly by those involved in such areas as the wine trade and shipping. Many of those who benefited were able to claim at least minor noble status, which gave them exemption from direct taxes.

Summary diagram: The social impact of inflation

Winners	Losers

• Entrepreneurs	• Fixed income earners, e.g.:
	  – Small landowners
	  – Lower clergy
	  – Government officials
	  – Farmers
	  – Workers in cities and towns
	• Unskilled labourers
	• Seasonal workers

←——————— Crown ———————→
←——————— Grandees ———————→

5 The impact of inflation on agriculture and industry

▶ *How were agriculture and industry affected by the changes taking place in the sixteenth century?*

Agriculture

The growing population of Spain needed to be accompanied by a corresponding increase in the food supply. The main staple was bread, and grain prices saw some of the highest price increases throughout the century. Securing enough grain could be only be done by one or more of the following measures:

- increasing production on the land that was already dedicated to wheat crops
- increasing production by allocating more of the land available to growing wheat
- finding new sources of wheat outside Spain.

Using the **tithe** returns, the historian Henry Kamen has shown that, in areas such as New Castile and Catalonia where cereals were produced, production rose steadily in 1460–1560, reaching its highest point in 1560–80 before going into decline. However, was this due to the introduction of improved farming methods or was it because of an increase in the amount of land available for growing cereals? It is clear that production on existing land did not increase. The evidence shows that there was no change in the amount of cereal grown from grain which had been sown. This indicates that no new techniques were introduced to improve crop yields. As production levels did increase, it must then mean that more land was being used for crops. As Florian de Ocampo wrote in

KEY TERM

Tithe One-tenth of annual production or earnings given to the Church.

1552, 'even mountains disappeared as everything in Castile was ploughed up for sowing'. This might be the poorer, less fertile lands, common lands, or royal lands (*baldios*) bought from the Crown.

The gains realised by expanding the area of arable lands were still not enough to meet the growing needs of the population and Spain had to import more, at first from areas of her own empire, in particular Sicily, and later from the Baltic countries of Europe. This was particularly the case in years of famine, as in the 1560s, 1570s and 1590s.

A time of chronic food shortages

The historian David Vassberg, who has researched this topic (1984), is quite clear over where the fault lay: 'the real problem was not meteorological but human: poverty was the result of man-made institutions that were inefficient and that did not permit the proper utilization of resources'. The inefficiencies to which Vassberg refers include:

- the unequal distribution of land
- the poor agricultural techniques such as the rotation methods, including leaving the fields to **lie fallow** for one or two out of three years
- the use of mules rather than oxen
- the difficulty of obtaining cash or credit for investment
- the high levels of rents and taxation that had to be paid.

It is no surprise, therefore, that agriculture found itself in great difficulties by the end of the sixteenth century. The situation was compounded by a series of bad harvests in the 1560s and 1570s. By the 1580s, most of Spain had to import wheat, not only from its usual suppliers, such as Sicily, but from as far away as the Baltic countries.

The sheep trade

It was not just grain crops that were critical in the farming economy. Sheep were particularly important to the textile industry and the export trade for wool had its main centres at Segovia, Toledo and Cuenca. The sheep trade was controlled by the sheep owners' guild, the **Mesta**. Each year flocks of sheep would be driven from their summer to their winter quarters. For many years the view of historians such as J. Klein dominated the debate about the sheep trade. Writing in 1920, Klein blamed the *Mesta* and the protection that it received from government for the damage trespassing sheep did to arable lands as they were moved to the winter quarters. This view is now discredited.

Vassberg (1984), among others, states that 'some historians have concluded that early modern Spanish agriculture was ruined by depredations of migratory flocks. That is simply not true.' The evidence for it is lacking. Certainly, in the first part of the sixteenth century the *Mesta* had been very powerful as they were allied to the wool exporters. The *Mesta* was also supported by the king

 **KEY TERMS**

Lie fallow The practice of leaving the soil unsown for a period of time to restore its fertility.

Mesta An influential guild of livestock owners, named after the communal grazing lands in Castilian villages.

as it was a source of loans to the Crown. When the demand for wool for the cloth industry declined in the second half of the sixteenth century, the Crown gradually withdrew its support of the *Mesta*. At the same time landowners began to enclose land for wheat growing.

Industry

Industry played a much smaller part than agriculture in the economic life of Spain. Spain possessed iron, lead and copper mines, and leather, pottery, soap and armaments industries. The main industry, however, was the textile industry, woollens and silks. From what little evidence is available it seems that the growth in the population, and demand from settlers in the New World, led to an increase in textile output, at least in the first part of the sixteenth century. However, Spain's high prices meant higher production costs for industry. In addition, the quality of cloth was generally poor. Foreigners who had bought Spain's wool were better placed to make quality products which could be sent back to Spain, and often on to the New World, at lower prices than the Spanish textiles but at higher prices than the raw wool which had been exported.

Not everything can be blamed on inflation, however. A number of factors hindered the development of industry:

- In many industries, the town guilds made the introduction of new practices difficult.
- People preferred to invest in government loans which brought higher returns than investing in industrial innovations which might have improved the quantity and quality of the goods produced.
- The war policies of the Crown meant a vastly increased need for weapons and other military supplies which Spain itself could not produce in sufficient quantities.
- The cost of moving goods around the country was high. Not only was there a poor road system but customs barriers existed between different parts of the country.
- Government policies on industry usually inflicted more damage than they provided help. Sometimes laws had to be abandoned, as in 1552, when legislation was introduced to prevent goods leaving Spain, unless destined for the New World. Then, when it was found not to improve matters, it was partially reversed in 1558. Similarly, a disastrous policy in 1548 had allowed foreign cloth to be imported and sold in Spain, thus competing cheaply with Spain's own manufactured cloth.

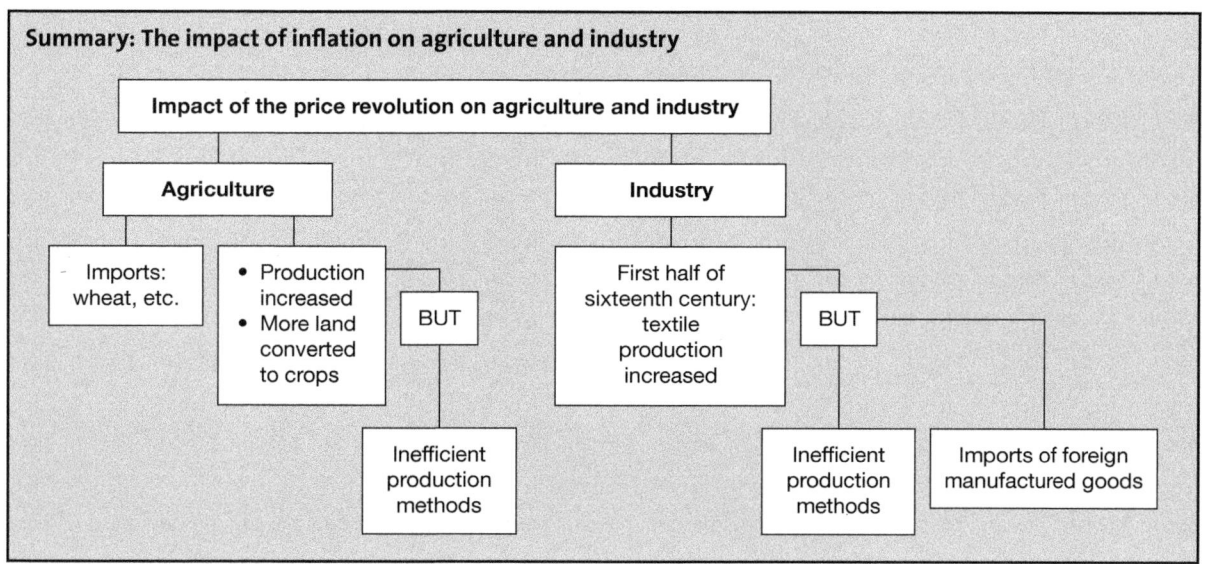

Chapter summary

In theory, Spain was a wealthy country, particularly from the mid-sixteenth century, when it should have been made rich by the treasure flowing in from the New World. In practice, this was an illusion. A large portion of the population was suffering from the effects of inflation, often made worse for them by taxes on ordinary foodstuffs. There was a lack of investment in agriculture and industry. Industry had declined in the face of foreign competition by the late sixteenth century. Much of the new wealth which came into Spain from the New World was immediately sent out of the country to repay the foreign loans that had been taken out to pay for the wars of Charles I and Philip II. By the end of the sixteenth century, Spain was struggling to survive.

Spain 1469–1598

 Refresher questions

Use these questions to remind yourself of the key material covered in this chapter.

1 What caused the price revolution?
2 When was inflation at its highest in Spain in the sixteenth century and when was it at its lowest?
3 Who was Martín de Azpilcueta and what were his views on inflation?
4 What was the root cause of inflation according to Tomás de Mercado?
5 What arguments for the causes of inflation were put forward by the twentieth-century historian Earl J. Hamilton? What was his evidence?
6 In what ways has Hamilton's work been challenged?
7 What other causes for inflation in sixteenth-century Spain have been suggested?
8 What segments of the population in sixteenth-century Spain were affected by the price revolution?
9 Which groups benefited from the effects of the price revolution?
10 What methods were attempted to increase food production in sixteenth-century Spain?
11 Why and how did the Spanish textile industry suffer at the end of the sixteenth century?

 Question practice

ESSAY QUESTIONS

1 'Spain's rising population, not imports of silver from the New World, brought about the price revolution c.1500–c.1570.' How far do you agree with this statement?
2 'The main cause of inflation in sixteenth-century Spain was the rise in population.' How far do you agree with this statement?
3 How accurate is it to say that the main impact of inflation in the years 1500–70 fell on peasant farmers and urban workers?
4 'It was the Crown which suffered most from the effects of inflation during the sixteenth century in Spain.' How far do you agree?

SOURCE ANALYSIS QUESTION

1 Assess the value of Source A (page 105) for revealing the reasons for the price revolution of the sixteenth century and its impact on Spanish society. Explain your answer, using the source, the information given about its origin and your own knowledge about the historical context.

Philip II: 1556–98. Spain: the heart of government

Philip II's reign was a long one – 42 years. It covered virtually the whole of the second half of the sixteenth century, a time of great change not only in the history of Spain but in the history of Europe. For Philip, as for his father, there were a number of challenges to be met in running the very different lands over which he ruled. This chapter looks at how successfully he did so (the analysis continues in Chapter 7). It also focuses on the personality, background and aims of Philip and how he dealt with key issues within Spain. These themes are developed in the following headings:

★ Philip's early life and character
★ The government of Spain
★ Finance
★ Religion and the Church
★ The revolts of Granada and Aragon

Key dates

1527	Philip born in Valladolid, Spain	1556	Charles I abdicated as King of Spain and transferred his Spanish possessions to Philip
1548–51	Philip visited Italy, Germany and the Netherlands	1557–62	Discovery, and elimination, of groups in Seville and Valladolid associated with Protestant ideas
1554	Philip spent approximately two years in England. Philip's sister Joanna took over government of Spain as regent during this time	1559	*Index of Forbidden Books* introduced into Spain
		1568–70	Revolt of the *Moriscos* in Granada – a major uprising which was put down with difficulty
1555	Philip left England to go to the Netherlands to meet with his father, Charles I	1591	Revolt in Aragon which was easily suppressed
	Charles I transferred his Burgundian territories to Philip and Spain	1598	Death of Philip

Philip's early life and character

▶ *What main principles would Philip follow in carrying out his role as king?*

From the time he was born in 1527 it was known that Philip II would one day follow in his father's footsteps. From the first, therefore, he was groomed to succeed to the Spanish Empire and, although his father was usually away from his side, fighting the many wars in which he was involved, he maintained contact with Philip. And as he grew older, Philip received regular advice from Charles by letter and appropriate experiences in government.

Early years

Philip II, the only son of Charles I, was born on 21 May 1527. Unlike his father, he was brought up and educated in Spain. From his birth, his connection with Spain was, therefore, far closer than with any other part of the lands he was to rule. Although his tutors taught him subjects such as mathematics, Latin, Greek, architecture and history, no effort was made to teach him foreign languages. This was to prove a handicap for Philip, who became fluent only in Castilian Spanish. He eventually came to understand Portuguese, French and Italian, but he was reluctant to speak them because of his poor pronunciation – a grave drawback for the ruler of a multilingual empire.

Like other princes he was taught the expected accomplishments of fencing, hunting and jousting, but, although he enjoyed riding, he seems to have derived most pleasure from dancing, playing the guitar and listening to music. He was an avid collector and reader of books, especially those of a religious nature. He also had an interest in nature study and a wide knowledge of birds, flowers and trees.

Preparations for Philip to become king

Philip's political training as a future king was not neglected. Although his father was often out of Spain, and was, therefore, not personally present to counsel him, he sent Philip a number of letters to guide him in his duties as a ruler. They contained advice that Philip was to try to follow throughout his life.

SOURCE A

From the correspondence between Charles and his son, Philip.

Above all be a friend to justice. Command your servants that they be moved neither by passion nor by prejudice, still less by gifts ... In your bearing, be calm and reserved. Say nothing in anger. Be easy of approach and pleasant of manner. Depend on no one but yourself. Make sure of all but rely exclusively on none. In your perplexities trust always in your Maker. Have no care but for Him [God].

? In Source A, what advice does Charles I give Philip on how he should conduct himself?

Chapter 6 *Philip II: 1556–98. Spain: the heart of government*

From the age of twelve, Philip attended meetings of the royal councils. Early in 1543 he was appointed regent in Spain in Charles's absence and he held this position until 1548. It was then that he visited the other areas of the empire which were to become part of his inheritance, so that he might see and be seen by his future subjects. A short visit to Italy was followed by a longer one to the Netherlands. Charles's confidence in his son's abilities increased. His letters show him beginning to ask Philip's opinion on various political matters. In 1555, in a moving ceremony at Brussels, Charles, worn out by his responsibilities as emperor, was finally able to abdicate to Philip his rights in the Netherlands and Franche-Comté, Castile, Aragon and the New World. It was now time for Philip, the prince 'who possesses many praiseworthy qualities', to take charge.

Character

In character Philip seems to have taken after his mother, Isabella, rather than his father. In public he was reserved and dignified, conscious of his position, and showed emotional self-control.

SOURCE B

From the reports filed by a Venetian ambassador.

[He was] white skinned and fair, very pleasantly built with a lip that hangs down a little … He is very sluggish by nature but very dignified. He listens to people patiently … accompanies his answers with an amiable smile. He has a good memory and is extremely pious. He loves repose and solitude, particularly in summer … He is never familiar with any of his servants, even with the most senior and intimate, but always preserves a gravity fitting to his royal dignity.

> What qualities for Philip's future role as king does Source B suggest?

In his private life, however, he showed affection with close relatives and friends. In the letters he wrote to his two young daughters, Philip wonders if the girls are looking after their young brother, Diego, or if Catherine (Catalina), the youngest, will suffer long-lasting effects from smallpox.

SOURCE C

From the personal letters Philip sent to his daughters from Portugal.

I think he will have managed to fill in the coloured letters; this is why I am sending you others … and I've got some more. Make sure that he occupies himself in filling them in, but little by little, so as not to tire himself, and let him sometimes copy them. He will learn more that way and I hope by this means acquire a good hand.

Your sister and the Count write me to the effect that you won't have any marks, I mean scars, the others don't matter; they were only afraid there might be one near your nose … but if there are only a few, as I pray, then that's nothing.

> In Source C, what do Philip's letters to his daughters reveal about his character?

Philip II

1527	Born in Valladolid, Spain
1543	Married Maria of Portugal, who died in 1545 giving birth to a son, Don Carlos
1554	Married Mary Tudor of England and became King of England
1556	Philip II became King of Spain
1558	Mary Tudor died
1559	Philip returned to Spain
1560	Married Elizabeth of Valois by whom he had two daughters
	Death of Elizabeth of Valois
	Death of Don Carlos, his eldest son
1570	Married his niece, Anne of Austria, by whom he had five children, of whom only Prince Philip (Philip III on the death of his father) survived to adulthood
1598	Died

Philip II's childhood and youth were designed to prepare him for becoming king and there is little doubt that the main influence on his life was his father, Charles I. Charles's advice to him was that he serve God, support the Inquisition and eradicate heresy wherever it might be found; to ensure justice; to pay attention to the finances of the country; and to ensure none of his advisers became too powerful. He was also to hold on to all the lands which he had inherited.

Philip married four times. His first marriage was to Maria of Portugal, which gave him a son, Don Carlos. Don Carlos, who was mentally unstable, died after Philip had had him imprisoned in his palace rooms. This led to the suggestion at the time, by Philip's enemies, that Philip had had Don Carlos killed. His second marriage to Mary Tudor was arranged by his father Charles I for political reasons. After her death, he married Elizabeth of Valois, the French princess. This resulted in the birth of two daughters. With no son to succeed him, he took his niece, Anne of Austria, as his fourth wife. She bore him five children, of whom only Prince Philip survived to adulthood. It was by her side that he was buried in 1598.

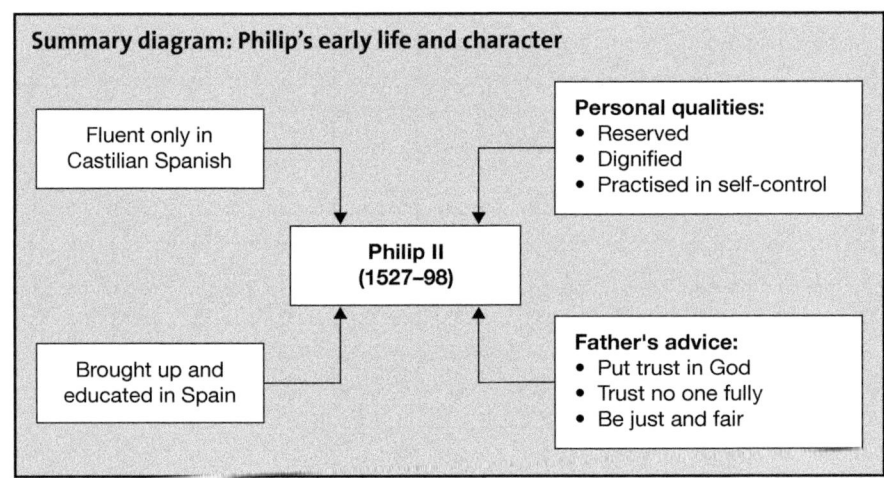

The government of Spain

> ▶ *What were the advantages and disadvantages in Philip's method of government?*
>
> ▶ *To what extent was the conciliar system effective?*

Much has been made of Philip II's style of government. He has, in fact, been referred to as the 'paper king'. In this he had very different views from those of his father. Whether his methods of working were more effective, however, is a matter of debate.

Philip II's method of governing

Philip's approach to governing his kingdoms was very different from that of his father. He was far less outgoing than Charles. He preferred to stay in one place rather than to be on the move with his secretaries and advisers around him, which he did not believe to be an effective way of governing. 'Travelling about one's kingdoms is neither useful nor decent', he wrote to his own son, the future Philip III. He established a permanent capital at Madrid, and rarely visited any of his territories outside Spain. Also unlike his father, he preferred to communicate in writing with his officials, rather than face to face. Philip was determined to know everything that was happening in his empire and to deal with all matters concerning its government himself. All important papers were meant to come to him for his consideration and signature. Often he would write comments on them in his spidery handwriting.

The issues with Philip's governing style

The king's own working style created major problems. The amount of written material he dealt with was enormous and, despite his ability to remember factual material well and his conscientious attitude to his work, he was unable to deal effectively with every matter that came to him. It is doubtful if any human being could. There is an account of one day in his reign when he read and signed 400 separate documents. Even this rate of work was not enough, and sometimes, through tiredness or eyestrain or sheer exhaustion, he had to give up. One can visualise him fighting to keep awake as he wrote: 'I have just been given this other packet of papers from you. I have neither the time nor the strength to look at it, and so I will not open it until tomorrow. It is already past ten o'clock and I have not yet dined. My table is full of papers for tomorrow because I cannot cope with any more now.'

Philip's way of governing meant that he was, in theory, the only person with complete knowledge about a matter on which a decision had to be made. No one had as much information as he did. His advisers and officials would only know

Spain 1469–1598

> **?** Study the portrait in Source D, which was sent to England before Philip II's marriage to Mary. What is the portrait of Philip intended to portray about him? How accurate a portrayal do you consider it likely to be?

SOURCE D

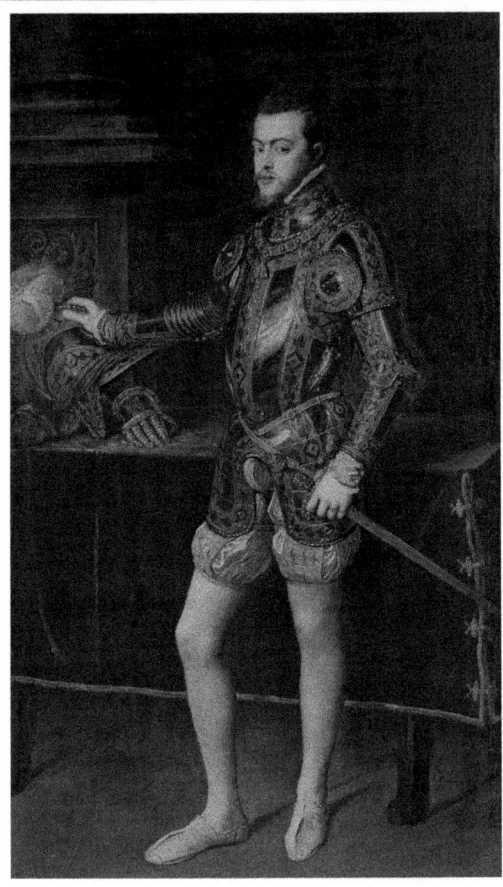

A 1550 portrait of Philip II by Titian.

about some aspects of any matter. Consequently, they could only give advice based on their limited knowledge. Lack of time and energy to fully investigate a matter put the king at risk if he made a bad decision or issued contradictory decisions, as those who worked closest to him were well aware.

SOURCE E

From the papers of Philip's personal secretary, Gonzalo Pérez.

His Majesty makes mistakes and will continue to make mistakes in many matters because he discusses them with different people, sometimes with one, at other times with another, concealing something from one minister and revealing it to another: it is little wonder that different and even contradictory decisions are issued.

> **?** Assessing Source E, why did Gonzalo Pérez consider that Philip made mistakes 'in many matters'?

Communication problems with the countries Philip ruled

Philip's wish to deal with all important matters himself also meant that there could be long delays in communicating with the more distant parts of the empire. Even if there were no delays, it took approximately two weeks for messages to travel from Madrid to Brussels in the Netherlands or to Milan in Italy, and at least another two weeks for a reply to be received. Two months was a short time for a letter to reach Mexico. By the time messages had been sent and replies had been received, the circumstances over which Philip had made a decision might well have changed and new orders might well be needed. However, once one action had been set in motion it was very difficult, if not impossible, to alter it in response to new circumstances. Sometimes, councillors felt forced to take decisions by themselves, although this undermined Philip's trust in them. The problem of communication in such a vast empire as Philip possessed was the source of many difficulties. The historian Helmut Koenigsberger, writing in 1984, asserts that the result was 'administrative chaos' in the empire.

Philip's problematic style of managing affairs

If Philip's personal style presented so many drawbacks, why did he persist in using it? The most obvious answer is that he was highly conscientious, wanting to do what was best for the people he governed. He thought that he could only do this by giving personal attention to every issue. A further explanation might be that Philip wished to ponder his decision at length because he was reluctant to trust anyone fully. His father's advice and his own experience made him distrustful. Philip showed on the death of one of his councillors that he felt he had allowed him too much power, 'I believed that it was wise to entrust many matters which concerned my royal office to [him] … And perhaps there were good reasons for it then. But experience has shown that it was not a good thing; and although it meant more leisure and less work for me, I do not think it should be allowed to continue.'

The need to think about issues for as long as Philip often did has been seen by others, then and now, as a sign of his inability to make decisions. Certainly Philip's appointment of Requesens as governor of the Netherlands shows him unable to make up his mind. For ten months after his appointment, Requesens did not know whether he was a permanent or a temporary governor, or what he was expected to do there. However, Philip could act decisively on occasions, as he did during the events leading up to his becoming King of Portugal.

Administration

Philip, as king, was forced to rely heavily on the advice he was given. He, therefore, tried to improve both the quality and quantity of the information upon which he based his decisions. Government became more centralised in some ways. In 1561 all central government offices were located in Madrid. A special depository was also set up for government papers so that these could be called on more easily when required.

Changes to the conciliar system

The conciliar system remained, but with modifications. By the end of Philip's reign there were fourteen central councils. The Council of State, officially the main council, continued to be a forum in which important nobles could offer advice to the king, although it seems to have had little power.

> **SOURCE F**
>
> **From a report given by a Venetian, 1557.**
>
> *At the court the opinion about this council is that it is not the source of such advice, deliberations, and performances as make for the honour and advantage of the king … for there seem to be no written rules or customs to produce order in its deliberations or decisions, nor is membership in it either convenient or dignified; and the result is a decline in the vitality of its discussions.*

? What criticisms are made about the Council of State in Source F?

At the beginning of the reign, the Council of State contained nobles from a number of countries over which Philip ruled. However, in 1559 Philip altered its membership. Castilian nobles replaced non-Castilian nobles. This preference for Castilians caused resentment in other parts of the empire. The new members mainly came from two rival noble families or their supporters. On the one side were the supporters of the Prince of Éboli and on the other the supporters of the Duke of Alba. The difference between the two groups centred mainly on a wish for power at court, with neither taking a particular line on issues. Rather, they

Leaders of the main factions at court

- *Ruy Gómez de Silva* (1516–73) was born in Portugal but came to Spain with his mother when Isabella of Portugal married Charles I. He became a trusted friend of Philip II, being created Prince of Éboli, and marrying into one of the most powerful Castilian families, the Mendozas. The self-effacing Gómez was completely loyal to Philip. A member of the Council of State, he led one of the two main factions at court.
- *Fernando Álvarez de Toledo* (1507–82). The third Duke of Alba was a Spanish noble and outstanding general and administrator who served both Charles I and Philip II. He fought in a number of campaigns including Tunis (1535) and held several important positions: governor of the duchy of Milan (1555–6), viceroy of the kingdom of Naples (1556–8) and governor of the Netherlands (1567–73). He was on a number of the councils, including the Council of State, and was the leader of one of the two main factions at court. In 1543, Charles I had warned Philip not to rely too heavily on Alba, for 'he has set his sights on great things and on rising as high as he can'. In 1578, he fell out of favour with Philip for letting his son make an unauthorised marriage, but this lasted only a short time. It became clear that he was the only choice to lead Spanish forces into Portugal in 1580, when Philip was vying for the Portuguese succession. At 73 years of age, Alba became viceroy and constable of the kingdom of Portugal until his death
- *Antonio Pérez* (1540–1611) was the son of Gonzalo Pérez. After his father's death in 1567, he became Philip's secretary. An extremely able and intelligent man, he led the Éboli faction after the death of Ruy Gomez. In 1579, Philip discovered that Pérez had been deceiving him by withholding letters sent to the king by his half-brother Don John from the Netherlands. Pérez was imprisoned but eventually escaped to Aragon, where his family came from. Here he became involved in the uprising of 1591–2 and escaped to France when it was defeated (see pages 144–5).

tended to put forward opposing views according to the problem being discussed at the time.

The regional councils were more important. They were reorganised to try to make them more effective. Each was to meet regularly at fixed times on fixed days. Five new councils were created, including a Council of Italy (set up in 1559 to deal with Naples, Sicily and Milan, matters which had formerly been dealt with by the Council of Aragon) and a Council of Portugal (1582). Each council was under a president with a secretary and dealt with executive, legislative and judicial matters, reporting to Philip on a daily basis. Philip did not usually attend these meetings.

A number of historians have pointed out the defects to be found in the conciliar system. The historian Geoffrey Woodward makes the point that problems were created because each council was dealt with separately, sending its reports directly to Philip and receiving orders from Philip. This meant that the information he received from them was incomplete and at times inaccurate. This situation, Woodward says, was made worse by the fact that Philip did not travel outside Spain after 1559 (except for three years when he was in Portugal). He, therefore, had no way of seeing for himself the truth of what he had been told. Another historian, John Lynch (1981), holds the view that the system 'probably reached its maximum efficiency in the reign of Philip II, yet still remained imperfect'.

Establishment of *juntas*

As the king grew older it took him much longer to deal with the ever-increasing business. This was especially so when he became ill in 1585 and was unable to do as much work as usual. As a result, the structure of government was changed in some respects. A system of *juntas* was set up. They were expected to discuss and advise the king on particular problems. They were not permanent bodies. Some might last for a few weeks, others for longer. Those who sat on the *juntas* were ministers and officials thought to be well informed about the problem being dealt with.

Even within the *juntas* themselves there was an inner group, consisting of the king, three of his closest advisers, on whose word he felt he could rely, and his private secretary, who, for many years, was the hardworking, loyal and indispensable **Mateo Vázquez**. This group was referred to as the *Junta* of the Night because of the time at which it usually met to discuss the business of the day and probably to decide on policy. Vázquez was a key figure in making this system work. As well as his position on the *Junta* of the Night he acted as the co-ordinator of all the work of the *juntas*.

Philip's secretaries

As Philip rarely attended meetings of the councils, he made great use of his secretaries. These were the men who worked most closely with the king. They

KEY FIGURE

Mateo Vázquez de Leca c.1542–91

Entered Philip's service in 1572 and became his private secretary in 1573 until his death.

KEY FIGURE

Gonzalo Pérez (c.1500–66)

A man of considerable learning who was appointed as personal secretary to Prince Philip in 1543. He remained in Philip's service from then until his death.

served as intermediaries between Philip and the councils, taking meeting summary reports to the king and relaying his views to the council. With Philip, the secretaries dealt with all important papers and requests. The principal secretary was a key position in the system. At the beginning of his reign this was **Gonzalo Pérez**. After his death in 1566 the post was divided into two between Gonzalo's son Antonio, who was part of the Éboli family faction, and Gabriel de Zayas, who was part of the Duke of Alba's faction.

Summary diagram: The government of Spain

Personal government	Attempts to improve the quality of advice	Conciliar system
• Philip communicated with officials and councils in writing rather than face to face • Used secretaries • Made all decisions personally	• All central government offices in Madrid • Depository for government papers	• Council of state (two rival factions) • Reorganisation of regional councils • System of *Juntas* established – 1585 onwards

Finance

▶ *How effective was Philip II in dealing with the financial problems of his reign?*

The financial position of the empire that Philip inherited from his father was to prove a key concern throughout his reign. He had to assume the debt accumulated by Charles, and had no option but to suspend payments on all his debts in January 1557. However, he was not in a position to cancel his debts completely. Had he done this, few bankers would have agreed to lend him money in the future. What he did was to come to an agreement with his creditors that he would pay off his old debts at a lower rate of interest, while continuing to receive fresh loans. It meant that the foreign bankers lending him money, especially those from Germany and Genoa, would be prepared to continue to deliver the money to whichever part of Philip's empire they were asked. Without this facility Philip would have had considerable difficulties in paying his armies. Further suspensions of payments took place in 1560, 1576 and 1596. In each case the old loans were renegotiated so that further new loans could be taken out with the bankers.

A poor financial start was not helped by the fact that Philip's territories, like most others in Europe at the time, were suffering from inflation (see Chapter 5). He, therefore, had to find increasing amounts of money to pay both for the ordinary expenses of government and for the cost of wars, which made major demands on his income.

State expenditure

Philip's ordinary expenditure in time of peace went on running the court, administering central and local government, funding the central courts of justice, and repaying the loans to bankers. He made efforts to bring down the expenses of his household, in which he met with some success. Where he did spend funds was in the public sphere. He wished to give status and prestige to the Spanish monarchy through the arts. Philip was able to call on works of art and artefacts from all over his empire. He also spent large sums on building palaces such as the Escorial and in furnishing them. Artists came from all over Europe to work for him. Among a number of these was **Titian**, who painted several portraits of the king. Many of his later works were designed for display in the public areas of Philip's palaces.

Savings were also possible on administrative costs as the major office holders were grandees, such as the Duke of Alba, who mainly spent their own funds in the service of the king. A few were given salaries to cut down on possible corruption, but other administrators were paid little. Spending on these areas would, however, have increased over the years of Philip's reign as a result of inflation.

For most of his reign Philip was engaged in waging war and this was his largest expenditure. Military and naval requirements were becoming increasingly costly. Not only had payments to be made to the fighting forces but money had also to be found for a wide range of armaments, and especially for the navy. These, too, were all affected by inflation. According to the work Henry Kamen (2005) has done on this area of expenditure, the total annual military expenditure of Castile in Spain, the Mediterranean and the Netherlands was under 2 million ducats before 1566; in the 1570s it had doubled to over 4 million ducats and by the end of his reign it was estimated to be five times higher (10 million ducats). It was only in this area that significant savings might have been made, but Philip was not prepared to do this.

Meeting the financial obligations of the empire

If Philip was not prepared to reduce his overall income more, how could he obtain enough funds to meet his needs? He would either have to increase his income and/or borrow. He did both.

Means of raising income

Philip had some success in increasing income, at least in Castile and the New World. Each part of the empire was supposed to raise enough money for its own needs. In addition, the king could, in theory, ask for money to meet the more general needs which concerned the whole of the empire. But most of his

 KEY FIGURE

Titian (c.1488–1576)
An outstanding Italian painter of portraits, landscape backgrounds and mythological and religious subjects; noted for his use of colour. He painted a number of portraits of Charles I and Philip II, and worked mainly for Philip for the last 26 years of his life.

territories had difficulty in raising money, even for their own requirements. The Netherlands, which had provided his father Charles with a great deal of income, ceased to do so from the 1570s when some states there revolted against Philip's rule. In fact, the reverse was true as more and more resources were needed to try to deal with the uprising there. Within Spain, the kingdom of Aragon was considered too poor to be able to contribute much. It was only from Castile and the New World that he could depend on obtaining more.

Raising money in Castile

In Castile there was little that the inhabitants could do to prevent Philip raising as much money as he wished. He was able to obtain subsidies from the *Cortes* at regular intervals and with little difficulty. The *alcabala* was increased during his reign. The rate at which it was levied was first doubled and later tripled. After the failure of the Armada in 1588 against England, the Castilian *Cortes* agreed to a tax called the *millones*. This would have to be paid by all, whatever their income. Hardly surprisingly, the fact that it had to be paid on everyday food such as meat and oil meant it became the most unpopular of all the taxes in Castile and hit the poorest most.

The receipts from customs duties were increased. New duties were imposed and the rates on salt, an essential item, were raised. Philip also regained control of the customs houses, which meant that the Crown received customs duties directly, instead of via tax farmers who had retained a significant proportion of what they collected.

Raising money from the Church

The Church also increased its contribution. The most important revenue from this source was the *cruzada*, which was paid regularly, and the amount collected from it doubled during the reign of Philip. The existing **subsidio** and the royal tithes also increased their yield. In addition a new tax, the **excusado**, was granted by the pope in 1567.

Raising money from the New World

Philip was particularly fortunate over the New World, from which his annual income increased fourfold between 1560 and 1600. By the end of the century revenues from the New World made up about twenty per cent of the Crown's total income, although this was not as much as some contemporaries seem to have imagined it to be. Philip received a similar amount from the various clerical sources and more from taxes levied in Castile. But it helped considerably in giving an extra boost to his income to help pay for the wars in which Spain was involved.

Other financial reforms

Philip also tried to ensure that he received all of the income which was due to him. The financial departments of the government were reformed to try to

KEY TERMS

Subsidio A clerical tax introduced in 1519 and regularly levied on rents, lands and other forms of income.

Excusado A tax on clerical property introduced in 1567 and usually paid as a lump sum by the Church.

make them more efficient. Attempts were made to prevent those in public office gaining an excessive amount of financial reward. At a time when such offices were low paid, a certain amount of corruption and bribery was acceptable. Excessive amounts were not. Attempts were therefore made to prevent this but had only limited success.

Borrowing

Yet there was never enough income for Philip to meet his expenses. He attempted, never with complete success, to bridge the gap by borrowing. As a result, he left long-term debts of about 68 million ducats to his successors – nearly three times the size of the debt he had inherited himself.

The economy

Raising money was made more difficult by problems in the economy. This was very much the result of Spain become part of a much wider economic network covering the Americas as well as Europe – areas over which it had little control, but also as a result of a lack of economic expertise on the Council for Finance. In addition, the wars in which Spain was engaged for much of Philip's reign created problems. Spain could not itself produce all the armaments needed or all the ships required. Journeys by sea were hazardous and investors were therefore reluctant to put money into new commercial ventures.

Summary diagram: Finance

Expenditure	Raising income			
	Castile	New World	Church	Other means
• Court • Administration • Justice • Loans • War	• Subsidies • Alcabela • Millones	Annual income increased fourfold	• *Cruzado* • *Subsidio* • Royal tithes • *Excusado*	• Reforms • Debt refinancing • Economies in the royal household

 # Religion and the Church

▶ *How successful were the Church reforms that were introduced in Spain during the reign of Philip II?*

There is no doubting Philip's personal faith and commitment. This drove him to follow his father's advice 'to serve God, uphold the Inquisition and suppress heresy'. At the same time, Philip wished to maintain his own control over the Church and not allow the papacy in particular, but any other foreigners as well, to interfere with that control.

The situation in 1556

Little had been done during the reign of Charles I to ensure that the Church in Spain was organised soundly and that clergy were capable of seeing to the spiritual education of the laity. The ordinary clergy tended to be uneducated and poorly paid. This led many of them to absent themselves from their religious duties and to hold a number of positions. The quality of the archbishops and bishops also varied. Appointments to these offices were usually held by members of the greatest noble families and provided a large income from the cities, castles and estates that they owned. Bishops were often non-residents employed in the service of the king. Thus, Fernando de Valdés, the Archbishop of Seville between 1546 and 1568, rarely visited his see during his tenure of office.

The organisation of the Church also needed reform. In some areas, particularly the towns, there were too many **parishes**. In other, mainly rural areas, there were few. There was often an overlap of **jurisdiction** between the churches, religious and monastic orders, lords, bishops, inquisitors and town authorities. A further difficulty was the fact that laymen had the right to appoint parish priests. With the organisation of the Church itself needing reform and with a generally poor level of education and ability among many of the clergy, it is not surprising that the ordinary people usually had poor knowledge of Christian beliefs and practice. Many people's faith was still rooted in pagan festivals and local rituals.

KEY TERMS

Parish An area overseen by a church and its priest.

Jurisdiction The extent of the right to administer justice and apply laws.

Jesuits Members of the Society of Jesus, founded by Ignatius Loyola in 1534.

However, some improvements to the Church had been made in Spain by 1556. These were carried out usually by small groups and individuals. They were not normally part of policies for the whole of Spain. One important group was the Society of Jesus (whose members were known as **Jesuits**). This religious group had been founded by the Spaniard Ignatius Loyola in 1534 and, in the beginning, was composed mainly of Spaniards. In its early days, it was supported by Philip and undertook missionary work among the ordinary people throughout Spain. It also appealed to powerful nobles within Spain, such as the Duke of Gandia, who became its third general and who was also important in bringing into existence what was to become the extremely important educational arm of the Jesuits.

Among individual figures who tried to improve the standards of both the clergy and laity was Luis de Granada (see page 133), who had great influence among all levels of society in both Spain and Portugal. Individual bishops also tried to introduce reforms. In 1540 the Bishop of Pamplona tried to introduce a number of reforms, including ordering priests to preach a sermon every Sunday. Although such individual work had some impact it did not meet the widespread need for reform.

Men of God

- *Ignatius Loyola* (1491–1556) was born into a powerful aristocratic family and became a soldier. During his convalescence after being wounded, he read works of devotional literature. This changed his life. After interrogation by the Inquisition on his beliefs he fled to France. With six other scholars he met in Paris, he founded the Society of Jesus. They took vows of poverty, chastity and obedience to the pope. In 1540 the Jesuits received official papal approval and soon became important in the mission of the Counter-Reformation. His main work, which governed the conduct of the Jesuits, was the *Spiritual Exercises*. This was considered to contain Illuminist content and withdrawn from circulation in the 1559 *Index of Forbidden Books*. He died in Rome and was canonised in 1622.
- *Luis de Granada* (1505–88) was born in Spain, where he lived until 1557 when he moved to Portugal. He became a Dominican friar and was famous for his preaching in both countries. He wrote and published many spiritual works, of which one particularly influential one was *The Book of Prayer*, which was published in 1554.
- *Fernando de Valdés* (1483–1568) was a Spanish churchman who held a succession of bishoprics up to 1546 when he became Archbishop of Seville (1546–66). Known for his extreme determination to rid Spain of all signs of heresy, Valdés was early in his career associated with the Inquisition and he became Inquisitor General 1547–66. In 1559 he was responsible for the arrest and imprisonment on charges of heresy of Bartolomé de Carranza, Archbishop of Toledo, who was one of the main adversaries of Valdés. In 1559 Valdés produced the *Index of Forbidden Books* which included the works of Erasmus. He directed the cases against Erasmians and the Lutherans of Valladolid and Seville (see pages 133–4). From 1565 onwards, however, Valdés fell out of favour at court and in 1566 he was replaced as Inquisitor General.

The elimination of heresy

Philip was determined to eliminate any signs of heresy within his kingdoms and relied on the Inquisition to accomplish this goal, for example in dealing with Erasmians and Illuminists and their association with Protestantism. The Inquisitor General Fernando de Valdés actively looked for any signs of heresy and took action against anyone suspected of Protestant views. Thus, in 1557, a group numbering some 130, including members of religious orders, was discovered in Seville. Another group, which included a former chaplain to Charles, was found in Valladolid. Members of that group were clearly Protestants.

At the time, Philip was in the Netherlands while his sister **Joanna** acted as his regent in Spain. Charles wrote to her on this issue in 1558.

 KEY FIGURE

Joanna of Austria (1535–75)

Daughter of Charles I, see was the widow of Prince John of Portugal and mother of King Sebastian of Portugal. Princess of Portugal 1552–4, she was regent of Spain in 1554–9 and contributed to religious, artistic and cultural affairs at the Spanish court.

SOURCE G

From Charles's letter of 1558 to Joanna on the subject of suspected Protestants, quoted in Henry Kamen, *The Spanish Inquisition*, Phoenix, 1997, pp. 94–5.

Believe me, my daughter, this business has caused and still causes me more anxiety and pain than I can express … I do not know whether it will be enough in these cases to follow the usual practice. Such people, if set free, are at liberty to commit the same offence, particularly if they are educated persons. One can imagine the evil consequences, for it is clear that they cannot act without armed organization and leaders, and so it must be seen whether they can be proceeded

What does Source G mention as reasons why Charles was so keen to have all signs of Protestantism, however small, completely eradicated?

against as creators of sedition, upheaval, riots and disturbance in the state. They would then be guilty of rebellion and could not expect any mercy. I wanted to introduce an Inquisition to punish the heresies that some people had caught from neighbouring Germany and England and even France … Finally an order was issued declaring that all people of whatever state and condition who came under certain specified categories were to be burnt and their goods confiscated … I do not know what the king my son had done since then, but I think that the same reason will have made him continue as I did, because I advised and begged him to be very severe in dealing with these people. Believe me, my daughter, if so great an evil is not suppressed and remedied without distinction of persons from the very beginning, I cannot promise that the king or anyone else will be in a position to do it afterward.

The message was clear. Those who were not true Catholics were to be treated as a threat to the state and the Church. A number of arrests were made in Seville and Valladolid and by 1562 both groups had been eliminated. There would be no further threat of Protestantism taking root in Spain. Further *autos de fé* took place during Philip's reign, often involving *Moriscos* and *conversos*. However, the main work of the Inquisition had changed its direction by the beginning of Philip's reign; its focus was now more on investigating and dealing with enforcing moral and Christian standards within the laity.

Censorship

An important part of the Inquisition's work was censoring heretical works. Again, Valdés was the driving force behind this. The censorship's main form was the Spanish *Index of Forbidden Books*, first published in 1559 (see Source H). It contained around 700, mainly foreign, works. The *Index* was regularly revised and extended, so that by 1583 it not only included the works of all known heretics but also included the names of many important figures in the Catholic Church, such as Fray Luis de Granada and Juan de Ávila. All books and manuscripts also needed a licence before they could be published and all bookshops and libraries were liable to being searched for circulating banned books.

In addition, a 1559 decree forbade Spanish students from going abroad to study at foreign universities. In practice, this ban never seems to have been a total one; Spaniards were still to be found in the various universities of Italy and the Netherlands during the second half of the sixteenth century.

For many years it was asserted by historians such as J.H. Elliott (1966) that the censorship imposed had at least some negative effect on the intellectual life of Spain. It was maintained that it contributed to the cultural isolation of Spain from the rest of Europe as freedom of speech and thought was stifled and writers were forced to conform or suffer the penalties. Elliott describes the censorship as Spain 'sealing itself off against the indiscriminate entry of foreign ideas'. This view has been disputed in more recent times. The historian Henry Kamen (2005) puts forward the view that Spaniards were still able to have access to a wide range of material. He maintains that it also did not prevent the development of Spanish culture. Spaniards went to the New World, engaged in trade with Europe and went on political missions to other parts of Europe. This exposed them to new ideas and thoughts which they then brought back to Spain.

SOURCE H

Cover of the *Index of Forbidden Books*, published in 1570.

> What impact was the work shown in Source H considered to have had on Spanish intellectual life?

Reforms of the Church: the Tridentine decrees

What Charles I had wanted was a direction for the whole of the Church in Spain. He had been disappointed by what he saw as a lack of urgency on the part of the papacy to introduce reforms into the Catholic Church throughout Europe. And it was only in 1545 that a council, the Council of Trent, was set up by Pope Paul III. Its main concerns were to condemn Protestantism, clarify the doctrines of the Catholic Church, deal with corruption within the Church and introduce reforms to improve the quality of the clergy. It convened three times in 1545–63, with the Spanish clergy playing an important role in its discussions.

The Council of Trent reinforced the traditional foundations of Catholic doctrine in a number of ways:

- The Latin **Vulgate** edition of the Bible was to be the official version of scripture.
- The mass was to become the most important aspect of Catholic worship.
- Variations in the **liturgy** were abolished and a new **missal** to be used by all was introduced.

The authority and the ability of the bishops were to be strengthened. Bishops were to:

- live in their **benefices** (except where official leave of absence was granted)
- hold meetings of the clergy in their areas
- visit their dioceses regularly
- preach regularly
- be responsible for ensuring the quality of those admitted to holy orders
- see that religious communities kept observance of their rule of life.

For their part, priests were to:

- receive more education; seminaries were to be set up to improve their training
- preach every Sunday
- provide for the Christian education of the laity
- keep parish records of baptisms, marriages and deaths
- remain within their parishes
- stop holding a number of parishes.

Pope Pius IV approved these recommendations in 1564 for introduction in all Europe. In the same year Philip approved their introduction into Spain. However, he also made it clear that, as leader of the Spanish Church, he, not the pope or his representatives, would be responsible for overseeing their implementation in Spain.

The impact of the Tridentine reforms in Spain

There were a number of stumbling blocks to the introduction of the Tridentine reforms in Spain. At the top, disputes between pope and king undermined the

> **KEY TERMS**
>
> **Vulgate** A late fourth-century Latin translation of the Bible.
>
> **Liturgy** The authorised form of public worship.
>
> **Missal** A book containing the prayers and customs of the Catholic Church.
>
> **Benefice** A Church appointment with a guaranteed amount of income and property.

leadership necessary to ensure that the reforms could be fully implemented. In particular, Philip would not allow any of his rights over the Church to be affected. He was genuinely committed to reform but wanted them to develop under his leadership and direction, not the pope's.

There was much opposition among clergy and laity. The powerful **cathedral chapters** were used to a great deal of independence and resented the new powers which the bishops had over them. The ordinary clergy were generally reluctant to commit to reform. Few seminaries for training of clergy were set up and regular meetings of Church councils and **synods** did not take place. In vast areas of the country local people remained wedded to their local customs, saints, processions and carnivals, and resisted all official orders to ban them.

Some improvements did take place, however. The calibre of bishops improved, although many of them, because of their abilities, were often needed by the Crown in the service of the government. This meant that they could not be in their dioceses for much of the time and could not oversee their clergy and laity closely enough. Where a bishop was determined on reform, changes did take place. One outstanding example was **Gaspar de Quiroga**, who set an example by his personal life, promoted education and welfare policies and worked to improve the standards of the clergy. Individuals such as St John of the Cross and St Teresa of Ávila continued their work of reform, started during the reign of Charles I (see page 87). Administrative changes were also made. A new archdiocese was established at Burgos in 1502 and a number of new dioceses were set up, mainly in Aragon.

However, it is telling that in the 1590s, at the very end of Philip's reign, the records of the Inquisition contain numerous complaints about many Spaniards' low level of Christian understanding.

Relations with the papacy

Charles I had had a difficult relationship with the papacy. Philip understood that it was better to have the pope on his side to support and finance his religious campaigns. The papacy, for its part, needed Philip to organise finance and lead the crusades against Protestants and Turks. However, relations between the two were generally difficult throughout Philip's reign. The two main causes of disputes between king and pope were over Philip's control over the Church in his kingdoms and foreign affairs.

First, Philip had considerable powers and control over the Church in his kingdoms. He had the right to appoint bishops and abbots. This meant that the Spanish clergy needed to be in favour with the king if they hoped for a promotion within the Church. Most appeals by clergy could only be heard in Spain. The Spanish Inquisition was also under the king's control. Philip was adamant that the pope should not interfere in any way with these rights that he had over the Church.

KEY TERMS

Cathedral chapter A group of clerics formed to advise a bishop.

Synod An assembly of the clergy (and sometimes laity) in a diocese.

KEY FIGURE

Gaspar de Quiroga (1512–95)

A prominent government official and priest who became Inquisitor General in 1573, Archbishop of Toledo in 1577 and cardinal in 1578. He was an important patron of the arts in the service of religion, and of artists such as El Greco.

>  **KEY FIGURE**
>
> **Bartolomé de Carranza (1503–76)**
>
> Appointed Archbishop of Toledo by Philip II in 155, he was a supporter of Church reform and made important contributions to the debates at the Council of Trent.

Relationships between king and pope reached a crisis point in 1559 over the case of **Carranza**, Archbishop of Toledo. This case had arisen when the Inquisitor General, Valdés, accused Carranza of heresy. It is likely that Valdés envied Carranza his successful career to date and was looking for ways to attack him. Unfortunately, Carranza had probably been unwise in making some pronouncements which might be misconstrued as heretical, although he was clearly no heretic. Valdés took the opportunity to pounce. Carranza was arrested by the Spanish Inquisition and kept in prison for over seven years while Philip and the Spanish Inquisition on the one side and the papacy on the other argued over his case.

Pope Pius V demanded that Carranza be sent to Rome to be tried there. He argued the papal right to try cases involving bishops and archbishops and felt that Carranza would not get a fair trial in Spain. The Spanish Inquisition refused to hand him over. Philip, for his part, felt that he needed to defend the Inquisition, which he saw as supporting him in preserving Catholicism in Spain. Even archbishops, he felt, must be held to account by the Inquisition for what they said and did. However, he was eventually forced to give way on this issue in 1566. The saintly Pius V refused to be browbeaten by Philip's representatives and withheld assent to the renewal of the *cruzada* in that year. This would have made Philip's financial situation very difficult and he gave way. Carranza was transferred to Rome but even then the Spanish managed to delay a decision on his case for a further ten years. After admitting a few minor errors, Carranza was at last released.

Philip, however, was able to establish his control in other ways. He asserted his right to have the final say on how the Tridentine decrees were implemented in Spain. In 1567 he ignored Pius V's edict banning bull fights. More importantly, in 1572 Philip refused to allow his subjects to appeal to Rome. As Philip was to say to his ambassador in Rome in 1578, 'Secular princes are not bound to carry out the mandates of the pope in temporal matters.'

As under Charles I, difficulties also arose, secondly in the area of foreign affairs. Throughout Philip's reign the Crown and the papacy differed over various policies in relation to foreign affairs. For example, they clashed over which methods to use in support of Catholicism in the Netherlands, and in policies involving the Protestant Elizabeth I of England. Philip was particularly incensed when Pope Paul IV decided to accept Henry IV as King of France, once he converted to Catholicism. Philip was still fighting Henry at the time. To the pope, Philip was putting Spanish interests ahead of those of the Church. For his part, Philip felt it was his duty to tell the pope what to do and, at the same time, resented what he saw as interference in Spanish affairs.

Summary diagram: Religion and the Church

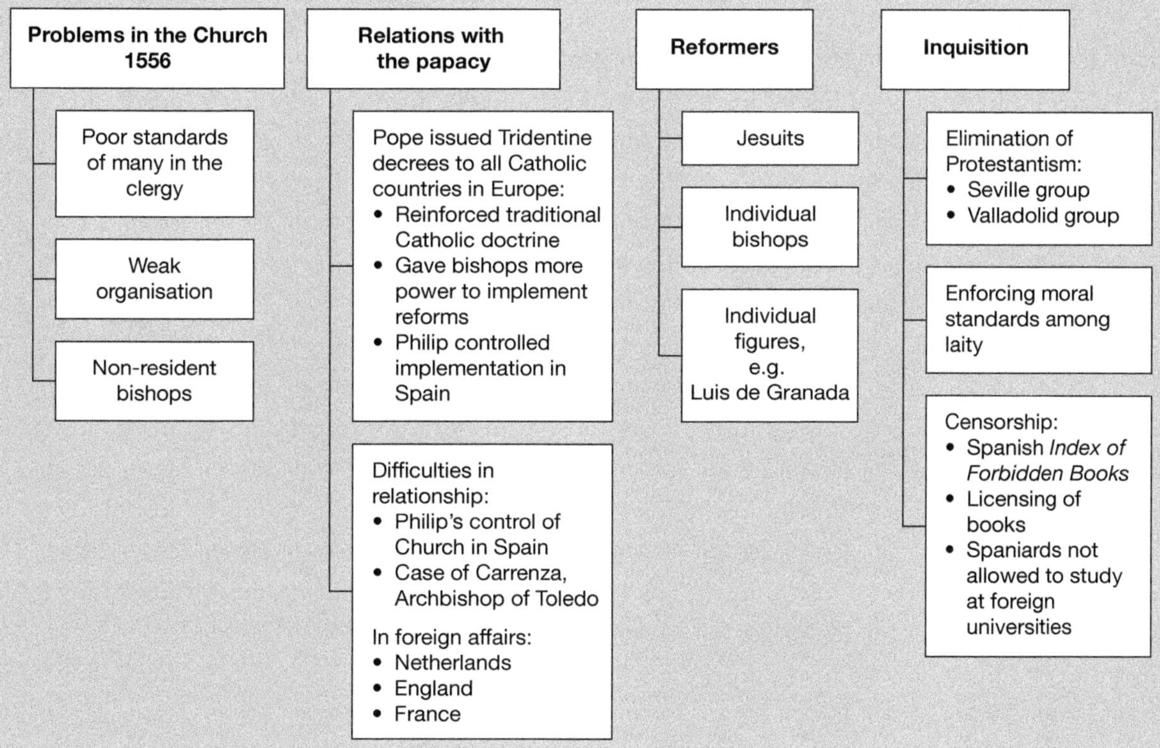

Problems in the Church 1556
- Poor standards of many in the clergy
- Weak organisation
- Non-resident bishops

Relations with the papacy
- Pope issued Tridentine decrees to all Catholic countries in Europe:
  - Reinforced traditional Catholic doctrine
  - Gave bishops more power to implement reforms
  - Philip controlled implementation in Spain
- Difficulties in relationship:
  - Philip's control of Church in Spain
  - Case of Carrenza, Archbishop of Toledo
- In foreign affairs:
  - Netherlands
  - England
  - France

Reformers
- Jesuits
- Individual bishops
- Individual figures, e.g. Luis de Granada

Inquisition
- Elimination of Protestantism:
  - Seville group
  - Valladolid group
- Enforcing moral standards among laity
- Censorship:
  - Spanish *Index of Forbidden Books*
  - Licensing of books
  - Spaniards not allowed to study at foreign universities

The revolts of Granada and Aragon

▶ *What were the causes of the rebellions in Granada and Aragon?*

During Philip's reign there were three rebellions in his empire. The most critical one, in the Netherlands, is covered in the next chapter. The other two took place in Spain: the revolt of the *Moriscos* took place in Granada in 1568–70 and the rebellion of Aragon in 1591–2. Both were defeated in the end.

The *Moriscos*

One internal threat that Philip had to deal with was the revolt of the *Moriscos* in Granada which broke out on Christmas Eve 1568. There had officially been no members of the Muslim faith in Spain since 1526 (see page 88). Those who had been Muslims before and who had remained in Spain had had to become Christians, known as 'new' Christians or *Moriscos*. In 1556 around 400,000

Moriscos lived in Spain, mainly in Aragon, Valencia and Granada, where they made up 50 per cent of the population.

Causes of the *Moriscos* revolt 1568

A number of reasons led to the revolt:

- the position of the *Moriscos* themselves
- government action towards the *Moriscos*
- the political situation in north Africa.

People forced into conversion are hardly likely to be sincere believers. Philip continued the policy of attempting to make *Moriscos* genuine converts through the teaching and the example of missionaries. This was a difficult task. Much depended on the quality of the clergy involved in the missionary work and this varied greatly. Some of the clergy put a great deal of effort into their task, but most seem to have done little. As long as the *Moriscos* attended mass and displayed the outward signs of the Christian religion, little more was expected of them.

It is not surprising, therefore, that most *Moriscos* retained at least some of the practices of their old faith. Arabic was still spoken by some. Circumcision was common. The *Moriscos* usually married within their own community, and generally followed their traditional way of life with its different diet and dress. Regular visits were made to the public baths around which their social lives centred. On the one hand, there was reluctance by the *Moriscos* to abandon their native culture, and on the other, a failure by the clergy in Granada to give the kind of Christian teaching which might have improved *Moriscos'* integration into Spanish society.

In Granada the practice had grown up too of *Moriscos* paying subsidies to avoid persecution. The Mondéjar family, hereditary captains-general of Granada, had also long offered some protection to the *Moriscos* living there. However, by the 1560s the family was not in favour at court and their advice to Philip was, therefore, ignored.

At the same time, government policy towards the *Moriscos* changed. The *Moriscos* experienced economic hardship as the government made the silk trade, the main means of income for many of them, more difficult. In particular, exports were banned and heavy taxes imposed. In 1560 a programme began to investigate the *Moriscos'* landholding rights. Those who could not provide proof of ownership either lost their land or had to pay a fine.

By then, Philip decided that the policy of ensuring that the *Moriscos* gradually became genuine Christians would have to be changed. Many of the Christian clergy had long been demanding that something more be done to deal with a group who seemed to be Christian in name alone. This demand cannot have failed to influence Philip, who was so committed to the Catholic faith. But of more concern to many in Spain, particularly the military commanders, was the security threat posed by the *Moriscos*. The *Moriscos* have been aptly described as a possible 'enemy within', prepared to help the Turks in their advances across the western Mediterranean or to support the Muslim **corsairs** from north Africa, who attacked villages and shipping along the coasts of Spain. The advance of the Turks into the western Mediterranean and their siege of Malta in 1565 only served to increase these fears.

At a time, therefore, when Philip was feeling that Christianity was on the defensive against the Muslim threat in the western Mediterranean, he was particularly concerned about any possible help that the Turks might receive from his own subjects. Although such fears were greatly exaggerated, there is certainly evidence of contact between *Moriscos* and Turks in north Africa and the Barbary corsairs. A major raid took place on Orgiba in Granada in 1565, when corsairs attacked Spanish troops and enabled several hundred *Moriscos* to leave Spain. There were also fears that the *Moriscos* might join with the Protestants in southern France in any attack on Spain. It appears to have been mainly for these reasons of security that the decision was made to take sterner measures against the *Moriscos* in Granada.

The new policy began in 1567. *Moriscos* in Granada were forbidden to use Arabic, to wear their distinctive dress, to read Moorish literature, or to follow any other of their traditional customs, including songs and dances. This decree was announced on the anniversary of the surrender of Granada, adding insult to injury. In many cases the new regulations were enforced harshly. Private and public baths were destroyed, including those of the **Alhambra**. The conciliatory approach was to be replaced by one of hardline coercion. The Inquisition increased its investigations into *Moriscos*. The Marquis of Mondéjar, captain-general of Granada and a major employer of *Moriscos*, tried in vain to safeguard them from the campaign by the Inquisition.

Driven to despair, large numbers of *Moriscos* joined a revolt which broke out near Granada on Christmas Eve 1568. The Marquis of Mondéjar had warned Philip as to what would happen at the imposition of the decree. His advice was ignored. As a result, Philip and his senior ministers totally underestimated what was likely to happen and the government was completely unprepared. Its best troops were fighting in the Netherlands and there was no clear plan of how to deal with the revolt, which was to continue for two years. The fighting was marked by cruelty and massacres on both sides, until the *Moriscos* were eventually defeated by government forces in 1570.

Crushing the revolt

The *Moriscos* were dealt with severely. An attempt was made to ensure that they did not live together as a group, but were spread throughout the Christian population. In this way, it was hoped, they would not present such a security

KEY TERMS

Corsairs Pirates, especially the privateers who operated along the Barbary Coast (north Africa).

Alhambra The fortress and palace of the Moorish rulers of Granada, built between the twelfth and thirteenth centuries.

threat and would be more likely to conform to a Christian way of life. All those not killed were expelled from Granada and sent to other areas of Castile. More than 100,000 were deported between 1570 and 1573 and around 20,000 died on the journey.

It was expected that the dispersal would solve the problem. In fact, it made it worse. The problem of the *Moriscos* was now spread throughout Castile instead of mainly Granada. Many *Moriscos* were now in areas of Spain in which they had rarely been seen before. The fears, suspicions and jealousies of many more 'old' Christians than before were now aroused and resentment against *Moriscos* became more widespread. The dispersal had also not dealt with the security threat that the *Moriscos* presented. Plots and conspiracies involving Turks and French Protestants are revealed in surviving letters, sent or received by *Moriscos*. A number turned to banditry or piracy.

Granada itself suffered economically. 'Old' Christians from northern Spain moved in and occupied the lands and homes of the vacated communities, but around a third of settlements remained empty and the population fell by over a quarter between 1561 and 1591.

The uprising had also revealed serious military weaknesses in Spain. There had been only 20,000 poor-quality troops and no effective local forces available to deal with the revolt. In addition, the coastal areas had been left defenceless. Such a long coastline would have been hard to defend under any circumstance. It was fortunate that the Turks had not given much support and that the Aragonese and Valencian *Moriscos* had not risen in revolt as well. To help protect the coast in the future, Philip ordered the building of 84 new forts in Granada.

The growing numbers of *Moriscos* continued to worry Philip. Some of his advisers urged him to expel them completely from the country. But Philip did not accept this advice. He was aware that there would be great opposition to such a move from those in Valencia who had many *Moriscos* working on their estates. Instead, the number of missionaries working among the *Moriscos* was increased. However, this had as little effect as before. The policy of assimilation had failed. Philip would not take the decision to force all *Moriscos* out of Spain, but that policy would be enacted during the reign of his son, Philip III.

Aragon

For the first part of his reign Philip paid little attention to the kingdom of Aragon. He rarely visited it and held few *Cortes* there. Nor did he press Aragon to vote him more money than it could easily pay. Part of his problem was the rights that Aragon possessed: since the reigns of Ferdinand and Isabella, Aragon had kept its *fueros*, or rights, protected by its office of *Justicia*.

SOURCE I

From a report by a Venetian ambassador, 1581.

The people of Aragon claim to be independent, as in effect they are, since they govern themselves almost as if Aragon were a republic. The king is the head of the state, but he does not inherit the position, they elect him to it. He appoints no official there except a viceroy, who has no part in governing the land or administering justice. These tasks are the responsibilities of officials elected in that kingdom. The viceroy has charge only of the armed forces, and the safety and defence of the region. His Majesty collects no revenue from this region unless he goes there to conduct a meeting of the Cortes, *in which case they grant him 600,000 ducats. They keep the rest of the taxes and duties and spend them for the benefit of their own land. They guard their liberties very jealously and bitterly contest each point so that the king and his ministers cannot enlarge their control over them. As a result they frequently and unnecessarily hinder measures which are not their business.*

> What does Source I tell you about the power that the king had in Aragon?

Philip probably felt, as his father had done, that the Aragonese had neither the men nor the money to assist him more than they did. And as we have already seen (see page 6), Aragon had a number of powers which made it a very different kingdom to govern compared with Castile.

Philip intervenes in Aragon

By the 1580s, however, Philip decided that he had to intervene more directly in the affairs of the kingdoms of Aragon. There were several reasons for this. He had failed in attempts to buy the county of **Ribagorza** on the border with France (see Figure 1.1, page 5) from the Duke of Villahermosa, the noble who held it. Philip felt he needed Ribagorza to improve security on the frontier with France. In addition, many **Huguenots** had settled just across the frontier in France. Philip feared that heresy would spread from France into Spain.

Philip also seems to have felt that he was failing in his duty as king to secure justice for his people. Banditry and lawlessness, as well as pirate raids along the coast, were reaching unacceptable levels in all three of Aragon's kingdoms. Silver convoys going from Castile to Italy were attacked and in 1582 one had been taken by bandits in Catalonia. The Duke of Villahermosa, like other landowners in Aragon, was hated by many of his **vassals**, who wanted Philip to intervene. They felt that conditions would improve for them under the control of the king. Personal hatred played its part. The Count of Chinon, a Castilian who was Philip's chief adviser on Aragon, was also urging the king to intercede, for personal reasons. The Duke of Villahermosa's son had had his wife, Chinon's sister-in-law, executed on a charge of infidelity. Chinon had then had the son executed for the crime (1573).

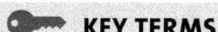

KEY TERMS

Ribagorza A county consisting of seventeen towns and 216 villages extending from Monzón to the Pyrenees.

Huguenots French Protestants.

Vassal Someone given land in return for supporting his master or lord.

Events leading up to the rebellion in Aragon

The first step Philip took was to send troops into Valencia in 1582 to defend the coast against a possible landing by north African pirates. Many complained that this was clearly against the privileges of the kingdom, as the entry of foreign soldiers was not allowed. Then a viceroy was sent to the kingdom of Aragon who was not a native of the country. This was the Marquis of Almenara, a Castilian. Tactless and pompous, he was also a cousin of the Count of Chinon. This appointment again aroused an outcry as it was claimed that all royal officials in the country should be Aragonese. Philip took the case to the *Justicia* on the grounds that this privilege did not apply to the office of viceroy. He argued that both Charles and Ferdinand had in the past appointed Castilians to this post. The *Justicia* found in his favour.

Soldiers from Aragon were then sent in to occupy Ribagorza, claiming that law and order had broken down in the area, and in 1591 the county became a possession of the Crown. Not surprisingly, many in Aragon harboured deep resentment over seeing what they held as their rights so trampled.

Anger in Aragon

To complicate matters, a minor rebellion broke out in Aragon in 1591. Antonio Pérez, Philip's disgraced former chief secretary, had escaped to Aragon from his place of imprisonment in Castile. Pérez claimed his right as a citizen of Aragon to be tried in the court of the *Justicia*. Philip tried to arrange for the case to be transferred to the court of the Inquisition. A riot broke out in Saragossa in which the Viceroy Almenara was wounded and later died. Philip's actions were seen by many as an infringement of the rights of the Aragonese. Others, particularly the lesser nobility, suspected that this was Philip's first step in taking away their local power. Still others felt resentful that they could not obtain offices or financial rewards from the king for themselves or their sons. Many grumbled that these rewards went to the Castilians alone. The Aragonese, or at least some of them, felt they would be better off if they were independent.

However, few joined in the rebellion, which was mainly confined to the town of Saragossa. Neither Catalonia nor Valencia wished to become involved. Most of the nobles in Aragon, and the rest of the population living in the towns and countryside, did not join in. In fact, the historian Henry Kamen (2005) queries whether it could be called a rebellion at all. The rebels took control of Saragossa, persuading, or perhaps forcing, the *Justicia* to support them.

Philip, with the advice of his councillors, decided to send in an army to crush the revolt, even though this was against the privileges of Aragon. The army dealt swiftly with the rebellion. It entered Aragon without resistance and even Saragossa did not put up much of a fight. The army easily overcame the small numbers of rebels, whose leaders were executed, including the *Justicia*. The Duke of Villahermosa, one of the few nobles to have sided with the rebellion, was imprisoned in Castile, where he died in mysterious circumstances. Antonio Pérez, however, fled to France, where he led a small force of rebels and Protestant allies back across the border. These were routed in 1592 by the royal forces with the support of many of the Aragonese, who were only too ready to rally round the Crown against a foreign invasion which included Protestants. The leaders were captured and executed, apart from Pérez, who escaped back to France.

The impact of the revolt and its consequences for royal power in Aragon

Philip's army was in Aragon. He was now in a position to impose a settlement on the kingdom which would have subjected it more closely to his authority. He knew that Aragon was on its own since the rebels had been unable to persuade Catalonia or Valencia to join with them. He could have reduced the powers of the *Justicia* and the *Cortes* to enable him to control the kingdom in the same way that he controlled Castile. But he did not.

Various reasons have been suggested by historians for this decision. For a number, such as the historian John Lynch (1981), it would not be in line with Philip's sense of fairness or justice. As no one in Catalonia or Valencia had played a part in the revolt, and as even in Aragon the majority of the people had distanced themselves from it, it may not have seemed 'just' to Philip to punish the majority for the faults of the few. Furthermore, many in Catalonia and Valencia had joined with him to repel the invasion from France. Another reason given by a number of historians, such as J.H. Elliott (1963), is that perhaps Philip had no intention of altering the traditional government of his kingdom. Kamen (2005) suggests that Philip had learnt lessons from his mistakes in the Netherlands (see pages 155–62). The kingdom of Aragon was not particularly rich and Philip may have felt that it was not worth the effort to impose his power if the Crown were to acquire so little in return.

Philip declared that his intention was 'only to keep their charter and not allow people to contravene it'. He generally kept to the traditional forms of government in Aragon, although he introduced a number of changes which increased his power there. At the *Cortes* of 1592 he was given the right to dismiss the *Justicia* when he wished. It was also clearly established that he was entitled to appoint a 'foreigner' as viceroy if he chase to do so. It was agreed that measures presented at the *Cortes* would become law if a majority of those present voted for them, rather than there being a need for unanimous agreement. The permanent committee of the *Cortes* also lost much of its say on how the revenues of Aragon should be spent. Apart from these prudent and moderate measures the constitution of the kingdom of Aragon remained unchanged. The reforms that took place were those deemed generally necessary to ensure more effective royal power and good government in Aragon.

No further revolts were to take place against the Habsburgs while they ruled Spain. This did not mean that all resentment had stopped. Complaints continued that Philip seldom visited the country and that non-Castilians had too little part in the government of Spain.

Summary diagram: The revolts of Granada and Aragon

The *Moriscos* revolt (Granada 1568–70)

Causes	Consequences
• Economic difficulties • Retention of traditional customs • Clergy demand for harsher methods to eradicate Moorish customs • Security risk	• *Moriscos* expelled from Granada • *Morisco* problem spread all over Castile • Economic problems in Granada • New coastal defences built in Granada • Advice that *Moriscos* should be expelled from Spain

The revolt in Aragon

Causes	Consequences

1. Philip's concerns
  • Fear of Protestant heresy spilling in from France into Ribagorza
  • Lawlessness
  • Count of Chinon urged Philip to intervene
  • Vassals of landowners would have preferred the Crown's overlordship
2. Aragonese fears of losing freedom
  • Philip sent troops to protect the coast
  • Castilian viceroy appointed
  • Troops took over Ribagorza
  • Aragonese nobles suspected a Castilian takeover
  • The Pérez case was seen as an infringement in local affairs
	Philip maintained a traditional form of government in Aragon, but increased his powers. He:
	• Gained the right to dismiss *Justicias*
	• Confirmed in his entitlement to appoint a foreign (Castilian) viceroy
	• Imposed majority voting in the *Cortes*
	• Wrestled control of spending away from the *Cortes*

Chapter summary

The image of Philip, the 'paper king', communicating with everyone in writing and thereby trying to keep on top of everything in his vast empire, is a compelling one. Without doubt the system was inefficient and could hinder decision-making, even if – to put a positive slant on it – it prevented any rash judgements being made. But somehow Philip managed to make it work for most of his reign.

Reforms were made to the conciliar system to try to make it more effective. There were, apart from the *Morisco* rebellion and a minor revolt in Aragon, few signs of the underlying problems that existed. In religion, any signs of Protestantism had been quickly extinguished by the Inquisition, but little had been achieved by the end of his reign to reform the Church in Spain. Philip's major failure was in finance. However much Philip tried to save money and to raise more, he was never able to obtain enough to support the needs of the wars in which he was engaged – as we shall see in Chapter 7.

Refresher questions

Use these questions to remind yourself of the key material covered in this chapter.

1. How did Philip's early life prepare him for kingship?
2. Why did Philip's method of working create problems for government?
3. How did Philip try to improve the conciliar system?
4. Why were Philip's secretaries so important?
5. How did Philip try to deal with state debts?
6. How successful was Philip in increasing income for the Crown?
7. What problems were to be found in the Church in Spain in 1556?
8. How effectively was 'heresy' dealt with?
9. In what ways did Philip assert his control over the Church in Spain?
10. What caused the *Morisco* revolt?
11. What were the results of the defeat of the *Morisco* revolt?
12. Why did Philip have concerns about Aragon in the 1580s?
13. What actions did Philip take which gave concern to at least some of the Aragonese?
14. How effectively did Philip deal with the minor rebellion in Aragon in 1591?

Question practice

ESSAY QUESTIONS

1. How far do you agree that the revolt in the kingdom of Aragon in the years 1591–2 shows both the weakness and strength of the King of Spain?
2. How successful were Philip II's policies in Spain 1556–98?
3. How significant was the revolt of Aragon (1591–2) in extending the authority of Philip II?
4. 'Philip II cannot be held responsible for more than a small part of what happened during his reign.' Assess the validity of this view with reference to events that took place in Spain in 1556–98.

5 How accurate is it to say that the expulsion of the Jews in 1492 had a greater social and economic impact on Spain than the rebellion in Granada in 1568?

6 'The reasons for the revolt in Aragon were radically different from those for the revolt in Granada.' How far do you agree with this statement?

SOURCE ANALYSIS QUESTION

1 Assess the value of Source 1 for revealing why the Spanish government was so concerned about the *Moriscos* and why the *Moriscos* in Granada revolted in 1568. Explain your answer using the source and your own knowledge about the historical context.

> **SOURCE 1**
>
> **From Francisco Muley, a *Morisco* nobleman, 'A Morisco Plea', 1567, quoted in Jon Cowans, *Early Modern Spain: A Documentary History*, University of Pennsylvania Press, 2003, pp. 105–7.**
>
> *When the natives of this kingdom converted to the faith of Jesus Christ, there was no condition that obliged them to give up their way of dressing or their language, nor the other customs they had concerning their festivals, zambras [flamenco dancing], and recreations. And to speak truthfully, the conversion was done by force, contrary to the provisions of the treaty signed by the Catholic monarchs [Ferdinand and Isabella] … Then, during the reign of Dona Juana, their daughter, it came to seem appropriate (to whom I do not know exactly) to order that we give up our* Morisco *clothing, but when certain drawbacks to this plan were pointed out, it was suspended. Now … the clergymen have taken up the issue … to harass us in many ways all at once. Anyone who looks at the new rules from a distance will think they would be easy to follow, but the difficulties they imply are very great … so that, in coming to share the pain of this miserable people, one will take pity on them with love and charity … I have often heard the ministers and prelates say that favours would be done for those who dressed in the Castilian style, but so far, of the many who have done so, I can see none who have been either bothered or favoured; we are all treated the same. If they find a knife on any one of them, they throw him in jail, and he loses his property in fines and penalties. We are persecuted both by ecclesiastical and secular authorities, and despite all this, we remain loyal vassals, obeying His Majesty, ready to serve him with our properties, and it can never be said that we have committed any treason from the day when we surrendered …*
>
> *Our weddings and festivals and the pastimes to which we are accustomed do not in any way prevent us from being Christian. I do not even see how these things can be considered Moorish ceremonies; good Muslims were never found doing these things, and the holy men left as soon as the* zambras *and the singing and music began … These* zambras *do not exist in Africa or Turkey; it is a local custom, and if it were a religious ceremony, it would have to exist in the same form everywhere …*

CHAPTER 7

Philip II: foreign policy and the New World

Philip had not inherited all the territory that his father had held. The title of Holy Roman Emperor and the Habsburg family lands had gone to Charles's brother Ferdinand and his family. However, the Spanish overseas empire grew considerably during Philip's reign, when Spain also acquired Portugal and its vast Portuguese empire.

Philip viewed his empire from the perspective of Madrid. He did not have first-hand evidence of what was taking place elsewhere. He had to rely on what he was told by inhabitants of the various regions visiting Madrid or the reports sent by his own advisers or representatives in the different territories. This often meant that he received only one view of what was happening in any part of his empire, a view which was frequently inaccurate and out of date by the time he received it.

This chapter looks at how Philip dealt with foreign policy issues and measures the impact that New World discoveries had on Spain. It concludes with an assessment of Philip's achievements during his long reign. These themes are developed under the following headings:

★ Philip's aims in ruling his empire
★ The foreign policy of Philip II
★ The New World
★ Spain in 1598

The key debate on *page 169* of this chapter asks the question: Was defending his empire the main consideration driving Philip's foreign policy?

Key dates

1559	Treaty of Cateau-Cambrésis. This made Spain the important European power in Italy	1580	Annexation of Portugal
1568	Netherlands in open revolt against Philip	1581	Philip became King of Portugal
1571	Battle of Lepanto: Don John of Austria defeated the Turkish fleet	1585	Treaty of Nonsuch: England pledges to support the rebellion in the Netherlands
	Turks captured Cyprus	1587	Farnese withdrawn from the Netherlands to support the proposed invasion of England
1572	Invasion by William the Silent in the northern provinces of the Netherlands	1588	Philip sent the Armada to invade England. This ended in failure
1578	The King of Portugal, Sebastian, presumed dead at the Battle of Alcazarquivir in northern Morocco	1590	Farnese sent to France to support the forces opposing Henry of Navarre
	Alexander Farnese, Duke of Parma, became governor general of the Netherlands and won back the southern states of the Netherlands for Spain	1598	Treaty of Vervins ended war with France
			Death of Philip

Philip's aims in ruling his empire

▶ *What did Philip wish to accomplish in foreign policy? How far did he achieve his aims?*

Philip's aims on the international stage were complex and not always clear. However, two important factors were fundamental to his actions: his wish to preserve and possibly extend the collection of lands over which he ruled, and his adherence to the Roman Catholic faith.

Foreign policy influenced by religion

Philip's religious views certainly played an important part in setting his aims for foreign policy. It is often difficult for us to understand, as we look back on the sixteenth century, just how much religion and religious belief mattered. They cannot be distinguished from political considerations. Few rulers even contemplated allowing more than one religion to be practised in their lands. Philip was, therefore, not unusual in his determination that in the empire he ruled there should only be one religion: Roman Catholicism. 'Before suffering the slightest damage to religion and the service of God, I would lose all my estates, and a hundred lives if I had them because I do not wish, nor do I desire, to be the ruler of heretics.'

Roman Catholicism needed to be defended not only against Protestantism but also against the threat of Islam. Defence against both was as fundamental to Philip's policies as it had been to his father's.

Enemies at the gate and enemies within

Beyond the defence of religion, Philip's principal aim in ruling his empire was to retain control of all his territories. He was determined to safeguard the interests of his family and his dynasty, and to hand his inheritance on to his successor undiminished.

The Netherlands were particularly vulnerable. From 1558, they were near to the strongholds of Protestant power in England and the Lutheran states in Germany. To the south, and separating them from Spain, lay France, by now a traditional enemy of Spain. To protect the Netherlands, Philip had to defend the routes which linked them with Spain both by sea and by land (see Figure 3.1, page 41). The sea route was frequently difficult, even in peacetime, due both to weather conditions and to piracy. Therefore, the land route, the 'Spanish Road' which started from Genoa, had to be kept open at all times. This meant that Philip had to ensure good relations with those rulers through whose territory the route passed.

Need for finance also meant that particular care had to be taken to ensure that the treasure fleets from America were able to make their journeys across the

Atlantic safely. A third major area of vulnerability was the Mediterranean, where there was intense rivalry with the Turks. The preservation of his sea routes in the Mediterranean and of his possessions there, particularly in Italy, was Philip's major concern at the beginning of his reign.

It is sometimes forgotten that even within the Iberian Peninsula there was considerable concern about security. There were fears for Roman Catholicism and concern for the 'purity of the faith'. A constant watch was kept on *Moriscos* and *conversos* to prevent them reverting to any aspect of their former faith, and to ensure that Protestantism did not enter the peninsula. Nor was the country itself considered safe from military attack. In 1590, the secretary of war was concerned about 'the miserable state of the monarchy, for which the only remedy and hope is to fortify Gibraltar, Perpignan, Navarre and the other frontiers … and to surround Madrid with fortresses, praying to God to give us the time, and in his mercy not punish us for our sins …'.

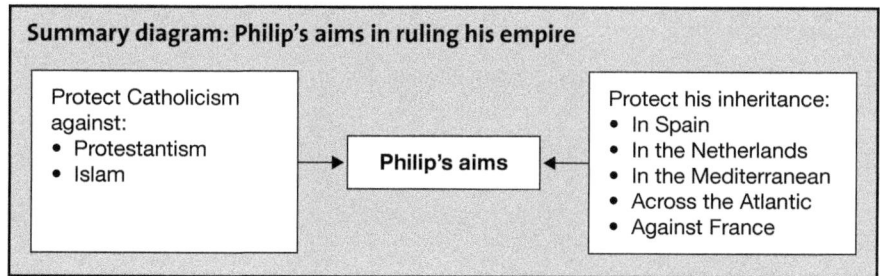

2 The foreign policy of Philip II

▶ What was Philip's stronger motivation in deciding policy: the preservation of his empire or religion?

▶ What factors made it difficult for Philip to achieve his aims?

Portugal

One of Philip's major aspirations was to unify the Iberian Peninsula. The opportunity for achieving this came in 1578 when his nephew, Sebastian, King of Portugal, died fighting the Moors at the Battle of Alcazarquivir in Morocco. Sebastian's heir was his great uncle Cardinal Henry, aged 66, ill in health and vowed to celibacy. It was unlikely that Henry would live for much longer, and it was not clear who would succeed him.

Philip's claim to the throne

There were several aspirants to the throne but Philip's claim, through his mother Isabella, was one of the strongest and one which he was determined to pursue.

By adding Portugal to his empire, Philip would unite under his rule all the kingdoms of the Iberian Peninsula. In addition, he would acquire an overseas empire to match his own. For one of the few occasions in his life Philip acted decisively. One of his councillors, a Portuguese, was sent with money to arrange any necessary bribes and to persuade the nobility in Portugal of the rightness of Philip's case. An army was made ready under the Duke of Alba, Philip's most experienced general, in case an invasion of Portugal proved necessary.

Philip had support in Portugal for his claim. Both the nobles and the clergy, particularly the religious order of the Jesuits, were favourable. Philip had gained the support of many of the nobles by his payment of their ransoms after the Battle of Alcazarquivir. Merchants hoping to gain a share in trade with the Americas were also in favour. The author of the letter quoted in Source A gives his views on Spanish possession of Portugal.

SOURCE A

From a letter written in Lisbon, capital of Portugal, to one of the banking houses in Germany, 1580.

... all the best people here are in favour of Spain, but dare not let it be seen ... When the King of Spain appears here with his army he will be better received than he expects ... I fancy the authorities set up in this country have an understanding with the Spaniards. I have no doubt that Spain will take possession of Portugal, as is fitting. I hope that then there will be better government and better business.

> Why does the writer of Source A think that Philip would be able to take possession of Portugal?

The people of the towns and most of the ordinary Portuguese opposed a takeover by Spain. Their hatred of the Spanish led them mainly to support another claimant to the throne, António, Prior of Crato, an illegitimate son of one of Cardinal Henry's brothers.

No decision as to his successor had been made when Henry died in 1580. Both António and Philip decided to pursue their claims. Philip acted swiftly and invaded Portugal before opposition could be organised. His forces quickly captured Lisbon and defeated António's army. António was forced to flee to France while Philip added Portugal to his empire.

Philip's relations with the Portuguese

Philip showed considerable skill in his dealings with the Portuguese in order to make himself acceptable as their new ruler. His entry to Lisbon shows the care he took over this. He wrote to his daughters that 'You will have heard that they want to dress me in brocade, much against my will, but they tell me it's the custom here.' He was prepared not only to wear Portuguese dress but also to cut his beard in the Portuguese fashion. He tried to learn the language and even thought about moving his capital to Lisbon, where he lived happily between December 1580 and February 1583.

Philip tried to make it clear that Portugal was not going to become a part of Spain but would be able to keep her own distinctive customs and laws. When he was recognised as king by the Portuguese *Cortes* in 1581, he swore to respect the laws of Portugal. He agreed to a number of measures which would enable Portugal to remain independent of Castile in every way. Only Portuguese were to hold office in their kingdoms and overseas possessions. The *Cortes* would not be required to meet outside Portugal. The country would retain its own coinage. A Council of Portugal was to be formed, like the other regional councils, to advise Philip on Portuguese affairs. Philip's representative in Portugal, the viceroy, was to be either Portuguese or a member of the Spanish royal family.

Philip's rule was generally accepted by the Portuguese. His first choice of representative was a wise one. The Archduke **Albert of Austria**, his favourite nephew, was a well-respected young man of 23. Under him Portugal prospered and was well governed. However, not everybody accepted Spanish rule. There were still many ordinary Portuguese who refused to accept that Sebastian was dead and who thought that he might some day return to drive out the Spanish intruder.

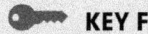

KEY FIGURE

Albert of Austria (1559–1621)
The son of the Holy Roman Emperor, Maximilian II, and Maria of Spain, daughter of Charles I. He became viceroy of Portugal and its empire from 1583 to 1593. He later became sovereign of the Habsburg Netherlands 1598–1621.

The importance of adding Portugal to Philip's empire

Philip's addition of Portugal to his empire has been considered to be probably the most successful exploit of his reign. For the first time since the Roman period, the Iberian Peninsula was under one Christian ruler. Philip had acquired another vast overseas empire. Possession of the Portuguese Azores gave the Spanish an important base for fleets sailing to Spain from the New World. Portugal was important strategically. It was now unlikely that it could be used as a base for foreign intervention, which had been a Spanish fear when the two countries had been separate kingdoms. The acquisition of Portuguese ports gave Philip a greater opportunity to involve himself in the affairs of northern Europe and, if necessary, to launch an attack on England. No wonder that England in particular should fear this great increase in Spain's power.

The Mediterranean

Philip, as the chief defender of the Catholic faith, could consider no cause more righteous than to fight the Turks and other Muslims. To the peoples of Spain, with their tradition of the Reconquest, the Turks and all Muslims were their natural enemies. However, Philip was rarely in a position to concentrate all his efforts on dealing with the Muslims. Problems in other areas of his vast empire, and a lack of money, prevented this. His methods were, therefore, mainly defensive; to fortify coasts, and to do whatever he could to help maintain the safety of those areas he ruled in the western and central areas of the Mediterranean.

There were three major concerns for Philip:

- The Turkish navy was in control of the eastern Mediterranean and posed a threat to its central and western areas. In nearly every year of Philip's reign fears were raised in all Christian areas along the coasts of the Mediterranean that a large Turkish fleet was on the offensive.
- Along the coast of northern Africa were bases such as Tunis and Algiers from which the Barbary corsairs were able to attack shipping and raid the coasts of Spain itself.
- Within Spain, as we have seen above, were the *Moriscos*, who might have co-operated with any Muslim invasion of Spain.

Protecting the Mediterranean against Islam 1560–5

In 1560 an expedition was mounted against Tripoli to help protect the central Mediterranean area. All that was accomplished, however, was the capture of one island, Djerba, which was soon lost again. Spanish failure here was a blow to its prestige. It also led Philip to revise his strategy against the Turks. He realised the need to possess a powerful navy if he was to have any real success against the forces of Islam. The next few years were to see the Spanish dockyards fully occupied in building the new fleet.

In 1563 Philip had an opportunity to test the effectiveness of the new fleet against the Barbary corsairs who were besieging the north African town of Oran, which was a Spanish outpost. The Spanish fleet was sent into action swiftly and efficiently. Here was another example of Philip acting decisively when necessary, and when he was in a position to do so. 'Let haste be made to save every possible hour', Philip wrote, 'for until the moment I see them [the ships] here, I cannot help but feel justifiable anxiety.' Oran was saved. Further successes followed. In 1565 Philip's viceroy in Naples won a victory over the Turks who were besieging the island of Malta, another important defensive position in the central Mediterranean. The victory was greeted enthusiastically by many.

SOURCE B

A contemporary view on the relief of the siege of Malta in 1565.

A hundred thousand years from now, the great king Philip of Spain will still be worthy of praise and renown, and worthy that all Christendom should pray as many years for the salvation of his soul, if God have not yet already given him a seat in Paradise for having so nobly delivered so many gentlemen in Malta, which was about to follow Rhodes into enemy hands.

> How far do you think this praise of Philip, as expressed in Source B, is justified?

The Battle of Lepanto 1571

More forceful methods were needed in 1570 after the Muslim governor of Algiers took Tunis from a supporter of Philip. This left the Spanish garrison at La Goleta isolated (see Figure 3.1, page 41). The Turks were also invading the island of Cyprus. A Holy League was formed in 1571, consisting of Venice,

Genoa, the pope, other Italian states and Spain, to send an expedition to help Cyprus. Such action was not a priority as far as Philip was concerned. His chief aim had been to regain Tunis and then conquer Algiers. In addition, he felt suspicious of the plans of Venice and the pope. However, not to have joined would have lost him support among the Italian states.

Eventually, the fleet of the Holy League, under the supreme command of **Don John of Austria**, Philip's illegitimate half-brother, set sail. Young and charismatic, Don John united the disparate forces under his control. The fleet sailed east across the Mediterranean and met the Turkish fleet at Lepanto, near the mainland of Greece. The sides were evenly matched. But victory came to the Christians when Don John broke the enemy in the centre of their formation and the Turkish admiral was killed. This settled the battle in the Christians' favour. Thousands of Turkish soldiers and sailors were killed or taken prisoner. Most of their ships were sunk or captured.

The initial rejoicing in Christian Europe was short lived. The victory was not followed up as it was late in the campaigning year and the victors themselves had suffered serious losses in men and ships. One Venetian was complaining only a few weeks after Lepanto, 'and not so much as an inch of ground gained'. This is to undervalue the victory. Although the Turks captured Cyprus a few months after Lepanto, never again was a large Turkish fleet seen in the western Mediterranean. The idea in Christian Europe of the invincibility of the Turks at sea was gone, as expressed by a Venetian contemporary: 'that day which was so happy for Christendom because all the world then learned how mistaken it had been in believing that the Turks were invincible at sea'.

KEY FIGURE

Don John of Austria (1547–78)
The illegitimate son of Charles I. He became a military leader in the service of Philip. He was commander-in-chief of the royal armies in the *Morisco* revolt and of the naval force which won the Battle of Lepanto. In 1577 he became governor general of the Netherlands.

The Turkish threat diminishes 1578–97

Little else changed in the following years in the Mediterranean. The Holy League broke up when Venice returned to its usual method of dealing with the Turks: negotiation rather than fighting. In 1573 the Spanish fleet would retake Tunis for a time, but it was soon lost again. Philip had neither the time nor the money to do more. He was by now fully involved in dealing with the Protestant challenge in England, France, and particularly in his own inheritance of the Netherlands. And while Philip looked to northern Europe, and turned his back on his interests in the Mediterranean, the Turks were becoming more concerned with the situation to the east and their fight against Persia. Both Spain and the Turks were, therefore, prepared to make peace in the Mediterranean, so a number of truces and treaties were arranged and regularly renewed during the remaining years of Philip's reign.

The Netherlands

Philip did not accomplish much against the Turks and their allies in north Africa, mainly because of his interests elsewhere in his empire and, particularly, from 1566, his growing involvement in the affairs of a key part of his empire, the **Netherlands**.

KEY TERM

Netherlands The name means 'Low Countries'. Up to 1581 the territories included most of present-day Belgium (including Flanders), the Netherlands, Luxembourg and parts of France and Germany.

Philip's decisions about what policies to follow in the Netherlands were among the most important of his reign and were to have repercussions for Spain over the next 100 years. However, Philip's own knowledge of the states was based on little personal understanding. Under his father, the Netherlands had believed themselves to be the centre of the empire. Charles had been born there and it was there that he abdicated his imperial responsibilities. Charles may have travelled to other parts of his empire frequently but those who lived in the Netherlands saw him as a ruler with genuine commitment to their well-being. Philip was different. Born and brought up in Spain, he had paid only three visits to the Netherlands. With less of the 'common touch' than his father, he does not seem to have made a great impression on his subjects there. This lack of understanding was to lead to mistakes in his dealings with the Netherlands.

Philip's aims in the Netherlands

In the past, a generally held view of Philip's aims in the Netherlands was that he wished to impose despotic rule over the Low Countries and make them a base from which to force the Protestant countries in Europe to reintroduce Catholicism. Most historians now consider this too extreme a view. On the other hand, many contemporaries, such as the Protestant Elizabeth I of England, felt that this was indeed Philip's intention, and it was, therefore, important in motivating the way in which other countries decided to act in regard to the Netherlands. It is now generally considered that Philip had two main aims: firm government in which his rights as the ruler were protected, and ensuring the position of Catholicism. The manner in which Philip achieved this, however, changed over time.

The Netherlands turn on Philip

In implementing these aims Philip made several mistakes at the beginning of his reign. He appointed his half-sister **Margaret, Duchess of Parma**, as his governor general. However, Margaret had spent most of her life in Italy and had little recent experience with the people of the Netherlands.

In addition, Philip ordered the creation of an inner advisory council made up of three known supporters of centrally controlled government. This provoked anger among the nobles in the Netherlands, particularly the rich and powerful **William I, Prince of Orange**. These nobles felt that their position gave them the right to advise Margaret themselves and feared that an attempt was being made to introduce a more centralised government, which would lead to a loss of their traditional power and prestige. It also went against the political tradition of the Netherlands, where all states were equal and government decisions were decided by majority rule or consensus. Philip caused further discontent by leaving a garrison of Spanish troops behind him in the Netherlands. Although these troops were later withdrawn, many of the nobles feared that they might return and impose Spanish authority more firmly over the country.

KEY FIGURES

Margaret, Duchess of Parma (1522–86)

An illegitimate daughter of Charles I. Brought up in the Netherlands, she lived in Italy from the age of eleven, marrying the Duke of Parma in 1538. From 1559 to 1567 she was governor of the Netherlands, and from 1578 to 1582 joint governor with her son Alexander Farnese.

William I, Prince of Orange (1533–84)

A member of the Council of State in the Netherlands, and later governor of Holland, Zeeland and Utrecht. He led the Dutch revolt, convinced that too many Spaniards were involved in governing the Netherlands. He was also opposed to the increasing persecution of Protestants.

Chapter 7 *Philip II: foreign policy and the New World*

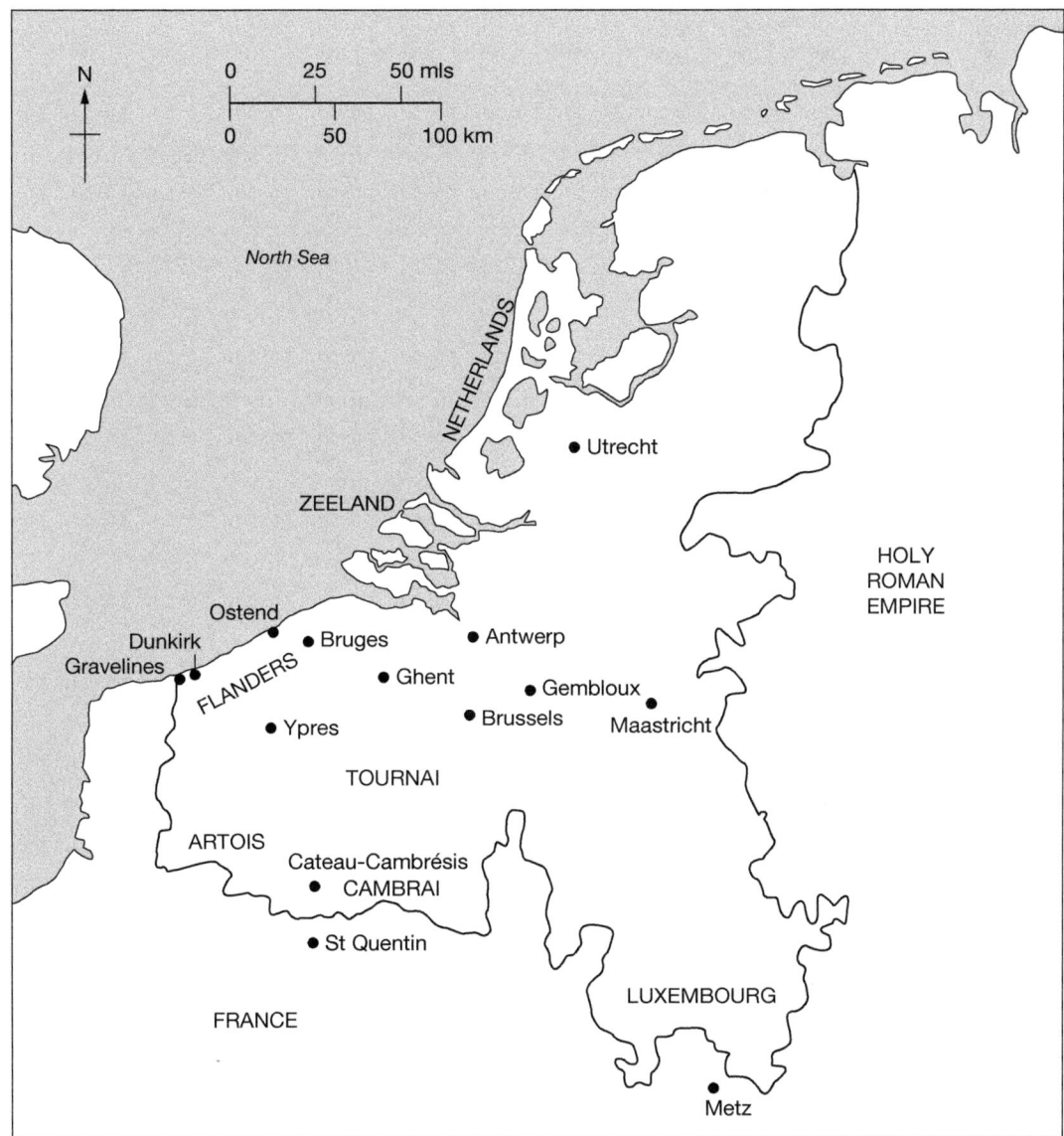

Figure 7.1 The Burgundian lands in the Netherlands during the reign of Philip II.

Having angered the nobles, Philip also created antagonism over his religious policies. He planned to increase the number of bishops in the Netherlands from four to eighteen. It was argued that this would make it easier for the bishops to provide for the religious needs of the people and to deal with heresy. But, at the same time, it would increase Philip's control over the Church in the Netherlands for he himself would decide who was to be appointed to a bishopric. The Crown's political power would also be enlarged, as the bishops would all have seats in local and national assemblies. Firmer attempts were also made to deal

KEY TERMS

Calvinism A more extreme branch of Protestantism. John Calvin was a Protestant reformer based in Geneva who prioritised issues of organisation as well as belief.

Iconoclast A destroyer of images, such as statues of saints.

with the growing threat of Protestantism, particularly in its more militant form of **Calvinism**. The Inquisition was increased in size, and further 'placards' or edicts against heresy were issued.

A policy of firmness: the Duke of Alba as governor general of the Netherlands

These policies aroused serious opposition and Philip's reactions show the working of the Spanish government at its most ineffective. Conflicting instructions were received by Margaret as to what to do, creating long delays while she awaited clarification from Madrid. Philip decided finally to make some concessions but before news of these had arrived in the Netherlands, matters there had got completely out of hand. Calvinists had rioted and seriously damaged Catholic churches – the so-called '**Iconoclastic** Fury' (1566).

Philip was horrified at what had been done 'against our Lord and His images'. The methods he then adopted were, however, to lead to a far more serious outbreak of trouble. In 1567 he gave in to the advice of the Duke of Alba and sent him to the Netherlands to deal firmly with what was considered in Madrid to be a rebellion, even though, by then, Margaret seemed to have matters under control and order was being speedily restored. On Philip's instructions, the Duke of Alba set up a 'Council of Troubles' which sentenced over 1000 people to death for their involvement in the 1566 riots and disturbances. However, Alba's orders from Philip to obtain money from the Netherlands in order to pay for the army stirred up further trouble. Alba tried to introduce a ten per cent sales tax, the 'Tenth Penny'. The unrest this aroused led to the second and more important outbreak of rebellion. By 1572 large areas of the northern Netherlands, particularly Holland and Zeeland, were in revolt against Philip, led by William of Orange.

Softening the policy: Requesens as governor general 1573

KEY FIGURE

Luis de Requesens (1528–76)

A Spanish politician and diplomat. He accompanied Don John at Lepanto. In 1572 he became governor of the Duchy of Milan and in the following year, 1573, became governor of the Spanish Netherlands.

The conflict which ensued over the remaining years of Philip's reign seems to show the king was often unclear as to what to do about the rebellion. Alba was recalled and replaced by **Luis de Requesens**, who had already served Philip well in both Rome and Madrid. Requesens made concessions to the rebels but these were too late to be effective and Philip would not consider toleration of religion or a reduction in his rights as ruler. 'On these two points on no account are you to give in or shift an inch' were his orders to Requesens in 1574.

Unfortunately, Requesens died in 1576. In the intervening period before Don John took up the position of governor, attacks were made on a number of loyal towns, including Antwerp, by unpaid, starving and mutinous Spanish troops. This 'Spanish Fury' led to a serious escalation of the revolt. When they saw that Spain could not protect them, the previously loyal southern states joined with the north to expel the Spanish. On his arrival from Spain, Don John, therefore, had no option but to make further concessions in the Perpetual Edict of 1577.

SOURCE C

An engraving showing the Duke of Alba with the bareheaded Prince of Orange. Produced by an anonymous Dutch artist, 1568–73.

> Referring to Source C, what do you think the attitude of the artist is towards Alba and Orange? What does this engraving tell you about the political tension in the Netherlands in the 1560s?

These included the withdrawal of all foreign troops from the country. However, the terms of the Edict were broken by the Calvinists in that they refused toleration of the Catholics. Fearing for his own personal safety, Don John gained Philip's agreement to call the Spanish army back to the Netherlands.

Victory in the south: the Duke of Parma becomes governor general 1578

The task now was to reconquer the whole of the Netherlands, not just a few states. The army returned under the command of **Alexander Farnese** – the son of Philip's half-sister Margaret, Duchess of Parma – and a victory was won at Gembloux. In 1578 Don John died and was replaced by Farnese, who had already shown his considerable political and military abilities at such battles as Lepanto. He was highly intelligent and of all Philip's governors in the Netherlands, he showed the most understanding of the problems there. He won the southern states back to Spain, convincing them that they had more to fear from an alliance with the Calvinist states than with Spain. By 1585, Maastricht, Dunkirk, Ypres, Bruges, Ghent, Ostend and Antwerp had been retaken and Farnese looked poised to secure the recovery of the remaining areas in revolt – the provinces of Holland, Zeeland and Utrecht.

KEY FIGURE

Alexander Farnese, Duke of Parma (1545–92)

Had a distinguished career in the service of his uncle, Philip II. He was extremely successful as governor general and won back the southern Netherlands for Philip.

> Look at Source D. What is the artist trying to show the viewer about Farnese?

SOURCE D

A portrait of Farnese, Duke of Parma, engraved by Crispin de Passe the Elder c.1580s.

Failure to win back the northern Netherlands

Farnese did not succeed in retaking the northern states for two main reasons:

- The first was that England officially became involved in the war. Help had been given to the rebels from the Protestant states in Germany, England and France from the early stages of the revolt, most of it unofficially. However, in 1585, Elizabeth I signed the Treaty of Nonsuch with the rebels, agreeing to give them military aid. Although this was not a great amount, it was enough to support their resistance to Farnese.
- The second, and more critical, reason concerns the decisions Philip took in regard to his relations with England and France. In 1585 when Farnese seemed at the point of reconquering the whole of the Netherlands, Philip decided that to do so must involve an invasion of England first. For two vital years, 1586 and 1587, Farnese was unable to fight in the Netherlands while he waited for the **Armada** to sail so that his troops could be taken over to England. Philip's decision to intervene in the affairs of France also had its consequences. In 1589 Farnese was ordered to enter France to fight alongside the Catholic rebels who were attempting to prevent the legitimate, but Protestant, Henry of Navarre becoming king (see page 165). These events gave the Calvinist rebels in the Netherlands time to improve their defences and to make several important gains. Farnese himself died in 1592.

KEY TERM

Armada A fleet of warships.

Philip's failures in the Netherlands

By the end of his reign, the failures in the Netherlands weighed on Philip. By 1592 the Calvinists had both France and England as their allies. Philip was also in further financial difficulties, declaring another bankruptcy in 1596. He was, therefore, forced to halt his campaign against the rebels. A new approach was attempted. Philip's daughter, Isabella, was given the Netherlands to rule with her husband, the Archduke Albert. Philip hoped that if he separated the Netherlands from the rest of his empire there would eventually be a reunion of all the states. But this plan failed. The northern states were by now a clearly distinct country that was already being referred to as the United Provinces (Holland). They would not be prepared to give up their political or religious independence for which many had fought so hard for so long.

Reasons why Philip failed to defeat the rebels in the Netherlands

Philip's failure to defeat the rebels in the Netherlands must have seemed improbable at the beginning of the disturbances in the 1560s. Spain, with its able commanders, its experienced fighting troops and the money from the New World, looked unbeatable. What then led to Spain's failures in the Netherlands? Some of these factors have already been mentioned: Philip's own hesitation and delays, his refusal to compromise on religion and his decision to commit his forces in England and France.

Involvement of foreign countries

The involvement of foreign countries gave the rebels support at critical times. Other factors must also be considered. The beliefs of the Calvinists helped to stiffen their resistance. Geographical factors also played an important part. There were delays and difficulties in sending men and money either overland or by sea to the Netherlands. Once there, fighting in the north was extremely difficult. Holland was 'the Great Bog of Europe', and comprised many islands separated from the mainland by the sea. To take each town usually required long sieges.

Lack of resources

Philip's lack of resources was crucial. He did not have the means to fight effectively in more than one part of his empire at any one time. In the early stages of the rebellion Philip had to direct his resources against the threat of Islam in the Mediterranean. It was only during periods when he could turn away from this threat that adequate resources could be sent to the Netherlands. From the 1580s, Philip also decided to fight first England and then France.

The most vital resource which Philip lacked was money. It was what led Alba to propose the 'Tenth Penny', which was a significant trigger in leading to a renewal of the revolt in 1572. And Alba was unable to deal with the revolt effectively as Philip could not send him enough money between 1570 and 1574. Things became even worse in 1576 when Philip repudiated all his debts. The bankruptcy meant that he was not able to send any money to the Netherlands to pay the troops. This led to the mutinies which frightened the loyal Catholic states of the south into joining with the northern states and united the whole of the Netherlands against Philip. What could be achieved when Spain's resources were concentrated on defeating the rebels is illustrated by Farnese's successes between 1578 and 1585.

Relations with England

Relations between Spain and England before Philip's reign had generally been cordial. To Spain, England presented a useful ally against France, its traditional enemy. In 1554, Philip had married Mary I of England on his father's wishes and had become, in title only, King of England. But he had not been popular in England and anti-Spanish feeling grew considerably there when Spain involved England in a war against France, in the process of which England lost Calais – something the English blamed on Philip. Following the death of Mary in 1558, her half-sister, Elizabeth I, succeeded to the throne. Philip was eager to maintain good relations, even though Elizabeth was considered by many to be a Protestant. This was mainly because he did not wish to see Elizabeth's closest relative, Mary, Queen of Scots, become Queen of England, even though she was a Catholic. Mary had close links with France and Philip feared that, as Queen of England, she might well form an alliance with France against Spain. Philip, therefore, supported Elizabeth at the beginning of her reign, offering her his hand in marriage and personally intervening to prevent the pope from excommunicating her in 1561.

Tension mounts

Relations between the two countries, however, were to become less friendly as England came to consider itself the protector of Protestantism in Europe. This is how it came to be involved in the affairs of the Netherlands. England also wished to participate in trade with the New World. Thus, it came into conflict with Spain in two important areas of Philip's empire.

English merchants attempted to trade with the New World either through smuggling or, when this failed, by piracy. A major exploit was **Francis Drake**'s round-the-world expedition of 1576–81, during which he seized large quantities of Spanish treasure. It was no secret that Elizabeth had given her unofficial support to Drake and this served to increase tension between the two countries.

It was, however, the earlier arrival of the Duke of Alba in the Netherlands in 1567 which most seriously affected relations with England, and led to the eventual outbreak of war. Elizabeth feared a Spanish armed presence only a few miles from England's own shores. In addition, England had close economic and religious links with the growing numbers of Protestants in the Netherlands. In 1568 Elizabeth confiscated Spanish ships on their way to the Netherlands. These

KEY FIGURE

Sir Francis Drake (c.1540–96)

English sea captain, privateer and politician under Elizabeth I of England. He carried out the second circumnavigation of the world 1577–80 and was second in command of the English fleet against the Spanish Armada 1588.

had had to land in England because of storms at sea. They had been carrying wool and money to pay for the Spanish troops in the Netherlands. From the early 1570s Elizabeth also provided help to the rebels in the Netherlands. She lent money to them, and paid for mercenaries to be sent there. In 1583 Elizabeth gave financial support and a temporary place at court to the Portuguese pretender to the throne, Don António.

The provocations were not all on Elizabeth's side, however. Philip himself sent a fleet to Ireland in 1580 in hope of encouraging an uprising there. This, however, failed. In 1583, Spain was also involved in a thwarted plot to assassinate Elizabeth.

At war 1585

Declaration of war became a certainty in 1585. From the point of view of the English, conditions had become far more serious. Philip seized all English ships in Spanish ports in retaliation for English piracies in the West Indies. In the Netherlands William of Orange had been assassinated in 1584 leaving the rebels without a leader for the moment. Farnese's successes, particularly the regaining of Antwerp in 1585, made it seem likely that all of the states would once again come firmly under Spanish rule. Elizabeth feared that if the Netherlands were to be defeated Philip would decide to invade the only major Protestant country remaining in Europe, England. Elizabeth's chief minister made the point, 'If he [Philip] once [should] reduce the Low Countries to absolute subjection, I know not what limits any man of judgement can set unto his greatness.' Convinced of the dangers to England, Elizabeth signed the Treaty of Nonsuch with the rebels, agreeing to send about 6000 soldiers and to lend them more money. The following year, 1586, she sent an English army.

The signing of the treaty spurred Philip into taking action. He ordered that an armada be prepared and made ready for an invasion of England. Some of his councillors, including Alba, did not feel such an attack would work, but Philip and the majority of his councillors did. It has been suggested by some historians in the past that Philip, now nearly 60 years old, was aware that his life might soon end and wished to lead a religious crusade on behalf of Catholicism against the Protestant Elizabeth while he still could.

On the other hand, the date of the change in his policy, 1586, probably indicates other reasons. There was news in that year of further incidents. The English captain Sir Francis Drake attacked Vigo and Bayone in northern Spain and, briefly, occupied Spanish fortresses. This was an affront to Philip's reputation. One of the commanders of the 1588 Armada who had been captured made this clear.

> What reason is given in Source E for Philip's decision to send the Armada to England?

SOURCE E

A report of a captured Spanish naval commander on why the Armada was sent to England.

The reason why the king undertook this war was that he could not tolerate the fact that Drake, with two or three rotten ships, should come to infest the harbours of Spain whenever it pleased him, and to capture its best towns in order to plunder them.

Drake sailed on across the Atlantic and made further raids in the Caribbean. Financiers fearful of losing the New World silver being shipped to Spain in the treasure fleets therefore became reluctant to lend money to Philip. Along with the Treaty of Nonsuch, such events lead historians nowadays to believe that political and economic considerations shaped his willingness to engage England in war. Certainly that is what the pope thought. He made the point that Philip was motivated by considerations of 'global strategy and revenge'.

The results of the failure of the 1588 Armada

The Armada of 1588 failed in its attempt to invade England. More than half its ships were destroyed and 15,000 men died. For Spain this was a serious defeat but not a decisive one. Philip had been unable to break either the alliance of the English with the rebels in the Netherlands or to invade England. But the failure did not put a complete end to such plans. Philip was able to build further armadas and attempts were made to invade Ireland, always a useful base from which to attack England, in 1596 and 1598. A second armada was sent directly against England in 1597. This too failed; scattered by the weather. The war was to drag on and continue until after Philip's death.

France

Towards the end of his reign Philip's attention turned principally to France rather than to England. When Philip came to the throne Spain had been at war with France. In spite of victories at St Quentin and Gravelines, the Spanish had not been able to defeat France decisively. Philip's financial difficulties at the time were serious and he had been ready to make peace in the Treaty of Cateau-Cambrésis (1559). In order to cement the peace, a marriage had taken place between Philip and Elizabeth of Valois, daughter of King Henry II of France.

After 1559, there was peace between France and Spain for some years. However, Philip became increasingly anxious about the growing number of Protestants in France. In 1562, the French wars of religion broke out, led by the Catholic family of Guise against their rivals for political power, the mainly Protestant Bourbon family. Philip's natural inclination during these wars was to support the Catholic cause, a feeling that was reinforced by fears that if France became Protestant it would present a serious danger to the Spanish Empire, both to the Netherlands and to Spain itself (see page 153).

Direct intervention in France

It was not until the 1580s that Philip decided to intervene directly in the struggle. In 1584 **Henry of Navarre**, a Huguenot, became heir to the French throne. This was a setback to Philip's hopes. It could have possibly led to the triumph of Protestantism in France and also to the implementation of an anti-Spanish policy there. Philip decided he must prevent Henry becoming king. He, therefore, signed the Treaty of Joinville with the French Catholic League, headed by the Guise family. In this he promised the League financial help, and both sides agreed to support each other in defending Catholicism. Five years later Henry III, the then King of France, was assassinated, leaving Henry of Navarre as his successor. In 1590, and again in 1592, Philip ordered Farnese to intervene in France from the Netherlands to prevent Henry becoming king. Spanish troops were also sent into Brittany. At the same time Philip put forward the claims to the French throne of Isabella, his eldest daughter by his marriage to Elizabeth of Valois. Her succession would ensure a Catholic ruler on the throne of France and bring the country under Spanish influence.

Failure of Philip's plans in France

The French were prepared to accept only a Frenchman as king. When Henry of Navarre converted to Catholicism in 1593, most of France supported him as king. In the same year he also received acceptance by the pope. The French rallied round their new king (crowned Henry IV) to expel the Spanish forces. A brief war ensued but neither side could achieve complete victory. However, when Philip became bankrupt for the third time in 1596, he decided that he must make peace. The Treaty of Vervins (1598), which ended the war, confirmed the main clauses of the Treaty of Cateau-Cambrésis.

Little had been achieved by Philip in France, although some historians have argued that his intervention preserved Catholicism there by forcing Henry IV to change his religion. This is now considered unlikely. Of more consequence was the effect of the intervention on Philip's policies in the Netherlands. Troops needed to ensure victory there had been sent into France and this may be said to have contributed significantly to Philip's failure in the Netherlands at the end of his reign.

KEY FIGURE

Henry of Navarre (1553–1610)

Baptised as a Catholic but raised in the Protestant faith by his mother, from whom he inherited the throne of Navarre in 1572. He became heir to the French throne in 1584. To secure support for becoming King of France he renounced his Protestant faith.

Spain 1469–1598

Summary diagram: The foreign policy of Philip II

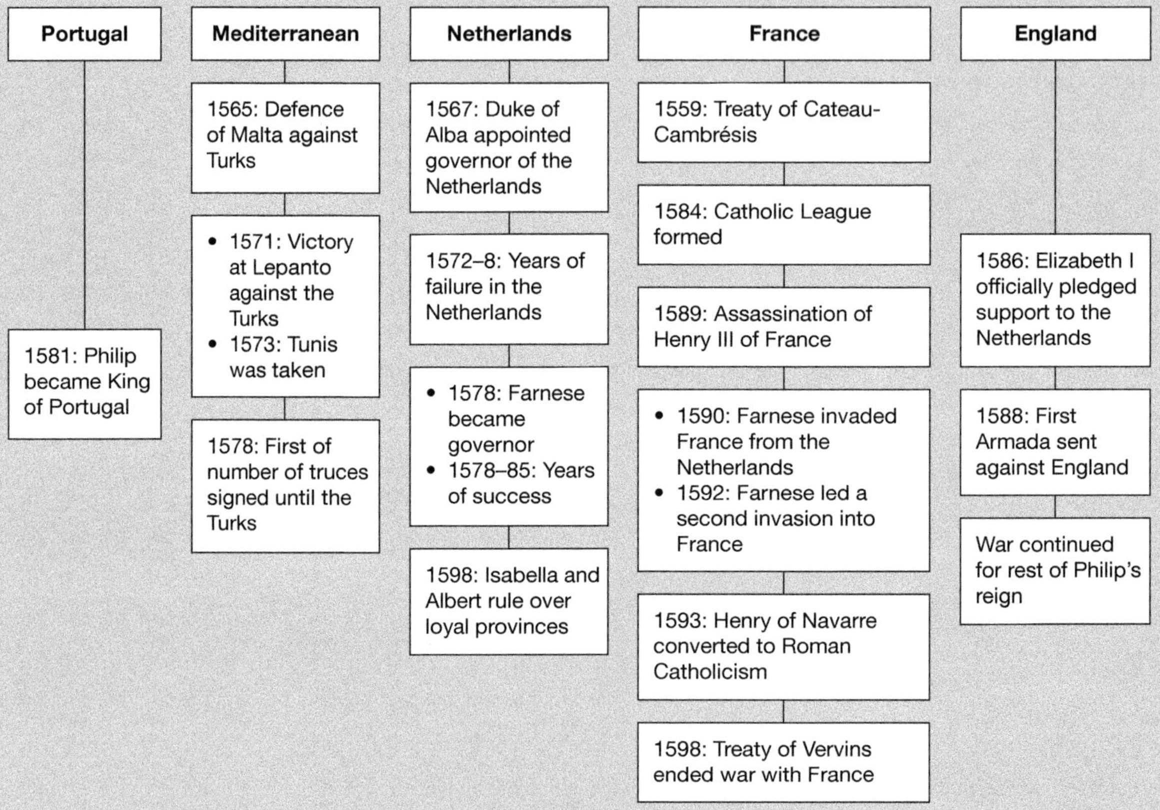

Portugal	Mediterranean	Netherlands	France	England
	1565: Defence of Malta against Turks	1567: Duke of Alba appointed governor of the Netherlands	1559: Treaty of Cateau-Cambrésis	
			1584: Catholic League formed	
	• 1571: Victory at Lepanto against the Turks • 1573: Tunis was taken	1572–8: Years of failure in the Netherlands	1589: Assassination of Henry III of France	1586: Elizabeth I officially pledged support to the Netherlands
1581: Philip became King of Portugal		• 1578: Farnese became governor • 1578–85: Years of success		1588: First Armada sent against England
	1578: First of number of truces signed until the Turks		• 1590: Farnese invaded France from the Netherlands • 1592: Farnese led a second invasion into France	War continued for rest of Philip's reign
		1598: Isabella and Albert rule over loyal provinces	1593: Henry of Navarre converted to Roman Catholicism	
			1598: Treaty of Vervins ended war with France	

 ## The New World

▶ *What were the advantages and disadvantages of the Spanish Empire extending to the New World?*

Further increases to the territories over which Philip ruled took place outside Europe. In South America the Spanish *conquistadors* advanced south from Paraguay and established Buenos Aires in 1580. In Asia, the Philippines, named after Philip, were taken over with little opposition in 1565. Added to this was the acquisition of the whole of Portugal's overseas empire in 1580 (see page 153).

The importance of the New World to Spain

Philip depended on receiving the riches which came from the New World, principally in the form of silver, but also as customs duties and the income from certain Crown monopolies such as the sale of playing cards. Later in his reign, the *alcabala* was introduced in both Mexico and Peru. It was obviously important that the silver arrived safely in Europe, although this was made difficult by attacks on the treasure ships. As early as the mid-1520s French privateers had seized part of a treasure fleet. A number of Spanish towns in the New World had been raided and plundered; shipping had been destroyed and further treasure had been taken. There had even been attempts to establish a French colony in Florida, but these had failed. From the mid-1550s the English became active in the area. Francis Drake made a number of daring raids on towns and shipping in the Caribbean and along the coast of Peru.

Safe passage across the Atlantic

During Philip's reign a convoy system was introduced to protect the twice-yearly treasure fleets as they made voyages across the Atlantic. Other ships patrolled in the seas near the Spanish coasts to protect the treasure as it arrived in Spanish waters. The scheme was expensive but it worked. From the 1560s, the fleets sailing to and from the New World consisted mainly of larger and more powerful ships sailing in convoy. Spain had asserted its position as the most powerful nation on the Atlantic crossing to the Americas. No complete treasure fleet was ever captured in the sixteenth century. The only losses were a few scattered ships, which had become separated from the main convoy. In addition, from 1588 groups of small, well-armed ships designed for speed so as to outrun any enemy were used successfully on the Atlantic route.

Adding Portugal to the empire also helped in policing Atlantic shipping as it gave Spain an additional base in the Azores to help protect the convoys.

Importing Spanish-style government to the New World

Philip was also concerned to see effective administration and justice in the New World. The problems involved were formidable, not the least of which was the distance between the New World and Spain. There was also the difficulty of ruling a population which was largely unfamiliar with European ways. Yet much was accomplished. The Council of the **Indies** was responsible for a number of changes aimed at improving the effectiveness of the government.

Viceroys were carefully selected from men of ability. An outstanding choice was **Toledo**, appointed viceroy to Peru in 1569, and who brought peace and prosperity to this area. Toledo introduced a number of reforms, including administrative and legal systems. And as a result of his policies the output of the silver mines at Potosí and the mercury mines of Huancavelica improved considerably.

Attention was also paid to the condition of the Indians. Attempts continued to be made to implement the laws, forbidding, among other things, the enslavement of Indians (see pages 54 and 97–8). As before, the intentions on the Crown's part were sincere but opposition from the Spanish settlers continued to make it difficult to put them into practice. Ordinances issued in 1573 condemned extreme violence against Indians but again, as with previous laws, had little effect on their well-being.

KEY TERM

Indies The term in use during the sixteenth century for the New World (the Americas).

KEY FIGURE

Francisco de Toledo (c.1520–84)

A Spanish noble who was viceroy of Peru from 1569 to 1581. He eventually lost Philip's confidence and was recalled to Spain, where he died in 1584.

The religious life of the New World was not neglected. From 1568 the first Jesuits arrived to support the work of conversion of the Indians to Christianity. The 1573 Ordinances referred to in the previous paragraph also allowed the missionaries to establish small-scale settlements to help in their work of Christianisation. This missionary work increased particularly in the 1580s.

The impact of the New World on Spain during Philip's reign

The New World continued to stimulate ideas in Spain (as in the rest of Europe). It led to necessary developments in map-making, geography and technical processes such as improved methods for extracting silver. Philip himself financed an expedition to study the plants and animals in the New World. Works by Spanish writers were also published, such as the *History of the Things of New Spain*.

In 1545 the large silver deposits of Potosí in present-day Bolivia were discovered. The more silver that was carried to Spain, the more ships were needed to carry it. This led to more shipbuilding, particularly on the Basque coast of Spain, but there was still a shortfall of ships and that meant the use of foreign ships. There were also technical developments in the ships sent across the Atlantic to improve the safety and speed by which the treasure arrived in Spain.

Silver imports to Spain increased greatly in the second half of the sixteenth century. The quantities of bullion tripled between the 1560s and 1590s. Trade between Spain and the Indies increased, including foreign goods channelled through Spain, since Spanish manufacturers could not meet the demand on their own. Some individuals became extremely wealthy from the import of silver and gold into Spain and often spent money on lavish buildings and works of art. However, much of the bullion went outside Spain to foreigners to repay loans or for the cost of goods. On the surface Spain seemed prosperous but in fact signs of problems lay underneath this incoming wealth.

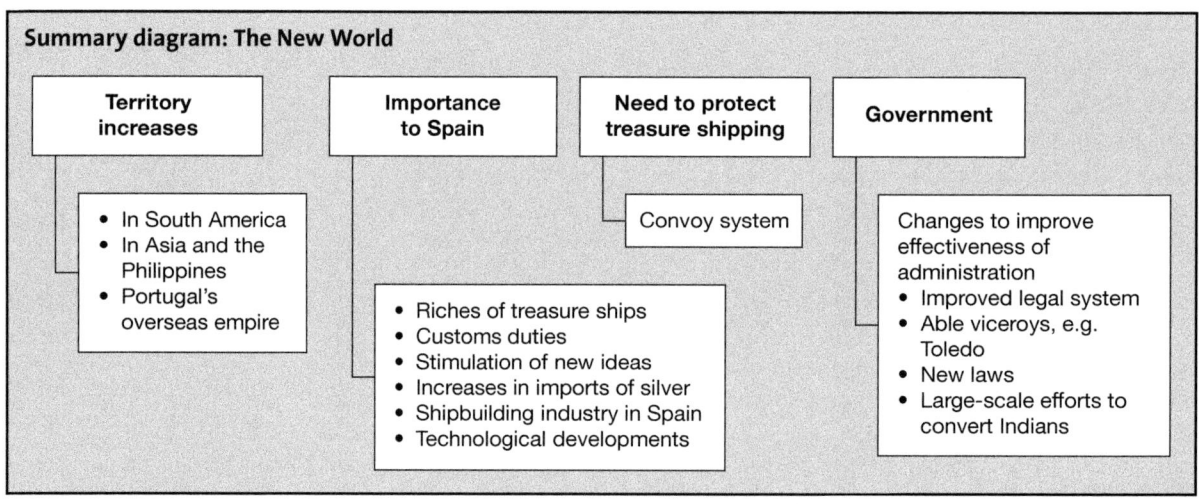

Summary diagram: The New World

Key debate

> ▶ Was defending his empire the main consideration driving Philip's foreign policy?

Much discussion has taken place among historians over the years as to the aims of Philip's foreign policy. Many of his contemporaries viewed him as wishing to dominate Europe, expanding his own lands and eliminating heresy. This Philip knew to be impossible. He had no grand vision and, in any case, was only too aware that he did not have the resources to fulfil such a vision.

John Lynch gives his view in Extract 1, noting where it could be argued that Philip was on the defensive, protecting Spain's interests, for example, in the Mediterranean, the New World and the Netherlands. However, Lynch dismisses the notion that Philip's policies towards France could be considered defensive. He also makes the point that if defence were the driving factor, then it should have been defence of the New World which took priority.

EXTRACT 1

From John Lynch, *Spain Under the Habsburgs*, Basil Blackwell, 1981, p. 366.

The entire reign was given to warfare on one front or another, for many years on two fronts at once – the Mediterranean and the Netherlands – and in the 1590's on three fronts at once – the Netherlands, England, and France. Spain was the only power in sixteenth century Europe capable of sustaining such an effort, but what did it gain her? In the Mediterranean Philip could legitimately claim to be fighting for survival. In the Low Countries he insisted he was merely defending his rightful inheritance, though against the United Provinces the argument was unrealistic. In the Atlantic and the Caribbean he was protecting his country's colonial, and, therefore, economic interests. But only in the imagination of the king himself could his war with France be regarded as a defensive war, unless it were conceded that he had to appropriate the whole of Europe in order to defend his interests. In the last fifteen years of his reign Philip proceeded on the assumption that war could gain him any objective he wanted, yet there was no order of priorities. The greatest source of Spain's power, and the greatest field for her religious and political ideals, was her empire in America. The logical procedure would have been to concentrate her efforts and resources on this front by cutting them elsewhere. As it was, the Netherlands were the biggest and most relentless drain on Spanish resources.

Henry Kamen says in Extract 2 that it could be argued that Philip's entire foreign policy was defensive. He then goes on to say that the only way Philip could have achieved this was by making Spain into a world power and then 'aggression' took over. In this, he seems to be implying that sometimes attack was the best form of defence. However, for Kamen, it was Philip's concern for religion and his dynasty that took priority. He maintains that religious considerations were a fundamental aspect of Philip's foreign policy and cites the example in particular of the Netherlands.

EXTRACT 2

From Henry Kamen, *Spain 1469–1714*, Pearson, 2005, p. 142.

It is plausible to maintain that Philip II's entire foreign policy was defensive. … But the requirements of defence meant that first in 1560 and then in 1580, in the Mediterranean and in the Atlantic, he was obliged to elevate Spain into a superpower, as the only way to maintain worldwide security. Once the Spanish system had been created, force and, therefore, aggression became an integral part of it, though there is no acceptable evidence or plausible reason to suggest that the king had expansionist dreams. Religious and dynastic considerations always remained fundamental, with the qualification that the king had his own view of what 'religion' entailed. When Philip disagreed with the papacy and France it was precisely because he felt their policies would not best serve the universal Church. At no point is the importance of the religious element clearer than in the Netherlands revolt, where all efforts at compromise with the Dutch ran into trouble because the Spaniards insisted on preserving the exclusive position of Catholicism.

> ? What do the two views in Extracts 1 and 2 bring out about Philip's direction in foreign policy? What examples could be used to support the arguments that it was or was not a defensive foreign policy?

Spain in 1598

> ▶ How successful was Philip at home and abroad over the course of his reign?

By 1598, when he died at the age of 71, Philip had ruled over his empire for 42 years. During that time his main aims seem to have been protecting and maintaining his empire, preserving and defending Catholicism, and ensuring good and just government in his lands. How much did he achieve by 1598?

Protecting and maintaining the Spanish Empire

Philip handed on to his son the territories that he had himself received from Charles I, and more. He had brought about the union of all the kingdoms in the Iberian Peninsula when he inherited Portugal. He had also acquired the vast Portuguese overseas empire made up, in theory, of Brazil, most of Africa, India, China, Japan and Indonesia. In practice, of course, Portugal merely attempted to retain exclusive trading rights in those areas; very rarely was any effort made to rule over them.

In addition to Portugal, his reign had seen the extension of the Spanish Empire in the New World. The northern states of the Netherlands, however, though they still in theory belonged to his empire, in practice, had been lost by the end of Philip's reign, and his instructions to his son not to give up his rights to any part of the empire were to create considerable difficulties for his descendants.

Preserving and defending Catholicism

Philip's success in religious matters was mitigated. He had certainly kept Protestantism out of the states which made up his empire, apart from the northern part of the Netherlands. Within the peninsula, a revolt by the *Moriscos* had been firmly put down, although his policies did not solve the religious and political threat the *Moriscos* seemed to represent. Philip had won significant victories against the forces of Islam, especially at Malta and Lepanto. However, his success was not complete: in the final years of his reign he had had to make truces with the Turks, and raids by Barbary pirates along the Spanish coast continued. Within Spain reforms to the Church had been limited during his reign, but Philip had started the reforms which were to lead to greater improvements during the reigns of his successors.

Ensuring good and just government

In considering this, one must remember the problems of distance and communication. These would have been insurmountable for anyone. There is no doubting Philip's conscientiousness. Whether his policies were effective is perhaps more debatable. He certainly showed wisdom in his dealings with Aragon and Portugal, even though there were complaints about the 'Castilianisation' of government, as there were throughout his empire. Finance surely has to be an issue in considering good government, and in this, one can only conclude that Philip was unsuccessful.

Philip's foreign wars against England and France expended considerable sums of money with little result, and in the process they exhausted Castile. The majority of the cost of the empire had fallen on Castile and by the end of Philip's reign signs of depression in agriculture and industry were already apparent. In addition, the financial burden that Philip left to his son was considerable.

Yet one must not exaggerate Philip's failures. Philip was the monarch of a vast empire, and for most of his reign the majority of his peoples seem to have been generally content with his rule. The despatch sent by the Venetian ambassador on Philip's death gives a final verdict in his favour.

SOURCE F

From a despatch sent by the Venetian ambassador on Philip's death, 1598.

The king is dead ... He was a prince who fought with gold rather than with steel, by his brain rather than by his arms. He has acquired more by sitting still, by negotiation, by diplomacy, than his father did by armies and by war. He was one of the richest princes the world has ever seen, yet he has left the revenues of the kingdom and of the crown burdened with about a million of debts. He owes to his good fortune rather than to the terror of his name the important kingdom of Portugal, with all its territories and treasure; on the other hand, he has lost Flanders ... Profoundly religious, he loved peace and quiet. He displayed great calmness, and professed himself unmoved in good or

What qualities and achievements of Philip's are mentioned in Source F? In your opinion, how balanced is the view of the writer?

bad fortune alike. He had vast schemes in his head: witness his simultaneous attack on England and on France ... On great occasions, in the conduct of wars, in feeding the civil war in France, in the magnificence of his buildings, he never counted the cost; he was no close reckoner, but lavished his gold without a thought; but in small matters, in the government of his household, he was more parsimonious than became his station. He held his desires in absolute control and showed an immutable and unalterable temper ... In short, he has left a glorious memory of his royal name, which may serve as an example, not only unto his posterity and his successors, but unto strangers as well ...

Summary diagram: Spain in 1598

Protecting and maintaining the Spanish Empire	Preserving and defending Catholicism	Good and just government
• Extended with the acquisition of Portugal and the Portuguese Empire • Success despite losing the northern states of the Netherlands	• Kept Protestantism at bay, except in the northern states of the Netherlands • *Morisco* revolt put down • Some significant victories against the Turks • Limited Church reforms enacted	• Philip's style of government probably ineffective • Complaints about the 'Castilianisation of government' • Signs of economic depression in agriculture and industry • Large financial debt passed on to Philip's heir • Parts of the empire still governed as separate individual entities

Chapter summary

Pious and hard working, Philip was a king who had taken defeat and victory in his stride and accepted God's will in each. His loss was regretted by some of his peoples, yet others were more critical. Dissatisfaction was expressed over rising taxes, economic and financial problems, and the constant wars. In spite of the costs, Philip achieved much in his foreign policy. He not only defended his empire but added to it, though the northern part of the Netherlands was in reality lost to him by the end of his reign. He became King of Portugal and acquired both the country and its overseas empire. His territories in the New World continued to grow. He had protected the Catholic faith against the Ottoman Empire and Spain against any possible external Islamic threat. These are large achievements. Where the religious aims of his foreign policy failed was in not preventing part of the Netherlands becoming Protestant. The key debate on page 169 looks at two historians' views of whether Philip's foreign policy was a purely defensive one. That is a question which promises to engender discussion for a long time to come.

Refresher questions

Use these questions to remind yourself of the key material covered in this chapter.

1 What security issues did Philip have to consider in regard to his empire?
2 How effectively did Philip deal with the future government of Portugal?
3 Why was the acquisition of Portugal so important to Philip?
4 How successfully did Philip deal with the threat of Islam?
5 What was the significance of the Battle of Lepanto?
6 What factors made dealing with the Netherlands a problem during the reign of Philip II?
7 Why did Farnese fail to win back control over the northern provinces of the Netherlands?
8 How did relations with England change during Philip's reign?
9 What motivated Philip's decision to send an armada against England?
10 Why did Philip decide to intervene in French affairs?
11 What had Philip's policies towards France achieved by the end of his reign?
12 What problems did Spanish ships encounter on cross-Atlantic journeys, and how successfully were they dealt with?
13 What improvements did Philip make to his naval forces and how effective were they?
14 How effective was government of the New World during Philip's reign?
15 What do you consider Philip's successes and failures to have been?

Question practice

ESSAY QUESTIONS

1 'In his foreign policy, Philip II achieved his aims of preserving his inheritance and defending the Roman Catholic faith.' Assess the validity of this statement.
2 How successful was Philip's foreign policy up to 1585?
3 Explain why Philip's policies were a success in Portugal but a failure in the Netherlands.
4 How far do you agree that Spanish foreign policy in the years 1474–1598 was driven by fear of France?
5 How far can the conquest of the Aztecs of 1521 be seen as the key turning point in the extension of the Spanish power in the New World in the years 1474–1598?
6 'The key factor in the expansion and maintenance of Spanish power in the years 1474–1598 was the calibre of her generals.' How far do you agree with this statement?
7 How far do you agree that the priorities for Spanish foreign policy changed significantly between 1474 and 1598?

INTERPRETATION QUESTION

1 Using Extracts 1, 2 and 3 (page 174), and your understanding of the historical context, assess how convincing the arguments in these three extracts are in relation to Philip's policies in regard to his empire.

EXTRACT 1
From John Lynch, *Spain Under the Habsburgs*, Basil Blackwell, 1981, p. 366.

The entire reign was given to warfare on one front or another, for many years on two fronts at once – the Mediterranean and the Netherlands – and in the 1590's on three fronts at once – the Netherlands, England, and France. Spain was the only power in sixteenth century Europe capable of sustaining such an effort, but what did it gain her? In the Mediterranean Philip could legitimately claim to be fighting for survival. In the Low Countries he insisted he was merely defending his rightful inheritance, though against the United Provinces the argument was unrealistic. In the Atlantic and the Caribbean he was protecting his country's colonial, and, therefore, economic interests. But only in the imagination of the king himself could his war with France be regarded as a defensive war, unless it were conceded that he had to appropriate the whole of Europe in order to defend his interests. In the last fifteen years of his reign Philip proceeded on the assumption that war could gain him any objective he wanted, yet there was no order of priorities. The greatest source of Spain's power, and the greatest field for her religious and political ideals, was her empire in America. The logical procedure would have been to concentrate her efforts and resources on this front by cutting them elsewhere. As it was, the Netherlands were the biggest and most relentless drain on Spanish resources.

EXTRACT 2
From Henry Kamen, *Spain 1469–1714*, Pearson, 2005, p. 142.

It is plausible to maintain that Philip II's entire foreign policy was defensive. … But the requirements of defence meant that first in 1560 and then in 1580, in the Mediterranean and in the Atlantic, he was obliged to elevate Spain into a superpower, as the only way to maintain worldwide security. Once the Spanish system had been created, force and, therefore, aggression became an integral part of it, though there is no acceptable evidence or plausible reason to suggest that the king had expansionist dreams. Religious and dynastic considerations always remained fundamental, with the qualification that the king had his own view of what 'religion' entailed. When Philip disagreed with the papacy and France it was precisely because he felt their policies would not best serve the universal Church. At no point is the importance of the religious element clearer than in the Netherlands revolt, where all efforts at compromise with the Dutch ran into trouble because the Spaniards insisted on preserving the exclusive position of Catholicism.

EXTRACT 3
From Geoffrey Woodward, *Philip II*, Longman, 1992, p. 73.

Philip's prime aim was to defend his dominions and not to give offence. His intention to preserve and secure his lands, people and faith by peaceful diplomacy was noted by Suriano, the Venetian ambassador, when he claimed in 1559 that Philip did not intend 'to wage war so that he can add to his kingdoms but to wage peace so that he can keep the lands he has'. If aggression was required, then it must be a 'just' war; this would not only enhance his reputation but also secure papal support. Philip's enemies of course, perceived him as an out-and-out aggressor. Historians are inclined to take an intermediate position. They acknowledge that Philip may have regarded attack as the best form of defence, but they also recognise that acts of apparent provocation occurred in the second half of his reign …

AQA A level History

Essay guidance

At both AS and A level for AQA Component 1: Breadth Study: Spain in the Age of Discovery, 1469–1598, you will need to answer an essay question in the exam. Each essay question is marked out of 25:

- for the AS exam, Section B: answer one essay (from a choice of two)
- for the A level exam, Section B: answer two essays (from a choice of three).

There are several question stems which all have the same basic requirement: to analyse and reach a conclusion, based on the evidence you provide.

The AS questions often give a quotation and then ask whether you agree or disagree with this view. Almost inevitably, your answer will be a mixture of both. It is the same task as for A level – just phrased differently in the question. Detailed essays are more likely to do well than vague or generalised essays.

The AQA mark scheme is essentially the same for AS and the full A level (see the AQA website, www.aqa.org.uk). Both emphasise the need to analyse and evaluate the key features related to the periods studied. The key feature of the highest level is sustained analysis: analysis that unites the whole of the essay.

Writing an essay: general skills

- *Focus and structure.* Be sure what the question is asking and plan what the paragraphs should be about.
- *Focused introduction to the essay.* Be sure that the introductory sentence relates directly to the focus of the question and that each paragraph highlights the structure of the answer.
- *Use detail.* Make sure that you show detailed knowledge, but only as part of an explanation being made in relation to the question. No knowledge should be standalone; it should be used in context.
- *Explanatory analysis and evaluation.* Consider what words and phrases to use in an answer to strengthen the explanation.
- *Argument and counter-argument.* Think of how arguments can be juxtaposed as part of a balancing act to give contrasting views.
- *Resolution.* Think how best to 'resolve' contradictory arguments.
- *Relative significance and evaluation.* Think how best to reach a judgement when trying to assess the relative importance of various factors, and their possible interrelationship.

Planning an essay

Practice question 1

> 'Charles I achieved little as King of Spain during the years 1529 and 1556.' To what extent do you agree with this view?

This question requires you to analyse what Charles I achieved as King of Spain. It gives particular dates, 'during the years 1529 and 1556', and it is important that the focus of your essay is on these dates. You must discuss:

- The areas in which you consider Charles I achieved little (your primary focus).
- Any other areas where you consider this view to be wrong; in other words, areas in which you consider he may have achieved a great deal (your secondary focus).

A clear structure makes for a much more effective essay and is crucial for achieving the highest marks. You need three or four paragraphs to structure this question effectively. In each paragraph you will deal with one factor. One of these *must* be the factor in the question.

A very basic plan for this question might look like this:

- Paragraph 1: areas of Charles I's policies in which you consider he achieved little.
- Paragraph 2: any areas of policy in which you feel Charles I achieved more than a little.
- Paragraph 3: a concluding summary of whether overall you consider that Charles I achieved little or not.

It is a good idea to cover the factor named in the question first, so that you don't run out of time and forget to do it. Then cover the others in what you think is their order of importance, or in the order that appears logical in terms of the sequence of paragraphs.

The introduction

Maintaining focus is vital. One way to do this from the beginning of your essay is to use the words in the question to help write your argument. The first sentence of question 1 (page 175), for example, could look like this:

It could be said that Charles I achieved little as King of Spain during the years 1529 and 1556 as a result of policy failings in a number of important areas. However, there were other areas of policy in which he achieved more.

This opening sentence provides a clear focus on the demands of the question, although it could, of course, be written in a more exciting style.

Focus throughout the essay

Structuring your essay well will help with keeping the focus of your essay on the question. To maintain a focus on the wording in question 1 (page 175), you could begin your first main paragraph with 'achieved little'.

Charles I achieved little as King of Spain during the years 1529 and 1556 in a number of areas, in particular, his financial policies, his preoccupation with his role as ruler of the Holy Roman Empire, his frequent absences from Spain, and the effects of the imports of gold and silver from the New World.

- This opening begins with a clear point that refers to the primary focus of the question (Charles I achieving little as King of Spain) while linking it to a factor or factors (the areas in which it could be argued that he achieved little, such as his financial policies).
- You could then have a paragraph for each of your other factors.
- It will be important to make sure that each paragraph focuses on analysis and includes relevant details that are used as part of the argument.
- You may wish to number your factors. This helps to make your structure clear and helps you to maintain focus.

Deploying detail

As well as focus and structure, your essay will be judged on the extent to which it includes accurate detail. There are several different kinds of evidence you could use that might be described as detailed. These include correct dates, names of relevant people, statistics and events. For example, for sample question 1 (page 175) you could use terms such as price inflation and regents as you are probably going to include a discussion of the financial situation and Charles's arrangements for ruling Spain during his absences from the country as part of your answer. You can also make your essays more detailed by using the correct technical vocabulary.

Analysis and explanation

'Analysis' covers a variety of high-level skills including explanation and evaluation; in essence, it means breaking down something complex into smaller parts. A clear structure which breaks down a complex question into a series of paragraphs is the first step towards writing an analytical essay.

The purpose of explanation is to account for why something happened, or why something is true or false. An explanatory statement requires two parts: a *claim* and a *justification*.

Study guide

For question 1 (page 175), for example, you might want to argue that one important area in which Charles I achieved little was in his economic and financial policies. Once you have made your point, and supported it with relevant detail, you can then explain how this answers the question. For example, you could conclude your paragraph like this:

Therefore, in finance Charles achieved little for Spain[1]. Although Charles was able to increase the amount of money that he received, it was never enough to match his outgoings[2]. For much of this period he was engaged in war, at considerable cost to Castile in particular. He constantly had to resort to loans at high rates of interest and, by the end of his reign, was on the verge of bankruptcy[3].

1 Claim.
2 Relationship.
3 Justification.

Evaluation

Evaluation means considering the importance of two or more different factors, weighing them against each other and reaching a judgement. This is a good skill to use at the end of an essay because the conclusion should reach a judgement which answers the question. For example, your conclusion to question 1 (page 175) might read as follows:

Clearly, Charles achieved little in a number of areas, particularly finance. However, in other areas he could be considered to have achieved more, such as in enforcing religious conformity to the Catholic faith. The development of the Spanish Empire in the New World was certainly no little achievement. Could any ruler have done more than he had done with such a large, and different, set of lands over which to govern? In the end though, Charles, by abdicating to withdraw to Yuste, must have known that he had achieved little overall in Spain during his reign as king.

Words like 'clearly' and 'however' are helpful to contrast the importance of the different factors.

Complex essay writing: argument and counter-argument

Essays that develop a good argument are more likely to reach the highest levels. This is because argumentative essays are much more likely to develop sustained analysis. As you know, your essays are judged on the extent to which they analyse.

After setting up an argument in your introduction, you should develop it throughout the essay. One way of doing this is to adopt an argument–counter-argument structure. A counter-argument is one that disagrees with the main argument of the essay. This is a good way of evaluating the importance of the different factors that you discuss. Essays of this type will develop an argument in one paragraph and then set out an opposing argument in another paragraph. Sometimes this will include juxtaposing the differing views of historians on a topic.

Good essays will analyse the key issues. They will probably have a clear piece of analysis at the end of each paragraph. While this analysis might be good, it will generally relate only to the issue discussed in that paragraph.

Excellent essays will be analytical throughout. As well as the analysis of each factor discussed above, there will be an overall analysis. This will run throughout the essay and can be achieved through developing a clear, relevant and coherent argument.

A good way of achieving sustained analysis is to consider which factor is most important.

Here is an example of an introduction that sets out an argument for question 1 (page 175):

As ruler of a large and diverse collection of lands, it is not surprising that Charles can be said to have achieved little as King of Spain during the years 1529–56[1]. There are critical areas in the running of a country where it can be clearly argued that he achieved little: his financial and economic policies, his preoccupation with his role as ruler of the Holy Roman Empire and his frequent absences from Spain[2]. However, there are also areas of policy where it could be argued that Charles achieved more, in some cases much more, than just 'a little'. Here one must consider such areas as the developments in the New World, the religious unity achieved, his relations with the nobility, the lack of any significant revolts against his rule in Spain and the appointment of his son, Prince Philip, as regent from 1543. However, it can be argued that all his achievements were undermined by his greatest failure – controlling his finances[3].

1 The introduction begins with a claim.
2 The introduction continues with another reason.
3 Concludes with an outline of the argument of the most important reason.

- This introduction focuses on the question and sets out the key factors that the essay will develop.
- It introduces an argument about which factor was most significant.
- However, it also sets out an argument that can then be developed throughout each paragraph, and is rounded off with an overall judgement in the conclusion.

Complex essay writing: resolution and relative significance

Having written an essay that explains argument and counter-argument, you should then resolve the tension between the argument and the counter-argument in your conclusion. It is important that the writing is precise and summarises the arguments made in the main body of the essay.

You need to reach a supported overall judgement. One very appropriate way to do this is by evaluating the relative significance of different factors, in the light of valid criteria. Relative significance means how important one factor is compared to another.

The best essays will always make a judgement about which was most important based on valid criteria. These can be very simple, and will depend on the topic and the exact question.

The following criteria are often useful:

- Duration: which factor was important for the longest amount of time?
- Scope: which factor affected the most people?
- Effectiveness: which factor achieved most?
- Impact: which factor led to the most fundamental change?

As an example, you could compare the factors in terms of their duration and their impact. A conclusion that follows this advice should be capable of reaching a high level (if written, in full, with appropriate details) because it reaches an overall judgement that is supported through evaluating the relative significance of different factors in the light of valid criteria.

Having written an introduction and the main body of an essay for question 1 (page 175), a concluding paragraph that aims to meet the exacting criteria for reaching a complex judgement could look like this:

Assessing whether Charles achieved little in Spain is a therefore a complex issue. It is only in the field of finance that one can make a clear claim for saying he achieved little. In other areas the situation is more nuanced. Charles's own frequent absences did not help his achievement in Spain. However, he did have able and skilled regents such as his son Prince Philip who is considered to have been a highly effective regent in Spain from 1543. Similarly, when looking at areas of much more achievement such as the developments in the New World, he was unable to deal effectively with problems, in particular from the gold and silver imports coming into Spain. In the final analysis, the fact that he abdicated and spent the rest of his life in a monastery in Yuste shows that he knew that he had achieved little.

Interpretation guidance

Section A of the examination for AQA Component 1: Breadth Study: Spain in the Age of Discovery, 1469–1598 contains extracts from the work of historians. This section tests your ability to analyse different historical interpretations. Therefore, you must focus on the interpretations outlined in the extracts. The advice given here is for both the AS and the A level exams:

- For the AS exam, there are two extracts and you are asked which is the more convincing interpretation (25 marks).
- For the A level exam, there are three extracts and you are asked how convincing the arguments are in relation to a specified topic (30 marks).

An interpretation is a particular view on a topic of history held by a particular author or authors. Interpretations of an event can vary, for example, depending on how much weight a historian gives to a particular factor and largely ignores others.

Interpretations can also be heavily conditioned by events and situations that influence the writer. For example, the American historian J.L. Motley, writing at the end of the nineteenth century and influenced by the Protestant and Dutch writers of the sixteenth century, was still attacking Philip II as a cruel, despotic, tyrant. Today, historians tend to look back with a more impartial judgement, seeing both the positives and the negatives, based more securely on primary sources.

The interpretations that you will be given will be largely from recent or fairly recent historians, and they may, of course, have been influenced by events in the period in which they were writing.

Interpretations and evidence

The extracts will contain a mixture of interpretations and evidence. The mark scheme rewards answers that focus on the *interpretations* offered by the extracts much more highly than answers that focus on the *information or evidence* mentioned in the extracts. Therefore, it is important to identify the interpretations:

- *Interpretations* are a specific kind of argument. They tend to make claims such as 'The Castilian nobility enjoyed substantial advantages under Charles'.
- *Information or evidence* tends to consist of specific details. For example: 'Charles exempted the nobility from the heaviest tax burden'.
- *Arguments and counter-arguments*: sometimes in an extract you will find an interpretation that is then balanced in the same paragraph with a counter-argument. You will need to decide with which your knowledge is most in sympathy.

The importance of planning

Remember that in the examination you are allowed an hour for this question. It is the planning stage that is vital in order to write a good answer. You should allow at least one-quarter of that time to read the extracts and plan an answer. If you start writing too soon, it is likely that you will waste time trying to summarise the *content* of each extract. Do this in your planning stage – and then think how you will *use* the content to answer the question.

Analysing interpretations: AS (two extracts)

The same skills are needed for AS and A level for this question. The advice starts with AS simply because it only involves two extracts rather than three.

> With reference to these extracts and your understanding of the historical context, which of these two extracts provides the more convincing interpretation of Charles's success in ruling Spain? (25 marks)

EXTRACT A

On why the Habsburgs were successful in Spain during the reign of Charles I. From Stanley G. Payne, *A History of Spain and Portugal*, volume 1, University of Wisconsin Press, 1973, pp. 184–5.

The Habsburg crown was successful in Spain during the reign of Carlos V [Charles I] because it accepted the institutional status quo of the Hispanic kingdoms, and because of the increasing Hispanization of the ruler himself, who eventually lost nearly all Flemish identification and came to associate himself more and more with the base of his empire Castile. If rebel movements such as the Comunero and Germania revolts were thoroughly suppressed, the Habsburg crown in return fully accepted the pluralistic 'Aragonese' structure of the united monarchy, and even extended this system to the new domains conquered in Italy. There were no efforts whatever in the sixteenth century to unify the various Hispanic states; the existing constitutional integrity of the separate principalities was fully respected.

EXTRACT B

On the relations of the nobility of Spain with Charles I. From Stewart MacDonald, *Charles V: Ruler, Dynast and Defender of the Faith 1500–58*, Hodder & Stoughton, 2000, p. 36.

The Castilian nobility enjoyed substantial advantages under Charles. Their pride was flattered and their self-interest satisfied as Charles increasingly loosened his ties with his Burgundian lands and put Spain at the centre of his empire. Castilian nobles found lucrative employment in the running of Charles's empire. In addition, Charles exempted the nobility from the heaviest tax burdens. The absenteeism of the monarch also provided opportunities for the nobility to consolidate and advance their own interests. As a result, it has been argued that Charles's partnership with the Castilian nobility was one of the major pillars of his success in ruling Spain. During the Comuneros revolt the nobility had proved their value to the Crown in the maintenance of effective royal government. In its aftermath, Charles was careful to avoid offending them. But the victory of the nobility over the Comuneros rebels brought them into a longer-term alliance with a monarchy much strengthened in its own right.

EXTRACT C

On the condition of Roman Catholicism in Spain and in regard to its foreign policy (only relevant for A level). From Helen Rawlings, *Church, Religion and Society in Early Modern Spain*, Palgrave, 2002, p. xiii.

By the end of the fifteenth century the Spanish Church had become firmly associated with the authoritarian power of the monarch and the repressive arm of the Holy Office [the Spanish Inquisition]. Spain's reputation as a major bastion of religious orthodoxy and racial intolerance was reinforced in the early sixteenth century as it took a leading role under Charles V ... in checking the spread of Protestant heresy through the lands of the Holy Roman Empire in northern and central Europe and in combating the onslaught of Turkish power in central and southern Europe.

Analysing Extract A (page 180)

From the extract:

- Increasing Hispanisation of Charles I.
- No efforts to unify the various Hispanic states.

Assessing the extent to which the arguments are convincing:

- Deploying knowledge that Charles lost nearly all his Flemish identification.
- Deploying knowledge that Charles came to associate himself more with Castile as the base of his empire.
- Suggesting that even though the rebel movements in Spain, the *comunero* and *Germania* revolts, were suppressed, there was no attempt to unite all Castile and Aragon into one country, Spain.
- Suggesting that there was no attempt to unite the new lands conquered in Italy with the rest of the Spanish possessions under one government.
- Deploying knowledge that each of the separate principalities kept their own constitutions.
- The extract omits references to other areas such as the relations between Charles and the nobility mentioned in Extract B.
- The extract comes from a general history of Spain written by a historian in 1973 and able to look back on the events described based on evidence accumulated by that date.

Analysing Extract B (page 180)

From the extract:

- The Castilian nobility enjoyed substantial advantages under Charles I.
- During the *comuneros* revolt, the nobility had proved its value in the maintenance of effective royal government.

Assessing the extent to which the arguments are convincing:

- Deploying knowledge to show the benefits that the nobles found from employment in the running of Charles's empire.
- Deploying knowledge that they were exempted from the heaviest tax burdens.
- Deploying knowledge that Charles was putting Spain at the centre of his empire (and agreeing here with Extract A).
- Suggesting that it was Charles's absence from Spain that gave the nobility opportunities to consolidate and advance its own interests.
- Suggesting that the nobility had played an important part in dealing with the *comuneros* revolt.
- Suggesting that because of its role during the *comuneros* revolt, Charles would be careful to avoid offending the nobility.
- Suggesting that both king and nobles had proved their importance in working together in the *comuneros* revolt.
- Suggesting negatives to Charles's success in Spain. That if the nobles did not pay the heaviest tax burdens, who did? That if Charles's absences meant the nobles could consolidate and advance their own interests, who might have lost out?
- The extract is written later than Extract A – 27 years – by when more evidence is likely to have been available.

Comparing the analysis of each extract should give the direction of an overall conclusion and judgement about which of the extracts is more convincing. In this case, though, there is a little overlap between the two extracts; the two extracts are dealing with different aspects of Charles's rule but it may be that Extract B is more convincing because of the amount of supporting evidence given to support the role of the nobility as one 'of the major pillars of his success in ruling Spain'.

The mark scheme for the AS exam

The mark scheme builds up from Level 1 to Level 5, in the same way as it does for essays:

- Do not waste time simply describing or paraphrasing the content of each source.

- Make sure that when you include your knowledge it is being used to advance the analysis of the extracts – not as knowledge in its own right.
- The top two levels of the mark scheme refer to 'supported conclusion' (Level 4) and 'well-substantiated conclusion' (Level 5).
- For Level 4, 'supported conclusion' means finishing your answer with a judgement that is backed up with some accurate evidence drawn from the source(s) and your knowledge.
- For Level 5, 'well-substantiated conclusion' means finishing your answer with a judgement which is very well supported with evidence, and, where relevant, reaches a complex conclusion that reflects a wide variety of evidence.

Writing the answer for the AS exam

There is no one correct way! However, the principles are clear. In particular, contextual knowledge should be used *only* to back up an argument. None of your knowledge should be standalone; all your knowledge should be used in context.

For each extract in turn:

- Explain the evidence given in the extract for Charles's success in ruling Spain, backed up with your own contextual knowledge.
- Explain the points in the extract where you have evidence that contradicts Charles's success in ruling Spain.

Then write a conclusion that reaches a judgement on which is more convincing as an interpretation. You might build in some element of comparison during the answer, or it might be developed in the last paragraph only.

Analysing interpretations: A level (three extracts)

For the AQA A level exam, Section A gives you three extracts (page 180), followed by a single question.

> Using your understanding of the historical context, assess how convincing the arguments in each of these three extracts are in relation to Charles's success in ruling Spain. (30 marks)

An analysis of Extracts A and B has already been provided for the AS question (page 181).

Analysing Extract C (page 180)

From the extract:

- Spain's reputation as a major bastion of religious orthodoxy and racial intolerance
- Association of the Spanish Church with the power of the monarch.
- Association of the Spanish Church with the Spanish Inquisition.

Assessing the extent to which the arguments are convincing:

- Deploying knowledge that Spain checked the spread of Protestantism.
- Deploying knowledge that Spain held back the attempts by the Turks to expand their power in central and southern Europe.
- Suggesting that the Spanish Church was working with Charles in an authoritarian way in Spain.
- Suggesting that the Spanish Inquisition was repressing all signs of religious dissent.

Writing the answer for A level

First, make sure that you have the focus of the question clear: in this case, the focus is on Charles's success in ruling Spain and how convincing the extracts are on that subject. Then you can investigate the three extracts to see how convincing they are.

You need to analyse each of the three extracts in turn. A suggestion is to have a large page divided into nine blocks as shown in the table below.

Extract's main arguments	Knowledge to corroborate	Knowledge to contradict or modify
A		
B		
C		

- In the first column, list the main arguments each extract uses.
- In the second column, list what you already know that can corroborate the arguments.
- In the third column, list what might contradict or modify (you might find that you partly agree, but with reservations) the arguments.
- You may find, of course, that some of your knowledge is relevant more than once.

Planning your answer

Decide how you could best set out a detailed plan for your answer:

- Briefly refer to the focus of the question.
- For each extract in turn set out the arguments, corroborating and contradictory evidence.
- Do this by treating each argument (or group of arguments) in turn.
- Make comparisons between the extracts if this is helpful. The mark scheme does not explicitly give credit for doing this, but a successful cross-reference may well show the extent of your understanding of each extract and add to the weight of your argument.
- An overall judgement is not required, but it may be helpful to make a brief summary, or just reinforce what has been said already by emphasising which extract was the most convincing.

The mark scheme for A level

For each of the three extracts, the mark scheme makes it clear that a good answer will:

- identify the arguments presented in each extract
- assess the extent to which the arguments are convincing, using your own knowledge
- take every opportunity to make a balanced answer wherever this is appropriate by corroborating and contradicting the arguments in each extract.

The mark scheme progresses as follows:

- Level 1: general comments about the three extracts or accurate understanding of one extract.
- Level 2: some accurate comments on the interpretations in at least two of the three extracts, but with limited comments or with description.
- Level 3: some supported comments on the interpretations, putting them in their historical context. Some analysis of the content of the extracts, but little attempt to evaluate them.
- Level 4: good understanding of the interpretations provided in the extracts, with knowledge to give a good analysis and some evaluation.
- Level 5: very good understanding and strong historical awareness used to analyse and evaluate.

Notice that there is no reference in the mark scheme to *comparing* the extracts or reaching a judgement about which is the most convincing.

STUDY GUIDE

Edexcel A level History

Sources guidance

Edexcel's Paper 3, Option 32: The Golden Age of Spain, 1474–1598 is assessed by an exam comprising three sections:

- Section A is a source analysis assessment. It tests your knowledge of one of the key topics in depth.
- Section B requires you to write one essay from a choice of two, again testing your knowledge of key topics in depth (see page 189 for guidance on this).
- Section C requires you to write one essay from a choice of two. Questions relate to themes in breadth and test your knowledge of change over a period of at least 100 years (see page 193 for guidance on this).

The sections of the exam relate to the sections of the paper in the following way:

Section A and Section B	Test your knowledge of the key topics in depth	Ruling Spain – newly united but still divided: • The Spanish Inquisition and the persecution of the Jews, 1478–92 • The accession of Charles and the revolt of the *comuneros*, 1516–29 • The price revolution and its impact, c.1500–c.1570 • The campaign for orthodoxy, 1558–70 • The crisis in Aragon, 1590–3
Section C	Tests your knowledge of the themes in breadth	Changes in Spanish influence and power, 1474–1598: • Changing geographical reach of Spanish power • Changing military and financial power

The following advice relates to Paper 3, Section A. Paper 3 is only available at A level, therefore there is no AS level version of this paper.

Paper 3 Section A questions

Section A of Paper 3 comprises a single compulsory question which refers to one source.

The question

The Section A question will begin with the following stem: 'Assess the value of the source for revealing …'. For example:

> Assess the value of Source 1 for revealing Ferdinand and Isabella's reasons for founding the Inquisition and why the Inquisition in Spain was feared. Explain your answer, using the source, the information given about its origin and your own knowledge about the historical context.

The source

The source will be a primary or contemporary source. That is to say, it will have been written in the period that you are studying: 1474–1598. The source will be around 350 words long. It will be accompanied by a brief passage which will set out the essential provenance of the source. An example is shown on the opposite page.

> **SOURCE 1**
>
> An extract from a letter from Hernando del Pulgar to the Archbishop of Seville, Don Pedro González de Mendoza, about how heresy was dealt with in Seville, *c.*1480. Hernando del Pulgar was a *converso* who was official historian and secretary to Ferdinand and Isabella. Cited in Helen Rawlings, *The Spanish Inquisition*, Wiley, 2005, pp. 57–8.
>
> *And he [King Ferdinand] gave principal charge of this Inquisition to a friar of upright life who had great zeal in the Faith, who was called Fray Tomas de Torquemada, confessor to the king and prior of the monastery of Santa Cruz of Segovia of the Order of St Dominic. This prior, who was the chief inquisitor, put other inquisitors in his place in all the other cities and towns of the kingdom of Castile, and Aragon, and Valencia, and Catalonia. These made inquisitions on the matter of heretical iniquity in every land and district where they were assigned; and in these places they set their charters and edicts, founded upon law, so that those who had engaged in Jewish practices or who were not in accord with the Faith, within a certain time might come to confess their faults and be reconciled with Holy Mother Church. And by these charters and edicts many persons of lineage appeared before the inquisitors and confessed their faults and the errors that they had committed in this crime of heresy. And these were given penances according to the degree of the crime that each one had incurred. These were more than fifteen thousand persons. And if some were guilty of that crime and did not come to be reconciled within the period of time that had been decreed, once there was information from witnesses of the error they had committed, then they were taken prisoner and trial was instituted against them, by means of which they were condemned as heretics and apostates and turned over to secular justice.*
>
> *Up to two thousand men and women were burned on various occasions in different cities and towns; and others were condemned to perpetual imprisonment, and to others was given as a penance that for all the days of their lives they should go marked with great red crosses placed on their clothing. And they as well as their children were declared unfit for all public office or responsibility … Some relatives of the prisoners and the condemned protested, saying that the inquisition and procedure was rigorous beyond what it ought to be and that in the manner in which the trials were conducted and in the execution of the sentences the ministers and executors showed that they had hatred for those people.*

Understanding the question

To answer the question successfully you must understand how the question works. The question is written precisely in order to make sure that you understand the task. Each part of the question has a specific meaning.

> Assess the value of the source[1] for revealing Ferdinand and Isabella's reasons for founding the Inquisition[2] and why the Inquisition in Spain was feared[3].

1 You must evaluate how useful the source could be to a historian. Evaluating the extent of usefulness involves considering its value and limitations in the light of your own knowledge about the source's historical context. Important information about the context of the source is included in the information given about the source.
2 The question focuses on two specific enquiries that the source might be useful for. The first is Ferdinand and Isabella's reasons for founding the Inquisition.
3 The second enquiry is why the Inquisition in Spain was feared.

In essence, you should use the source, the information about the source and your own knowledge of the historical context to make a judgement about how far the source is useful to a historian engaged in two specific enquiries. Crucially, you must consider both enquiries;

an answer which only focuses on one of the enquiries is unlikely to do well.

Source skills

Generally, Section A of Paper 3 tests your ability to evaluate source material. Your job is to analyse the source by reading it in the context of the values and assumptions of the society and the period from which it came.

Examiners will mark your work by focusing on the extent to which you are able to:

- Interpret and analyse source material:
  - At a basic level, this means you can understand the source and select, copy, paraphrase and summarise the source to help answer the question.
  - At a higher level, your interpretation of the source includes the ability to explain, analyse and make inferences based on the source.
  - At the highest levels, you will be expected to analyse the source in a sophisticated way. This includes the ability to distinguish between information, opinions and arguments contained in the source.
- Deploy knowledge of historical context in relation to the source:
  - At a basic level, this means the ability to link the source to your knowledge of the context in which the source was written, using this knowledge to expand or support the information contained in the source.
  - At a higher level, you will be able to use your contextual knowledge to make inferences, and to expand, support or challenge the details mentioned in the source.
  - At the highest levels, you will be able to examine the value and limits of the material contained in the source by interpreting the source in the context of the values and assumptions of the society from which it is taken.
- Evaluate the usefulness and weight of the source material:
  - At a basic level, evaluation of the source will be based on simplistic criteria about reliability and bias.
  - At a higher level, evaluation of the source will be based on the nature and purpose of the source.
  - At the highest levels, evaluation of the source will be based on a valid criterion that is justified in the course of the essay. You will also be able to distinguish between the value of different aspects of the source.

Make sure your source evaluation is sophisticated. Avoid crude statements about bias, and avoid simplistic assumptions such as that a source written immediately after an event is reliable, whereas a source written years later is unreliable.

Try to see things through the eyes of the writer:

- How does the writer understand the world?
- What assumptions does the writer have?
- Who is the writer trying to influence?
- What views is the writer trying to challenge?

Basic skill: comprehension

The most basic source skill is comprehension: understanding what the source means. There are a variety of techniques that you can use to aid comprehension. For example, you could read the sources included in this book and in past papers. In this context you could:

- Read the sources out loud.
- Look up any words that you don't understand and make a glossary.
- Make flash cards containing brief biographies of the writers of the sources.

You can demonstrate comprehension by copying, paraphrasing and summarising the sources. However, keep this to the minimum as comprehension is a low-level skill and you need to leave room for higher-level skills.

Advanced skill: contextualising the sources

First, to analyse the sources correctly you need to understand them in the context in which they were written. Source 1 (page 185) reflects a contemporary's view. Your job is to understand the values and assumptions behind the source.

- One way of contextualising the source is to consider the nature, origins and purpose of the source. However, this can lead to a formulaic essay.
- An alternative is to consider two levels of context. First, you should establish the general context. In this case, Source 1 was written in about 1480, a few years after the Inquisition had been introduced into Castile (in 1478). Second, you can look for specific references to contemporary events, people or debates in the source. For example, when considering the reasons why the Inquisition was feared, the details in the source can be put in context in the following way:
    - If *conversos* did not come forward to confess their faults then they could be accused by 'witnesses of the errors they had committed' … 'in this crime of heresy'. It was the secrecy in regard to what happened which was so feared: the Inquisition worked in secret and accusers were not named. This made it difficult for those accused to defend themselves. Accusations could be, and in fact were, often malicious.
    - 'They were taken prisoner and trial was instituted against them, by means of which they were condemned as heretics and apostates': once the *conversos* had been taken prisoner and brought to trial the most likely, indeed probable, verdict was a guilty one. It was very difficult for a defendant to prove his or her innocence. Not only were the accusers not named but the courts worked in secret.
    - 'The inquisition and procedure was rigorous beyond what it ought to be': it was seen as unjust; not only were the accusers not named but the courts worked in secret. In addition, there was no right of appeal against the verdict.
    - 'Up to two thousand men and women were burned on various occasions in different cities and towns'; these figures were probably not accurate. The writer of the source is writing in the 1480s, shortly after the introduction of the Inquisition. He, like others of his contemporaries, gives high figures for the number of deaths. Later, twentieth-century historians put the numbers far lower. Henry Kamen suggests that 2000 may have been executed in the whole of Spain during the first 50 years of its existence. But it was what people thought and feared would happen that was critical. Those found guilty were paraded in an *auto de fé* and those who were to be executed were then handed over to the secular authorities for execution, which usually took place elsewhere.
    - 'Others were condemned to perpetual imprisonment, and to others was given as a penance that for all the days of their lives they should go marked with great red crosses placed on their clothing': there were a range of penalties which *conversos* lived in fear of.

Use context to make judgements

- Start by establishing the general context of the source:
    - Ask yourself, what was going on at the time when the source was written, or the time of the events described in the source?
    - What are the key debates that the source might be contributing to?
- Next, look for key words and phrases that establish the specific context. Does the source refer to specific people, events or books that might be important?
- Make sure your contextualisation focuses on the question.
- Use the context when evaluating the usefulness and limitations of the source.

For example:

Source 1 is valuable to a historian investigating why the Inquisition was so feared because it highlights a number of the reasons for that fear. First, it mentions that people could be taken prisoner and brought to trial based on 'information from witnesses of the error they had committed'. As these witnesses were not named, it was difficult for the accused to defend themselves. Accusations could be, and in fact were, often malicious. Second, it refers to the manner in which the trial itself was conducted as showing 'hatred' for the conversos. Everything seemed against the accused in regard to the trial and it was likely, indeed probable, that the verdict would be a guilty one. It was very difficult for a defendant to prove their innocence. Not only were the accusers not named but the courts worked in secret. In addition, no one could appeal against the verdict. Third, it refers to the penalties that could be given and which generated fear among the conversos: penances, imprisonment (sometimes 'perpetual') and, for a number, death. Those found guilty suffered the indignity of being paraded in the auto de fé. Those who were to be executed were then handed over to the secular authorities for execution, which usually took place elsewhere. The source refers to 'up to two thousand men and women were burned on various occasions in different cities and towns'. These figures, however, were probably not accurate. The writer of the source is writing in the 1480s, shortly after the introduction of the Inquisition. He, like others of his time, gives high figures for the number of deaths. Later twentieth-century historians put the numbers far lower. For example, Henry Kamen suggests that 2000 may have been executed in the whole of Spain during the first 50 years of its existence. But it was what people thought and feared would happen that was critical, and this is what the source brings out. The whole process of the Inquisition was designed to instil fear and this is what the writer of this source shows was achieved.

This answer makes use of inferences from details in the source to uncover a variety of motives, showing that the passage is of considerable use for this enquiry. Significantly, in order to do well it would also have to deal with the other enquiry: Ferdinand and Isabella's reasons for founding the Inquisition.

Essay guidance (1)

The following advice relates to Paper 3, Section B. Paper 3 is only available at A level, therefore there is no AS level version of this paper.

Essay skills

In order to get a high grade in Section B of Paper 3 your essay must contain four essential qualities:

- focused analysis
- relevant detail
- supported judgement
- organisation, coherence and clarity.

This section focuses on the following aspects of exam technique:

- Section B: the nature of the question.
- Planning your answer.
- Writing a focused introduction.
- Deploying relevant detail.
- Writing analytically.
- Reaching a supported judgement.

Section B: the nature of the question

Section B questions are designed to test the depth of your historical knowledge. Therefore, they can focus on relatively short periods, or single events. Moreover, they can focus on different historical processes or 'concepts'. These include:

- cause
- consequence
- continuity and change
- similarities and differences
- significance.

These different question focuses require slightly different approaches:

Cause	1 How far were Isabella's concerns about Jewish *conversos* responsible for the foundation of the Inquisition in the years 1478–80?
Consequence	2 How accurate is it to say that the main impact of inflation in the years 1500–70 fell on peasant farmers and urban workers?
Continuity and change	3 To what extent was Charles I more successful in his relations with the Spanish people between 1522 and 1529 compared with 1517–20?
Similarities and differences	4 How accurate is it to say that the expulsion of the Jews in 1492 had a greater social and economic impact on Spain than the rebellion in Granada in 1568?
Significance	5 How significant was the revolt of Aragon (1591–2) in extending the authority of Philip II?

Some questions include a 'stated factor'. A common type of stated factor question would ask how far one factor caused something. For example, for question 1 in the table:

> **How far were Isabella's concerns about Jewish *conversos* responsible for the foundation of the Inquisition in the years 1478–80?**

you would be expected to evaluate the importance of 'Isabella's concerns about Jewish *conversos*' – the 'stated factor' – compared to other factors.

Planning your answer

It is crucial that you understand the focus of the question. Therefore, read the question carefully before you start planning. Check the following:

- The chronological focus: which years should your essay deal with?
- The topic focus: what aspect of your course does the question deal with?

- The conceptual focus: is this a causes, consequences, continuity/change, similarity/difference or significance question?

For example, for question 5 (page 189) you could point these out as follows:

How significant[1] was the revolt of Aragon[2] (1591–2)[3] in extending the authority of Philip II[4]?

1 Conceptual focus: significance, specifically to the extension of the authority of Philip II.
2 Topic focus: revolt of Aragon.
3 Chronological focus: 1591–2.
4 Topic focus: the position of the Crown in Aragon.

Your plan should reflect the task that you have been set. Section B asks you to write an analytical, coherent and well-structured essay from your own knowledge, which reaches a supported conclusion in around 40 minutes:

- To ensure that your essay is coherent and well structured, it should comprise a series of paragraphs, each focusing on a different point.
- Your paragraphs should come in a logical order. For example, you could write your paragraphs in order of importance, so you begin with the most important issues and end with the least important.
- In essays where there is a 'stated factor', it is a good idea to start with the stated factor before moving on to the other points.
- To make sure you keep to time, you should aim to write three or four paragraphs plus an introduction and a conclusion.

Writing a focused introduction

The opening paragraph

The opening paragraph should do four main things:

- answer the question directly
- set out your essential argument
- outline the factors or issues that you will discuss
- define key terms used in the question – where necessary.

Different questions require you to define different terms, for example:

A level question	Key terms
'The reasons for the revolt in Aragon were radically different from those for the revolt in Granada.' How far do you agree with this statement?	Here it is worth defining the notion of 'radically different'
'Spain's rising population, not imports of silver from the New World, brought about the price revolution c.1500–c.1570.' How far do you agree with this statement?	In this example, it is worth distinguishing between Spain's rising population and imports of silver from the New World
How accurate is it to say that it was the religious conviction of Isabella and Ferdinand that accounts for the intensification of persecution of Spanish Jews in the period 1478–92?	In this example the key terms which need defining are 'religious conviction' and 'intensification'
To what extent can Charles I be held personally responsible for the revolt of the *comuneros*?	In this example the key terms which need defining are 'personally responsible' and '*comuneros*'

Below is an example introduction in answer to the following question:

'The reasons for the revolt in Aragon were radically different from those for the revolt in Granada.' How far do you agree with this statement?

The reasons for the revolt in Aragon were radically different from those for the revolt in Granada[1]. A major element, and one where there was a clear radical difference, in the revolt by the Moriscos in Granada, in contrast to the revolt in Aragon, was religion. The Morisco revolt can be dated back to 1502 when the Mudéjars in Castile were officially forced to become Christians or leave the country. From then on, those in the country were known as Moriscos. However, there had been a complete failure to assimilate the Moriscos into Spanish society.

In Aragon, in complete contrast, the reasons for the revolt were very different. At its heart was the question of its *fueros* (traditional privileges), which it guarded jealously**[2]**. Although there were a number of differences between the two revolts which could be described as fundamentally different, similarities can be found. For example, in both revolts, the government feared that foreign powers might intervene on the side of the rebels**[3]**.

1 The essay starts with a clear focus on the question.
2 This sentence simultaneously defines 'radically different' and provides an initial answer to one of the ways in which there were radical differences.
3 This sentence addresses the 'How far' part of the question and provides an initial answer to the second part of the question.

The opening paragraph: advice

- Don't write more than a couple of sentences on general background knowledge. This is unlikely to focus explicitly on the question.
- After defining key terms, refer back to these definitions when justifying your conclusion.
- The introduction should reflect the rest of the essay. Don't make one argument in your introduction, then make a different argument in the essay.

Deploying relevant detail

Paper 3 tests the depth of your historical knowledge. Therefore, you will need to deploy historical detail. In the main body of your essay your paragraphs should begin with a clear point, be full of relevant detail and end with an explanation or evaluation. A detailed answer might include statistics, proper names, dates and technical terms. For example, if you were writing a paragraph about the nature of the revolt in Granada you might include the royal decree of 1567 which banned Moorish literature, songs and other traditional customs, and the fears generated by possible links between *Moriscos* and the Turks in north Africa and elsewhere.

Writing analytically

The quality of your analysis is one of the key factors that determines the mark you achieve. Writing analytically means clearly showing the relationships between the ideas in your essay. Analysis includes two key skills: explanation and evaluation.

Explanation

Explanation means giving reasons. An explanatory sentence has three parts:

- a claim: a statement that something is true or false
- a reason: a statement that justifies the claim
- a relationship: a word or phrase that shows the relationship between the claim and the reason.

Imagine you are answering question 1 in the table on page 189:

> How far were Isabella's concerns about Jewish *conversos* responsible for the foundation of the Inquisition in the years 1478–80?

Your paragraph on Isabella's concerns about Jewish *conversos* should start with a clear point, which would be supported by a series of examples. Finally, you would round off the paragraph with some explanation:

Therefore, Isabella's concerns about Jewish conversos were one reason for the foundation of the Inquisition in the years 1478-80**[1]** because**[2]** she was determined to ensure that there were no signs of Judaism among the conversos and she felt that to ensure this she needed to introduce the Inquisition into Castile**[3]**.

1 Claim.
2 Relationship.
3 Reason.

Make sure of the following:

- The reason you give genuinely justifies the claim that you have made.
- Your explanation is focused on the question.

Reaching a supported judgement

Finally, your essay should reach a supported judgement. The obvious place to do this is in the conclusion of your essay. Even so, the judgement should reflect the findings of your essay. The conclusion should present:

- a clear judgement that answers the question
- an evaluation of the evidence that supports the judgement.

Finally, the evaluation should reflect valid criteria.

Evaluation and criteria

Evaluation means weighing up to reach a judgement. Therefore, evaluation requires you to:

- summarise both sides of the issue
- reach a conclusion that reflects the proper weight of both sides.

So, for example, for question 1 in the table on page 189:

> How far were Isabella's concerns about Jewish *conversos* responsible for the foundation of the Inquisition in the years 1478–80?

the conclusion might look like this:

In conclusion, Isabella's concerns about Jewish conversos were largely responsible for the foundation of the Inquisition in the years 1478–80 because she was determined to ensure that the conversos were following Christian practices and that there should be no element of Judaism in their customs[1]. Clearly, other elements played a part[2]. Both Isabella and Ferdinand wanted to gain more control over the Church in Castile. There was also the fact that the conversos were resented and envied for their position in society and, in some cases, their wealth[3]. However, Isabella does seem to have been genuinely pious and to have been horrified by the warning given to her about the conversos when visiting Seville in 1478. Establishing an Inquisition in Spain would help her to fulfil her religious aims. In addition, her concern at what seemed from what she was told was a serious problem – the fact that many conversos were still practising Jews – lends weight to the view that it was her concerns about the conversos which were largely responsible for the foundation of the Inquisition[4].

1. The conclusion starts with a clear judgement that answers the question.
2. This sentence begins the process of weighing up the different factors involved in the reasons for the introduction of the Inquisition by acknowledging that other factors also played a part.
3. The conclusion summarises the part played by other factors, such as gaining more control over the Church in Castile.
4. The essay ends with a final judgement that is supported by the evidence of the essay.

The judgement is supported in part by evaluating the evidence, and in part by linking it to valid criteria. In this case, the criteria are Isabella's aims in regard to religious matters and other aims which she and Ferdinand had, and how serious or not was the matter of the *conversos* still following the Jewish faith and therefore whether action needed to be taken.

Essay guidance (2)

The following advice relates to Paper 3, Section C. Paper 3 is only available at A level, therefore there is no AS level version of this paper.

Essay skills

Section C is similar in many ways to Section B. Therefore, you need the same essential skills in order to get a high grade:

- focused analysis
- relevant detail
- supported judgement
- organisation, coherence and clarity.

Nonetheless, there are some differences in terms of the style of the question and the approach to the question in Sections B and C. Therefore, this section focuses on the following aspects of exam technique:

- Section C: the nature of the question
- planning your answer
- advice for Section C.

Section C: the nature of the question

Section C questions focus on the two themes in breadth:

- Changing geographical reach of Spanish power, 1474–1598.
- Changing military and financial power, 1474–1598.

Questions can address either theme or both themes. There are two questions in Section C, of which you must answer one. However, you are not guaranteed a question on both themes, therefore you have to prepare for questions on either of the themes.

Section C questions are designed to test the breadth of your historical knowledge, and your ability to analyse change over time. Therefore, questions will focus on long periods, of no less than 100 years.

Section C questions have a variety of forms. Nonetheless, they have one of two essential foci. They will focus on either:

- the causes of change: for example, the factors, forces or individuals that led to change

or

- the nature of change: the ways in which things changed.

Significantly, the exam paper may contain two causes of change questions or two nature of change questions: you are not guaranteed one of each.

Finally, questions can focus on different aspects of change over time:

- Comparative questions: ask you to assess the extent of change and continuity of an aspect of the period.
- Patterns of change questions: ask you to assess differences in terms of the rate, extent or significance of change at different points in the chronology.
- Turning point questions: ask you to assess which changes were more significant.

Comparative question:	'The key factor in the expansion and maintenance of Spanish power in the years 1474–1598 was the calibre of her generals.' How far do you agree with this statement?
Patterns of change question:	How far do you agree that the priorities for Spanish foreign policy changed significantly between 1474 and 1598?
Turning point question:	How far can the conquest of the Aztecs of 1521 be seen as the key turning point in the extension of Spanish power in the New World in the years 1474–1598?

Planning your answer

It is crucial that you understand the focus of the question in order to make an effective plan. Therefore, read the question carefully before you start planning. Different questions require a different approach. Here are suggestions about how to tackle some of the common types of question:

> 'The key factor in the expansion and maintenance of Spanish power in the years 1474–1598 was the calibre of her generals.' How far do you agree with this statement?

This is a comparative question which focuses on the causes of change. In this case, you should examine the significance of 'calibre of her generals', the stated factor, and compare it to other possible causes of change.

> How far do you agree that the priorities for Spanish foreign policy changed significantly between 1474 and 1598?

This is a patterns of change question which focuses on the significance of change. Here you should examine the changes in the priorities for Spanish foreign policy during the period 1474–1598, assessing whether these priorities changed significantly.

> How far can the conquest of the Aztecs of 1521 be seen as the key turning point in the extension of Spanish power in the New World in the years 1474–1598?

This is a turning point question which focuses on the nature of change. Therefore, you should examine the significance of the stated turning point, and compare it to two or three other turning points from the period 1474–1598. Significantly, you should not just focus on the conquest of the Aztecs of 1521, you must consider other possible turning points. Additionally, when considering how far an event was a turning point you must consider both the changes it caused and the ways in which things stayed the same.

Advice for Section C

In many ways a Section C essay should display the same skills as a Section B essay (see page 189). However, Section C essays focus on a much longer period than Section B essays and this has an impact on how you approach them.

The most important difference concerns the chronology. In order to answer a Section C question properly you must address the whole chronology, in this case the period 1474–1598. In practice, this means choosing examples from across the whole range of the period. Specifically, it is a good idea to have examples from the early part of the period, the middle of the period and the end of the period. For example, if you were answering the question:

> How far can the conquest of the Aztecs of 1521 be seen as the key turning point in the extension of Spanish power in the New World in the years 1474–1598?

The question states a possible turning point from 1521: the middle of the period. Therefore, if you are considering other possible turning points you should choose one from the early part of the chronology and one from towards the end to make sure you cover the whole period.

Equally, if you are dealing with the question:

> How far do you agree that the priorities for Spanish foreign policy changed significantly between 1474 and 1598?

you should analyse examples for the priorities of Spanish foreign policy throughout the whole period, assessing how far there was significant change. This could include developments such as:

- early: Africa and the conflict with France in Italy during the reign of Ferdinand and Isabella
- middle: Africa and the conflict with France in Italy during the reign of Charles I but then moving to northern Europe
- late: some focus on the Mediterranean and the Ottoman threat but the main focus now in other areas, particularly the Netherlands, England and France.

In so doing, you would be addressing the full chronological range of the question.

STUDY GUIDE

OCR A level History

Essay guidance

The assessment of OCR Units Y206 and Y236: Spain 1469–1556 depends on whether you are studying it for AS or A level:

- for the AS exam, you will answer one essay question from a choice of two, and one interpretation question, for which there is no choice
- for the A level exam, you will answer one essay question from a choice of two and one shorter essay question, also from a choice of two.

The guidance below is for answering both AS and A level essay questions. Guidance for the shorter essay question is at the end of this section. Guidance on answering interpretation questions is on page 200.

For both OCR AS and A level History, the types of essay questions set and the skills required to achieve a high grade for Unit Group 2 are the same. The skills are made very clear by both mark schemes, which emphasise that the answer must:

- focus on the demands of the question
- be supported by accurate and relevant factual knowledge
- be analytical and logical
- reach a supported judgement about the issue in the question.

There are a number of skills that you will need to develop to reach the higher levels in the marking bands:

- understand the wording of the question
- plan an answer to the question set
- write a focused opening paragraph
- avoid irrelevance and description
- write analytically
- write a conclusion which reaches a supported judgement based on the argument in the main body of the essay.

These skills will be developed in the section below, but are further developed in the 'Period Study' chapters of the *OCR A level History* series (British Period Studies and Enquiries).

Understanding the wording of the question

To stay focused on the question set, it is important to read the question carefully and focus on the key words and phrases. Unless you directly address the demands of the question you will not score highly. Remember that in questions where there is a named factor you must write a good analytical paragraph about the given factor, even if you argue that it was not the most important.

Types of AS and A level questions you might find in the exams	The factors and issues you would need to consider in answering them
1 Assess the reasons why there was unrest in Spain in the years 1519–24.	Weigh up the relative importance of a range of factors as to why there was unrest. See below.
2 To what extent was Charles's major success in domestic policy dealing with religion in the years 1522–59?	Weigh up the relative success of a range of issues, including comparing the success of religion with other factors, such as finance, relations with the nobility, and government and administration.
3 'The Inquisition was the most successful religious policy of Ferdinand and Isabella.' How far do you agree?	Weigh up the relative importance of a range of religious policies, including comparing the success of the Inquisition with other religious policies, to reach a balanced judgement.
4 How successful were the Catholic monarchs in enforcing royal authority within Aragon and Castile in the years 1474–1505?	This question requires you to make a judgement about how successful the Catholic monarchs were in enforcing royal authority within Aragon and Castile during specific years, 1474–1505. You need here to think about how successful they were in a number of issues such as: • Their ability to enforce law and order • Their management of the nobility • Their ability to control the towns • The success of their peripatetic style of government.

Planning an answer

Many plans simply list dates and events – this should be avoided as it encourages a descriptive or narrative answer, rather than an analytical answer. The plan should be an outline of your argument; this means you need to think carefully about the issues you intend to discuss and their relative importance before you start writing your answer. It should, therefore, be a list of the factors or issues you are going to discuss and a comment on their relative importance.

For question 1 in the table, your plan might look something like this:

- Inherited problems from Ferdinand and Isabella, the power of the nobility and towns, the situation in Castile after the death of Isabella.
- Charles's early actions as king: his delay in arriving in Spain to take up his position, his failure to speak Spanish, and seen as a foreigner, his mishandled demands for money from the *Cortes*, his leaving Spain in 1516 when he was elected Holy Roman Emperor.
- Hostility to Burgundian dominance, court and advisers, leaving a Burgundian, Adrian of Utrecht, in charge when he left Spain in 1516; fear of commercial competition from Flanders and damage that might occur to the Castilian wool trade.

The opening paragraph

Many students spend time 'setting the scene'; the opening paragraph becomes little more than an introduction to the topic – this should be avoided. Instead, make it clear what your argument is going to be. Offer your view about the issue in the question – what was the most important reason for the unrest in Spain in the years 1519–24 – and then introduce the other issues you intend to discuss. In the plan you may wish, for example, to argue that Burgundian dominance was the most important reason. This should be made clear in the opening paragraph, with a brief comment as to why – perhaps that it threatened Castile economically, through hitting the wool trade, and politically because of Charles's reliance on Burgundians as advisers and awarding them important Spanish offices. This will give the examiner a clear overview of your essay, rather than it being a 'mystery tour' where the argument becomes clear only at the end. You should also refer to any important issues that the question raises. For example:

There are a number of reasons why there was unrest in Spain, including underlying tensions and problems arising from Ferdinand and Isabella's rule, and Charles's absences[1]. *However, the most important reason was the fear of Burgundian dominance, both politically and economically*[3]. *Charles's chief adviser was a Burgundian nobleman, the Lord of Chièvres, William de Croÿ; Burgundians held the majority of positions in his household; and they were also given important Spanish offices – Adrian of Utrecht for example received the bishopric of Tortosa. Economically, there were fears that competition from the Flemish cloth trade would damage Castile's fragile textile industry*[3].

1 The student is aware that there were a number of important reasons.
2 The answer offers a clear view as to what the student considers to be the most important reason – a thesis is offered.
3 There is a brief justification to support the thesis.

Avoid irrelevance and description

It is hoped that the plan will stop you from simply writing all you know about why there was unrest and force you to weigh up the role of a range of factors. Similarly, it should also help prevent you from simply writing about the events of the two major revolts. You will not lose marks if you do that, but neither will you gain any credit, and you will waste valuable time.

Write analytically

This is perhaps the hardest, but most important skill you need to develop. An analytical approach can be helped by ensuring that the opening sentence of each paragraph introduces an idea, which directly answers the question and is not just a piece of factual information. In a very strong answer it should be possible to simply read the opening sentences of all the paragraphs and know what argument is being put forward.

If we look at question 3, on the success of the Inquisition (see page 196), the following are possible sentences with which to start paragraphs:

- The policy of religious conformity, largely driven by the Inquisition, created intolerance and replaced the traditional *convivencia*.
- It was victory in Granada that was the high water mark of the religious policies of the reign of Ferdinand and Isabella.
- The most successful aspect of Ferdinand and Isabella's religious policy was the decision to make all Jews in Castile and Aragon convert to Christianity or to emigrate.
- Reform of the Church itself in Spain was limited.
- The most successful aspect of Isabella's religious policy was the expulsion of the Jews and *Mudéjars* from Castile.
- The Inquisition was particularly important in bringing about religious unity.

You would then go on to discuss both sides of the argument raised by the opening sentence, using relevant knowledge about the issue to support each side of the argument. The final sentence of the paragraph would reach a judgement on the role played by the factor you are discussing in the success or otherwise of their religious policies. This approach would ensure that the final sentence of each paragraph links back to the actual question you are answering. If you can do this for each paragraph you will have a series of mini-essays, which discuss a factor and reach a conclusion or judgement about the importance of that factor or issue. For example:

The victory against the Moors in Granada appeared to bring religious unity to the Iberian peninsula by destroying the final bastion of Islam, but in practice this was far from the case[1]. *However, although the Moors were defeated, the 200,000 who stayed under Castilian rule were allowed to keep their customs, laws and properties, as well as their Islamic faith, which undermines the argument that Isabella wanted to impose religious uniformity throughout her country and suggests that perhaps she had other more pressing religious concerns,* such as the Jews, or that she realised that the large number of Mudéjars in Granada would make such a policy unenforceable[2].

1 The sentence puts forward a clear view that the victory appeared to bring religious unity, but in practice did not.
2 The claim that it was a success is undermined by evidence of the terms granted to the Moors and the possibility that Isabella had other religious priorities.

The conclusion

The conclusion provides the opportunity to bring together all the interim judgements to reach an overall judgement about the question. Using the interim judgements will ensure that your conclusion is based on the argument in the main body of the essay and does not offer a different view. For the essay answering question 1 (see page 196), you can decide what was the most important factor in the causes of unrest, but for questions 2 and 3 you will need to comment on the importance of the named factor – religion or the Inquisition – as well as explain why you think a different factor is more important, if that has been your line of argument. Or, if you think the named factor is the most important, you would need to explain why that was more important than the other factors or issues you have discussed.

Consider the following conclusion to question 2 (on page 196): 'To what extent was Charles's major success in domestic policy dealing with religion in the years 1522–59?'

Although it can be argued that Charles's religious policy was his most successful domestic policy given the religious stability of the state, the country was still troubled by three religious problems: the new fear of Protestantism and continuing worries about former Jewish and Islamic groups[1]. However, most of the religious issues were managed during his reign, whereas the economic and financial problems grew worse, so that his son Philip had to suspend all payments from the Castilian treasury shortly after becoming king. Government appeared to be largely successful and, after the unrest of Charles's early years as king, stability followed for the rest of his reign. Charles had established his authority over the towns and the Cortes of Castile and built up a good working relationship with the nobility. The conciliar system, despite corruption, worked reasonably well. On balance, given Charles's sincere religious views and the importance that he gave to ensuring that Protestantism was unable to take a hold in Spain, one could maintain that 'Charles's major success in domestic policy was dealing with religion[2].

1 This is a strong conclusion because it considers the importance of the named factor – religious success – but weighs that up against a range of other factors to reach an overall judgement.
2 It also compares his success in religion with other issues to produce a balanced conclusion.

How to write a good essay for the A level short answer questions

This question will require you to weigh up the importance of two factors or issues in relation to an event or a development. For example:

> Which of the following was of greater importance in considering whether Ferdinand and Isabella deserved their title of 'Most Catholic Monarchs'?
>
> i) The Conquest of Granada
>
> ii) The establishment of the Inquisition
>
> Explain your answer with reference to both i) and ii).

As with the long essays, the skills required are made very clear by the mark scheme, which emphasises that the answer must:

- analyse the two issues
- evaluate the two issues
- support your analysis and evaluation with detailed and accurate knowledge
- reach a supported judgement as to which factor was more important in relation to the issue in the question.

The skills required are very similar to those for the longer essays. However, there is no need for an introduction, nor are you required to compare the two factors or issues in the main body of the essay, although either approach can still score full marks. For example, an opening paragraph could be:

The conquest of Granada had a significant impact on the reputation of Ferdinand and Isabella as deserving the title 'Most Catholic Monarchs'. And, of course, it was for this reason that the Pope had given Ferdinand and Isabella the title. The conquest, or rather Reconquest, was welcomed throughout Christendom for its victory over the last part of the Iberian Peninsula under the control of the Moors. At last there was a victory against some of the feared (in Christian Europe) forces of Islam. Now, at long last the Peninsula was under the control of Christian monarchs[1]. However, the settlement after the war allowed Muslims, or rather Mudéjars as they were now called, to keep their own customs, laws and Islamic faith. It was only at the end of the century that there was a drive to force Mudejars to become Christians and not till 1502 that they were forced into conversion or emigration and then only in Castile, not in Aragon[2]. However, it must also not be forgotten that many of those involved in the war were among the earliest discoverers and settlers in the New World, with one of its important aims of bringing Christianity to those who already lived in the Americas[3].

1 The answer explains some of the reasons why the conquest of Granada was so important in considering that Ferdinand and Isabella were deserving of the title 'Most Catholic Monarchs'.
2 The implications of this development are considered.
3 The wider implications are hinted at and this could be developed and contrasted with the religious ideals and the actuality of what happened when exploration and development of the New World took place.

The answer could go on and argue how the conquest of Granada was not wholly for religious reasons but had political aspects as well.

Most importantly, the conclusion must reach a supported judgement as to the relative importance of the factors in relation to the issue in the question. For example:

Both of the issues had a significant impact on the reputation of the two monarchs as both policies appeared to be strengthening Catholicism in the peninsula and helped to achieve religious stability[1]. However, the willingness of Isabella and Ferdinand to allow the Moors to retain their faith, as well as customs, laws and property, suggests that they were pragmatic and may not be completely deserving of the title. It was not until 1502 that the policy of convivencia ended, and then only completely in Castile, not in Aragon. The impact of the Inquisition had been limited to start with to conversos, and then expanded to include Moriscos and any signs of Protestantism within Spain. As far as Spain itself is concerned, Ferdinand and Isabella are perhaps most deserving of the title of Catholic Monarchs for their introduction of the Inquisition which preserved traditional Catholicism within Spain. As far as the wider world of Christianity is concerned their initial support of the exploration of the New World led eventually to the conversion of thousands to Christianity and therefore had far more impact in the long term[2].

1 The response explains the relative importance of the two factors and offers a clear view.
2 The response reaches a supported judgement as to the relative significance of the two events.

Interpretation questions

How to write a good essay

The guidance below is for answering the AS interpretation question OCR Unit Y236 Spain 1469–1556. Guidance on answering essay questions is on page 195.

The OCR specification outlines the two key topics from which the interpretation question will be drawn. For this book these are:

- Isabella and Ferdinand: government.
- Isabella and Ferdinand: religion.

The specification also lists the main debates to consider.

It is also worth remembering that this is an AS unit and not an A level historiography paper. The aim of this element of the unit is to develop an awareness that the past can be interpreted in different ways.

The question will require you to assess the strengths and limitations of a historian's interpretation of an issue related to one of the specified key topics.

You should be able to place the interpretation within the context of the wider historical debate on the key topic. However, you will *not* be required to know the names of individual historians associated with the debate or to have studied the specific books of any historians. It may even be counter-productive to be aware of particular historians' views, as this may lead you to simply describe their view, rather than analyse the given interpretation.

There are a number of skills you need to develop if you are to reach the higher levels in the mark bands:

- To be able to understand the wording of the question.
- To be able to explain the interpretation and how it fits into the debate about the issue or topic.
- To be able to consider both the strengths and weaknesses of the interpretation by using your own knowledge of the topic.

Here is an example of a question you will face in the exam:

> Read the interpretation and then answer the question that follows:
>
> 'The Spanish Church formed another instrument for forging Spanish unity and creating a strong monarchy.'
>
> From: V.H.H. Green, *Renaissance and Reformation*, 1964.
>
> Evaluate the strengths and limitations of this interpretation, making reference to other interpretations that you have studied.

Approaching the question

There are several steps to take to answer this question:

1 Explain the interpretation and put it into the context of the debate on the topic

In the first paragraph you should explain the interpretation and the view it is putting forward. This paragraph places the interpretation in the context of the historical debate and explains any key words or phrases relating to the given interpretation. A suggested opening might be as follows:

The interpretation puts forward the view that the Church in Spain played a vital role in bringing about unity between the different kingdoms and strengthening the power of the monarchy under Isabella and Ferdinand. The interpretation also suggests that there was a range of factors that helped to bring about unity[1]. In raising the issue of 'forging Spanish unity', the interpretation puts forward the view that 'Spain' was not unified, but there was a desire and a deliberate policy to bring it about and suggests that the Church would play a crucial role in this development[2]. The debate centres around the extent to which Spain was unified by the end of the reigns of Ferdinand and Isabella, with other interpretations suggesting that there was no attempt to unify the kingdoms[3].

1. The opening two sentences are clearly focused on the given interpretation. They clearly explain that there was more than one factor in bringing about unity and that the Church also helped to strengthen royal authority, but there is no detailed own knowledge added at this point.
2. The second sentence suggests that the idea of unity was a policy pursued by Ferdinand and Isabella, in which the Church played a vital role.
3. The last sentence begins to place the concept of the unity of Spain in the wider historical debate and suggests that this historian's emphasis on it might contrast with other views.

In order to place Green's view in the context of the debate about the unity of Spain and the strengthening of royal authority within the kingdoms, you could go on to suggest that there are a wide range of factors that could be considered, including religion, the political institutions of councils and *Cortes*, and the contrast here between Castile and Aragon, the economic barriers, and the personal nature of the unity based only on the marriage of the two monarchs.

2 Consider the strengths of the interpretation

In the second paragraph consider the strengths of the interpretation by bringing in your own knowledge that supports the given view. A suggested response might start as follows when considering the strengths of the view:

There is some merit to the interpretation as it acknowledges that there was more than one 'instrument' in bringing about unity and that the monarchy was strengthened, particularly after the civil war of the late fifteenth century[1]. *The Church did help to create a sense of unity as the conquest of Granada brought the whole of the Iberian Peninsula under Christian monarchs and a new archbishopric was created in Granada. The monarchs also secured further powers from the Pope over the Church in Spain. In particular, they acquired the right to nominate all bishops. In this way they were able to strengthen their control over the Church. The inquisition was established throughout all the kingdoms of Spain – the one visible sign of an institution that was common to, and therefore united, all parts of the country. It was also completely in the control of the monarchs and thereby strengthened their powers*[2]. *These events therefore helped to bring together the two issues mentioned in the interpretation of creating unity and a strong monarchy*[3].

1. The answer clearly focuses on the strength of the given interpretation.
2. The response provides some support for the view in the interpretation from the candidate's own knowledge. There is some detailed and precise knowledge, but this could be developed in the remainder of the paragraph.
3. The final sentence links together the two issues of unity and strength mentioned in the interpretation.

In the remainder of the paragraph you could show how these two factors were linked and how this question of 'unity and a strong monarchy' was seen in other religious policies of the reign: the expulsion of the Jews from both Castile and Aragon, and the expulsion of the *Mudéjars* from Castile (but not from Aragon).

3 Consider the weaknesses of the interpretation

In the third paragraph consider the weaknesses of the given interpretation by bringing in knowledge that can challenge the given interpretation and explains what is missing from the interpretation. A suggested response might start as follows when considering the weaknesses of the view:

However, there are a number of weaknesses in the interpretation[1]. *Most importantly, it fails to explain that neither Ferdinand nor Isabella desired to achieve a unitary state and recognised the limits to their powers outside their own kingdoms. They never used the title 'Kings of Spain' and therefore the interpretation might be ascribing to them something that they did not even consider as possible*[2]. *The interpretation also fails to consider other methods that helped to strengthen the monarchy, although it does hint that there were other factors*[3].

1. The opening makes it very clear that this paragraph will deal with the weaknesses of the interpretation.
2. It explains clearly the first weakness and provides evidence to support the claim. The evidence is not detailed and could be developed, but the answer focuses on explaining the weakness, rather than providing lots of detail.
3. Although more detail could have been provided about the other factors that helped to create a strong monarchy, or whether the monarchy was strong, this could be developed in the remainder of the paragraph.

Answers might go on to argue that the lack of unity was evident from the succession question following the death of Isabella, when Ferdinand was prevented from becoming regent of Castile and had to leave for his own realm of Aragon. The answer might discuss other examples showing a lack of unity such as the lack of central government – the Council System, the individual *Cortes*, the economic divisions; and, in regard to the question of whether there was 'strong monarchy', the concessions that had had to be made to the nobility, and the difficulties over finance – two important weaknesses. The paragraph might therefore suggest that the interpretation provides a partial answer which needs further development.

There is no requirement for you to reach a judgement as to which view you find more convincing or valid.

Assessing the interpretation

In assessing the interpretation you should consider the following:

- Identify and explain the issue being discussed in the interpretation: the development of Spanish unity and a strong monarch, and the role of the Church in that process.
- Explain the view being put forward in the interpretation: the interpretation is arguing that Spain became more unified and the monarchy strengthened, at least in part because of the Church.
- Explain how the interpretation fits into the wider debate about the issue: the extent of the unity of Spain and the strength of the monarch by the time of Charles I's accession in 1516 and the role of various institutions in that process.

In other interpretations you might need to:

- Consider whether there is any particular emphasis within the interpretation that needs explaining or commenting on, for example, if the interpretation says something is 'the only reason' or 'the single most important reason'.
- Comment on any concepts that the interpretation raises, such as 'total war', 'authoritarian system', 'liberalisation'.
- Consider the focus of the interpretation, for example, if an interpretation focuses on an urban viewpoint, what was the rural viewpoint? Is the viewpoint given in the interpretation the same for all areas of society?

In summary, this is what is important for answering interpretation questions:

- Explaining the interpretation.
- Placing the interpretation in the context of the wider historical debate about the issue it considers.
- Explaining the strengths *and* weaknesses of the view in the extract.

Glossary of terms

Alcabala   A sales tax, usually ten per cent.

Alhambra   The fortress and palace of the Moorish rulers of Granada, built between the twelfth and thirteenth centuries.

Arable   Land that can be ploughed and is suitable for growing crops.

Aragon   In the mid-fifteenth century, the Crown of Aragon consisted of three kingdoms, Aragon, Catalonia and Valencia. In this book the term 'Crown of Aragon' is used to mean all three kingdoms. References to the kingdoms of Aragon, Catalonia or Valencia mean the individual kingdoms.

Armada   A fleet of warships.

Arquebuse   An early musket.

Artillery   Large military weapons built to fire projectiles far beyond the range of an infantry's small arms.

Audiencia   A court of appeal.

Auto de fé   A public ceremony (literally an 'act of faith') at which the Inquisition announced its sentences for those found guilty. The burning of any heretics took place after such ceremonies and was carried out by the secular authorities.

Basque countries   Consisted of Vizcaya, Guipuzcoa, Alava and Navarre and were in the western end of the Pyrenees. In the mid-fifteenth century Navarre, the main Basque country, was partly in Spain and partly in France.

Benefice   A Church appointment with a guaranteed amount of income and property.

Blasphemy   Action or offence of speaking in an insulting or disrespectful way towards God.

Bullion   Amount of gold and silver valued by weight, before it is minted into coins.

Calvinism   A more extreme branch of Protestantism. John Calvin was a Protestant reformer based in Geneva who prioritised issues of organisation as well as belief.

Castile   In the mid-fifteenth century the Crown of Castile occupied the area from Burgos in the north to Toledo in the south, equivalent to the modern-day provinces of León, Madrid and La Mancha.

Cathedral chapter   A group of clerics formed to advise a bishop.

Comuneros   The city dwellers who organised themselves to defend the rights of their communities against the government. The term is often associated with a rebellion or revolt. (Spanish for members of a community.)

Comunidad   Many of the towns in Castile joined together in a league to rebel against the imposition of Habsburg authority.

Conquistador   A conqueror, especially one of the Spanish conquerors of Mexico and Peru in the sixteenth century.

Conversos   Jews who converted to Christianity, many forcibly, to avoid persecution or expulsion from Spain or Portugal.

Convivencia   The coexistence of Christians, Jews and Muslims in medieval Spain.

Corregidores   Crown governors appointed to Castilian towns.

Corsairs   Pirates, especially the privateers who operated along the Barbary Coast (north Africa).

Cortes   The parliament in each of the kingdoms in Castile and Aragon (called *Corts* in Catalonia).

Cruzada   A tax, or money offering, which was earmarked for the Christian crusades against Muslims.

Debasement   Lowering the value of currency, particularly in connection with the reminting of coins. A coin is debased if its gold, silver, copper or nickel content is reduced.

Ducat   A variety of gold and silver coins that became widely used in western Europe. One ducat was worth 375 *maravedís*.

Encomienda   A land grant given to an individual in return for his services to the Crown. Settlers receiving these grants also received a specified number of natives from a particular community.

Erasmist   Follower of Erasmus and his doctrine.

Excusado   A tax on clerical property introduced in 1567 and usually paid as a lump sum by the Church.

Frontiersmen Christian men who lived on the frontier of Christian and Muslim Spain; they had to fight to defend and extend Christian lands.

Fueros Aragonese laws and privileges.

Fuggers A politically influential banking family from Germany with trading links throughout Europe. The loans they made to Charles I enabled him to become Holy Roman Emperor.

Germanía 'Brotherhood'. It was a Christian brotherhood of armed volunteers formed to defend the Valerian coast against Muslim pirates.

Grandee A Spanish nobleman of the highest rank. During the reign of Charles I the number of grandees was limited to 25.

Habsburgs Rulers of Austria and the Netherlands (including modern-day Belgium and Netherlands), they also held the elected position of Holy Roman Emperor, with control over a large number of states of various sizes which made up the Holy Roman Empire.

Hermandad A local peace-keeping force (plural *Hermandades*).

Huguenots French Protestants.

Iberian Peninsula The land mass occupied by today's Spain and Portugal. It is separated from France by the Pyrenees Mountains and from Africa by the Strait of Gibraltar.

Iconoclast A destroyer of images, such as statues of saints.

Illuminist Someone who believed in direct communion with God.

Indies The term in use during the sixteenth century for the New World (the Americas).

Indulgences The remission granted by the Church of the temporal punishment due to sins already forgiven, for example, penitents who had been given a great number of prayers to recite as their (earthly) punishment could have this reduced by receiving an indulgence.

Inflation A sustained increase in the price of goods and services, resulting in money losing value.

Inquisition An organisation that was responsible for finding and punishing people who did not follow Catholic beliefs and practices.

Jesuits Members of the Society of Jesus, founded by Ignatius Loyola in 1534.

Junta A council.

Jurisdiction The extent of the right to administer justice and apply laws.

Juros Bonds (paid as annuities) issued by the Crown to cover the costs of its military campaigns.

Justicia Aragonese law officer in charge of courts and justice, appointed by the Crown for life.

Knights Hospitallers Catholic religious and military order based on Rhodes during this period.

Laity People who are not clergy.

Letrados Lawyers, usually with two academic degrees and ten years' legal experience.

Lie fallow The practice of leaving the soil unsown for a period of time to restore its fertility.

Liturgy The authorised form of public worship.

Maravedís A copper coin which was the lowest measure of Castilian money and the most used.

Mayorazgo The inheritance of an estate by a single person.

Mendoza family One of the most powerful families in Spain, a number of whose members held important positions in government during the fifteenth and sixteenth centuries.

Meseta The vast highland plateau that occupies the interior of Spain at an average elevation of 600 metres.

Mesta An influential guild of livestock owners, named after the communal grazing lands in Castilian villages.

Millones A tax on basic foods – wine, meat, olive oil and vinegar – introduced in 1590.

Missal A book containing the prayers and customs of the Catholic Church.

Moors Muslims who invaded in the eighth century and established a rule that lasted until the fifteenth century in Andalusia.

Moriscos Name given to the Muslims who converted to Christianity. They were suspected of secretly practising their ancestral religion as they usually retained their traditional diet and dress, and used the Arabic language.

Glossary of terms

Mudéjars   Muslims living under Christian rule.

Netherlands   The name means 'Low Countries'. Up to 1581 the territories included most of present-day Belgium (including Flanders), the Netherlands, Luxembourg and parts of France and Germany.

New World   A name for the Americas, especially during the time of first exploration and colonisation of the region by Europeans; also called the Indies in contemporary sources.

'Old' Christians   People of Catholic faith with no Jewish ancestry.

Order of the Golden Fleece   An order of chivalry founded in the fifteenth century by a Duke of Burgundy and headed by the king. Members of the order had a number of privileges.

Ordinances   Decrees issued by the monarchs.

Ottoman Empire   The former Turkish (and largely Muslim) Empire in Europe, Asia and Africa, which lasted from the late thirteenth century until the end of the First World War.

Papal bull   A document issued by a pope. It is named after the metal seal (*bulla*) which it bears as a mark of authenticity.

Parish   An area overseen by a church and its priest.

Patrimony   An inheritance or legacy handed down to someone.

Peso   New World bullion was normally reckoned in *pesos*. The New World silver *peso* was valued at 272 *maravedís* and the gold *peso* at 450 *maravedís*.

Pikemen   Foot soldiers who carried pikes – long weapons (about 4.9 m) topped with a metal point.

Pogrom   The officially ordered persecution and massacre of a minority group, especially Jews.

Polyglot Bible   A version of the Bible that contains side-by-side versions of the same text in a number of different languages.

Pragmaticas   Laws which the two monarchs had issued without going through the *Cortes* of Castile but which still had to be obeyed by the inhabitants of Castile.

Privateering ships   Privately owned armed ships authorised by a government to take part in war.

Real   A unit of currency fixed at a value of 34 *maravedís* in 1497.

Reconquest   (*Reconquista* in Spanish.) A succession of military campaigns to reclaim Iberian lands from Muslim occupiers. The Reconquest started in the eighth century and ended in 1492 with the capture of Granada.

Regent   Ruler of a kingdom during the absence, childhood or illness of the king or queen.

Religious orders of knights   Christian military monastic organisations formed to defend and expand the Christian lands of Spain against the Muslims.

Ribagorza   A county consisting of seventeen towns and 216 villages extending from Monzón to the Pyrenees.

See   The area of a bishop's ecclesiastical jurisdiction.

Servicio   A sum of money to be raised by taxation.

Sisa   A tax on food.

Speculator   A person who makes risky investments in anticipation of prices going up in order to resell at a profit.

Subsidio   A clerical tax introduced in 1519 and regularly levied on rents, lands and other forms of income.

Synod   An assembly of the clergy (and sometimes laity) in a diocese.

Tercio   A new type of infantry formation used by the Spanish armies from 1534.

Tithe   One-tenth of annual production or earnings given to the Church.

Trebuchet   A type of catapult used as a siege engine.

Usury   The lending of money at unreasonably high rates of interest.

Vassal   Someone given land in return for supporting his master or lord.

Viceroy   An official who runs a country or state in the name of, and as a representative of, a king or queen.

Vulgate   A late fourth-century Latin translation of the Bible.

Witchcraft   Practice and belief in magical skills. Usually such powers were considered to be evil and associated with the Devil.

Further reading

Chapter 1

Books relevant to the whole period

J.H. Elliott, *Imperial Spain 1469–1716* (Edward Arnold, 1963)
Still extremely relevant with good coverage of the period

Henry Kamen, *Spain 1469–1714: A Society of Conflict* (Pearson Longman, 2005)
A standard work from one of the best writer–researchers on Spain

General texts on religion and the Inquisition

Henry Kamen, *The Spanish Inquisition: A Historical Revision* (Yale University Press, 2014)
A detailed and scholarly work that gives a balanced view

Helen Rawling, *Church, Religion and Society in Early Modern Spain* (Palgrave, 2002)
Short and useful book with good insights

Helen Rawling, *The Spanish Inquisition* (Blackwell, 2006)
Concise and insightful with good coverage of the various debates on the topics

General text on the New World

J.H. Parry, *The Spanish Seaborne Empire* (University of California Press, 1990)
Gives a good broad coverage

Chapter 2

John Edwards, *Ferdinand and Isabella, Profiles in Power* (Pearson Longman, 2005)
Very readable account of the two monarchs; includes a helpful chronology

John Edwards, *The Spain of the Catholic Monarchs 1474–1520* (Oxford University Press, 2000)
Up-to-date work with detailed coverage of the reign

J.N. Hillgarth, *The Spanish Kingdoms 1250–1516, volume II: 1410–1516: Castilian Hegemony* (Oxford University Press, 1978)
Authoritative and clearly written; out of print but available second-hand and in some libraries

P.K. Liss, *Isabel, The Queen* (Oxford University Press, 1992)
One of the few biographies on Isabella in English, accurate and enjoyable

Geoffrey Woodward, *Spain in the Reigns of Isabella and Ferdinand, 1474–1516* (Hodder & Stoughton, 1997)
A more in-depth look at the issues touched on in this book

Chapter 3

G. Mattingly, *Renaissance Diplomacy* (Jonathan Cape, 1970)
Useful insights into the use of ambassadors by the two monarchs; out of print but available second-hand and in some libraries

Chapter 4

Stephen Haliczer, *The Comuneros of Castile. The Forging of a Revolution, 1475–1521* (University of Wisconsin Press, 1981)
Most of the works on the *Comunidades* are in Spanish. This one, in English is well worth reading. It considers the mistakes made by Charles I's government but also traces the roots of this revolt to the policies of Ferdinand and Isabella. Out of print but available second-hand and in some libraries

John Hemming, *The Conquest of the Incas* (Mariner Books, 2003)
One of the best books on this topic, comprehensive and easy to read

John Lynch, *Spain Under the Habsburgs, volume 1, Empire and Absolutism 1516–1598* (Basil Blackwell, 1981)
A lively and detailed account of both the reign of Charles and that of Philip

H. Soly, editor, *Charles V 1500–1558 and his Time* (MercatorFonds, 1999)
A good range of articles, particularly rich in illustrations

Hugh Thomas, *The Conquest of Mexico* (Pimlico, 1994)
A detailed, stimulating account and interesting to read

Further reading

Chapter 5

Earl J. Hamilton, *American Treasure and the Price Revolution in Spain* **(Harvard University Press, 1934)**
For those who wish to read in detail the result of Hamilton's researches into the price revolution

Henry Kamen, *Spain 1469–1714: A Society of Conflict* **(Pearson Longman, 2005)**
Written in 2005 this is based on more recent research than John Lynch. It also covers the price revolution and the economy and social change during the sixteenth century

John Lynch, *Spain Under the Habsburgs, Volume One, Empire and Absolutism 1516–1598* **(Basil Blackwell, 1981)**
This covers the price revolution and its social and economic effects, agriculture and industry including some useful information on ship building in the sixteenth century. Some of his conclusions need to be treated with caution

Chapter 6

Henry Kamen, *Philip of Spain* **(Yale University Press, 1997)**
A sympathetic view of Philip and an enjoyable read

Geoffrey Parker, *Imprudent King: A New Life of Philip II* **(Yale University Press, 2014)**
A scholarly and detailed account, based on recent research, by an author who has written extensively on Philip II

Geoffrey Parker, *Philip II* **(Little, Brown, 1978)**
This earlier work by Geoffrey Parker is easy to read and gives an illuminating personal view of Philip

Peter Pierson, *Philip II of Spain* **(Thames & Hudson, 1981)**
Gives good coverage of the main points of Philip's reign; out of print but available second-hand and in some libraries

Geoffrey Woodward, *Philip II* **(Routledge, 1992)**
Gives a sound overview of the reign and includes a collection of documents, glossary and bibliography

Chapter 7

Neil Faulkner, editor, 'The Dutch War of Independence' pages 26–42 in *Military History Monthly***, Issue 52 (Current Publishing, 2015)**
Includes useful maps for the events in the Netherlands from 1566, and information on the Spanish *tercio*, supported with illustrations

Julian Humphrys, 'Clash of oars' pages 56–60 in *History Revealed***, Issue 19 (Immediate Media, 2015)**
Includes a clearly labelled drawing of Don Juan's flagship at the Battle of Lepanto, as well as information on how the battle was fought – and won. This is also supported with illustrations

Index

Adrian of Utrecht 65, 68, 69, 71
Agriculture 2, 110, 114–16
Alba, Duke of, *see* Toledo, Fernando Álvarez de, Duke of Alba
Albert of Austria 153, 161
Alcabala 25, 27, 84, 130, 166
Alfonso V, King of Portugal 17
Aragon 3, 4, 5, 6
   and foreign policy 40–1, 42, 43, 44, 45
   and Inquisition 30–1
   and Spanish Empire 12
   audiencia 26–7
   comparison with Castile 6, 143
   Cortes 6, 27, 68–9, 81
   Council of 26, 78–9, 82, 83, 127
   dislike of *Hermandad* 24, 27, 57
   exclusion from New World 54, 58
   expansion 4–5
   in fifteenth century 6
   income from 28, 85, 130, 171
   Justicia 6, 26, 142–5
   lack of economic unity 6
   rebellion against Philip 139, 142–6, 171
   revolt of Catalonia 16
   unity with Castile 57–8, 59–60
   see also Ferdinand of Aragon; *Germania* revolt; *Moriscos*
Armada 130, 160, 163–4
Avila, John of 87
Azpilcueta, Martín de 105–6

Barbarossa, Hayreddin 94
Barbary corsairs 92, 94, 141, 154
Battles
   Alcazarquivir 151, 152
   Landriano 92
   Lepanto 154–5, 159
   Mühlberg 95
   Pavia 91
   Toro 17
   Villalar 71
Bodin, Jean 107

Bourbon, Duke of 92
Bravo, Juan 71
Bull Inter Caetera 51, 53

Carranza, Bartolomé de 133, 138
Castile 2, 3, 4, 5, 6
   and New World 54, 58, 79
   appointments of *corregidores* 24, 57
   comparison with Aragon 6, 143
   conciliar system 26, 78–9
   conquest of Granada 29, 41
   Cortes 6, 27, 68, 69, 81–2, 83, 104
   importance 5, 8, 23, 77
   income from 28, 40, 69, 83, 84, 100, 129–30
   inflation 104–5
   introduction of Inquisition 30–1
   law and order 26–7
   military expenditure 129
   military orders 25
   population growth 111
   relations with France 40, 42
   relations with Portugal 40, 42
   succession 16–17, 56, 58, 65, 99
   unity with Aragon 57–8, 59–60
   see also Cisneros, Cardinal Francisco Ximénez de; *Comuneros* revolt; Granada War; Isabella of Castile; Muslims
'Catholic Monarchs', *see* Ferdinand and Isabella
Catholicism 7–8
   Islamic threat 7, 8, 11, 15, 19–22, 40, 45–6, 77, 88–9, 90, 94–5, 150, 153–5, 161, 171
   Protestant threat 11, 77, 87–8, 89, 99, 100, 133–4, 136, 137, 150, 151, 156, 158, 171
   reforms of Church in Spain 86–7, 136–7
   security in Spain 87–9, 100, 138, 150–1, 171

   see also Heresy; Holy Roman Empire; Spanish Inquisition
Censorship 133, 134–5
Charles I of Spain (Charles V, Holy Roman Emperor) 10, 57, 66
   acceptance in Spain 67–9, 75–6
   and Catholicism 66, 77, 86–9, 90, 95, 100
   as Holy Roman Emperor 11, 66, 77, 99
   death and succession 99
   development of New World 96–8
   early life 65–6
   evolution of government in Spain 76–83
   foreign policy 90–5
   raising income 83–6
   relations with pope 89
   ruler of a united Spain 57–8, 65
   see also Comuneros revolt; *Germania* revolt; Holy Roman Empire; Religion
Christians, *see* Catholicism; Protestantism
Cisneros, Cardinal Francisco Ximénez de
   as regent 56–7, 65, 67–8, 70
   improvements in education, training and practices of clergy 29–30, 87
   policy towards Muslims 33–4, 46
Cobos, Francisco de los 80, 82
Columbus, Christopher 50–2, 53, 54, 55
Comuneros revolt 70–2, 73–5, 76
Conciliar system 26, 78–9, 82, 126–7
Conquistadors 96–7
Conversos 7, 29, 30, 31–3, 134, 151
Council of the Inquisition 57, 79
Córdoba, Gonzalo Fernandez de 11, 44, 47
Corregidores 24, 57, 60, 70, 72, 74

Index

Cortes 6, 27, 28, 57, 68–9, 71, 72, 73–4, 80–2, 83, 84, 104, 105, 130, 142, 143, 145, 153
Cortés, Hernán 76, 96–7, 98
Council of Trent 136
Crown of Aragon, *see* Aragon
Croÿ, William de, Lord of Chièvres 67, 91

Don John of Austria 11, 66, 155
Doria, Andrea 92, 94
Drake, Sir Francis 162, 163, 164, 167

Elizabeth I of England 138, 156, 160, 162–3
England
   and Protestantism 138, 150, 155, 160, 161, 162–3
   betrothal of Catherine of Aragon to Prince Arthur 48, 53
   Philip II's marriage to Mary 122, 124
   trade in New World 162
   war with Spain 153, 160, 163–4, 171
   see also Elizabeth I of England; Treaties, Nonsuch
Erasmus, Desiderius 87, 88, 133

Farnese, Alexander, Duke of Parma 11, 156, 159–60, 162, 163, 165
Ferdinand I, Holy Roman Emperor 66, 94, 99–100
Ferdinand and Isabella
   and New World 50–4, 96
   and Spanish Church 29–30
   as a 'New Monarchy' 59–60
   as 'Catholic Monarchs' 21, 24, 26, 27, 60, 65
   death of Ferdinand 56–7
   death of Isabella 55–6
   expulsions of Jews and Muslims 32–4
   financial management 27–8
   foreign policy 40–9
   government 22–4, 26
   law and order 26–7
   marriage partnership 18–19, 40, 57
   personal presence 23
   qualities 17–18
   relations with nobility 25
   unity of kingdoms 57–8, 59–60, 70
   see also Cisneros, Cardinal Francisco Ximénez de; Granada War; *Hermandades*; Spanish Inquisition
Ferdinand of Aragon 15
   marriage to Isabella of Castile 8, 15
   see also Ferdinand and Isabella

Food supplies 2, 115, *see also* Inflation
France 2, 3, 5
   concerns over Habsburgs 10
   debasement of coinage 107, 110
   marriage alliances 48, 164
   plans for expansion in Italy 43–4
   relations with Spain 40–1, 42–4, 49, 67, 90–1, 143, 145, 150, 169–70
   wars of religion 164–5
   see also Henry of Navarre

Gattinara, Mercurino 72, 76–7, 91
Germania revolt 72–3, 75, 88
Granada, *see* Granada War; *Moriscos*, revolt
Granada, Luis de 132, 133
Granada War 19–22, 28, 29

Habsburgs 8–11, 41
   marriage alliances 9, 48
   see also individual rulers
Hamilton, Earl J. 108–10
Henry IV of Castile 16
Henry of Navarre 138, 160, 165
Heresy 31, 79, 100, 122, 131, 133–4, 138, 143, 157–8, 168
Hermandades 20, 23–4, 26, 57
Holy Roman Emperors, *see* Habsburgs
Holy Roman Empire 44
   communication 91
   German states 66, 95
Huguenots 143, 165

Iberian Peninsula 2, 3, 5, 41
   as a Roman province 4
   frontiers 41–2
   kingdoms 4
   Muslim conquest 4
   Philip II's desire for unification 151–3, 170
   Reconquest 4, 19–20, 40
   see also individual countries and regions
Index of Forbidden Books 133, 134–5
Industry 110, 111, 116
Inflation 84, 104, 128–9
   effect of New World treasure 105–7, 108–11
   evidence 104
   impact 112–13, 114–16
Inquisition, *see* Spanish Inquisition
Isabella of Castile 16
   fight for Crown of Castile 16–17
   marriage to Ferdinand of Aragon 8, 15–16
   see also Ferdinand and Isabella
Islam
   war against 90, 94–5, 150, 154–5, 161, 171
   see also Moors; Muslims
Islamic states, trade routes 51
Italy, and Spanish Empire 5, 10, 11, 91–4, 95, 121, 125, 127, 134, 151, *see also* Naples

Jesus, Teresa of 87
Jews 8
   expulsion 32–3, 57
   growing hostility from Christians 7–8, 29, 30
   see also Conversos
Joanna of Austria 133
Joanna of Portugal 16–17
Joanna, Queen of Castile 48, 56–7
John II of Aragon 16

Juntas 127
Juros 28, 84

Lannoy, Charles de 91, 92
Lara, Alonso Manrique de 88
Las Casas, Bartolomé 98
League of Cognac 92
Loyola, Ignatius 87, 132, 133

Maravedís 27–8, 52, 68, 107, 108
Margaret, Duchess of Parma 66, 156, 158, 159
Margaret of Austria 65, 66
Mary of Hungary 66
Mendoza, Iñigo Lopez de 22
Mercado, Tomás de (on laws of demand) 106–7
Meseta 2, 3, 5
Moors 7, 8, 15, 19–22, 40, 45–6, 88–9, 151, *see also* Muslims
Moriscos 33–4, 57, 88–9, 100, 134, 151, 154
  revolt 139–42, 171
Mudéjars, see Muslims
Muslims 4, 8
  expulsion 33–4, 57
  hostility towards 7, 29, 46, 137, 153–5
  threat to Catholicism 11, 77, 90
  see also Germania revolt; Granada War; Islam, war against; *Moriscos*; Ottoman Empire; Reconquest

Naples 43–5, 90
Navarre 3, 4, 5, 10, 42, 49, 91
Netherlands 5, 41, 67
  income from 84, 99, 130
  Protestantism 8, 99, 150, 164–6, 171
  war against Philip 141, 155–62, 169–70
  see also Habsburgs
New World
  discoveries 10, 19, 52, 55
  government 97, 167
  importance to Spain 166–8
  income 85, 98, 105

  passage across Atlantic 42, 167
  religious missionaries 67, 87, 97–8
  Spanish expansion 51, 52–5, 58, 76, 97–8
  treatment of native Indians 98
  see also Columbus, Christopher; *Conquistadors*

Ottoman Empire 8, 11, 41, 45, 49, 51, 92, 94

Padilla, Juan de 71
Papacy
  acceptance of Henry of Navarre's conversion 165
  relations with Charles 77, 85, 89, 91–2, 94
  relations with Philip 130, 137–8, 164
  support to Ferdinand and Isabella 20, 21, 29, 43, 53, 60, 65
  see also Catholicism; Spanish Inquisition
Peace of Cambrai 93
Pérez, Antonio 126, 128, 144, 145
Pérez, Gonzalo 124, 126, 128
Peris, Vicent 72
Philip I, King of Castile 10, 48, 56
Philip II of Spain 10, 122, 124
  achievements 170–2
  administration 125–7
  as ruler of Portugal 151–3
  character 121, 124–5
  death 170
  defending Mediterranean against Islam 153–5
  early life 120–1
  financial management 128–31
  foreign policy aims 150–1, 169–70
  importance of New World 166–8
  loss of Netherlands 155–62
  method of government 123–4
  rebellions in Aragon and Granada 139–46
  relations with England 162–4
  relations with France 164–5
  relations with pope 137–8

  religious reforms 131–7
  secretaries 127–8
  succession 99–100
Population
  New World Indians 98
  Spanish 4, 5, 110–11, 140, 141, 142
Portugal 2, 3, 4, 5, 9, 10
  and Turks 45
  and War of Succession 17, 45
  empire 45, 52–3, 153, 167, 170
  marriage alliances 17, 48, 66, 76, 122
  relations with Spain 40, 41, 42, 78
  succession of Philip to throne 125, 126, 151–3, 170, 171
  see also Treaties, Tordesillas
Protestantism 7–8
  fear of attack on Spain 141, 142, 145, 155
  threat to Catholicism 11, 77, 87–8, 89, 99, 100, 133–4, 136, 137, 150, 151, 156, 158, 171
  see also England; France, wars of religion; Huguenots; Netherlands
Pulgar, Hernando del 18

Quiroga, Gaspar de 137

Reconquest 4, 7, 20, 34, 45–6, 153
Religion 7–8
  see also Catholicism; *Conversos*; Jews; Muslims; Protestantism; Reconquest
Religious orders of knights 4, 25, 45
Requesens, Luis de 125, 158

'Sack of Rome' 77, 92
Sheep trade 115–16
Silva, Ruy Gómez de, Prince of Éboli 126, 128
Spain
  borders 2
  family tree of rulers 9
  geography 2–3
  location 2

military forces 11, 12, 20, 27, 30, 47–8, 49, 130, 160, 163–4
start of overseas empire 4–5
unity of monarchy 57
use of term 'Spain'/'Spanish' 3
Spanish Empire 4–5, 10, 11, 12, 41, 49, 90
communication 91, 124–5
expansion into New World 51, 53–5, 76, 97–8
government of 78–9, 82, 97
income and financial obligations 84–6, 129–30
manageability 99
nature of 12
protecting and maintaining 170
see also individual countries, states, rulers and religions
Spanish Inquisition
and *conversos* 31–2, 134
and *Moriscos* 34, 134, 141
and papacy 137–8
elimination of heresy 133–5
elimination of Protestantism 87–8, 158
enforcing moral and Christian standards 32, 134, 137
establishment of 30–1
see also Council of the Inquisition
Suleiman I 8, 11
Supply and demand 106–7, 111

Tavera, Juan Pardo de 82
Taxes 6, 24, 27–8, 29, 70, 80–1, 84–6, 98, 99, 113, 130, 140
Titian 129
Toledo, Fernando Álvarez de, Duke of Alba 11, 126, 128, 129, 152, 158–9, 161, 162, 163
Toledo, Francisco de 167
Torquemada, Tomás de 31, 32
Treaties
Alcaçovas 42, 45
Augsburg 95
Barcelona 42
Cateau-Cambrésis 164, 165
Joinville 165
Madrid 91
Medina del Campo 48
Nonsuch 160, 163, 164
Noyon 67, 91
Tordesillas 51, 53
Vervins 165
Villafafila 56
Tridentine decrees 136–7
Turkey 151, 153–4, 155, 171, *see also* Battles, Lepanto; Ottoman Empire
Turkish Empire, *see* Ottoman Empire

Valdés, Fernando de 133, 134, 138
Vázquez, Mateo de Leca 127

William I, Prince of Orange 156, 158, 163

Acknowledgements:

Basil Blackwell, *Spain Under the Habsburgs* by John Lynch, 1981. Edward Arnold, *Imperial Spain 1469–1716* by J.H. Elliott, 1963; *Renaissance and Reformation* by V.H.H. Green, 1964. *Estudios Americanos*, 'Actitudes del español en la época de Carlos V' by J. Sanchez Montes, 1951. George Allen & Unwin, *History of the Reign of Ferdinand and Isabella the Catholic*, edited and abridged by C. Harvey Gardiner by William H. Prescott, 1962. Hodder & Stoughton, *Spain in the Reigns of Isabella and Ferdinand, 1474–1516* by Geoffrey Woodward, 1997; *Charles V: Ruler, Dynast and Defender of the Faith 1500–58* by Stewart MacDonald, 2000. Longman, *Philip II* by Geoffrey Woodward, 1992. Macmillan, *Spain In the Fifteenth Century* by R. Highfield, 1972. Oxford University Press, *The School of Salamanca* by Marjorie Grice-Hutchinson, 1952. Palgrave, *Church, Religion and Society in Early Modern Spain* by Helen Rawlings, 2002. Pearson, *Spain 1469–1714* by Henry Kamen, 2005. Phoenix, *The Spanish Inquisition* by Henry Kamen, 1997. Routledge, *Early Economic Thought in Spain, 1177–1740* by Marjorie Grice-Hutchinson, 1978. University of Miami Press, *The Council of the Santa Hermandad* by Marvin Lunenfeld, 1979. University of Pennsylvania Press, *Early Modern Spain: A Documentary History* by Jon Cowans, 2003. University of Wisconsin Press, *A History of Spain and Portugal* by Stanley G. Payne, 1973. Wiley, *The Spanish Inquisition* by Helen Rawlings, 2005.

Every effort has been made to trace all copyright holders, but if any have been inadvertently overlooked the Publishers will be pleased to make the necessary arrangements at the first opportunity.